Red Hole in Time

Muriel Marshall

NUMBER NINE
ESSAYS ON THE AMERICAN WEST
sponsored by the
Elma Dill Russell Spencer Foundation

Red Hole in Time

MURIEL MARSHALL

TEXAS A&M UNIVERSITY PRESS
COLLEGE STATION

The paper used in this book meets the minimum requirements
of the American National Standard for Permanence
of Paper for Printed Library Materials, Z39.48-1984.
Binding materials have been chosen for durability.

Frontispiece: Boy Rock, unfazed by government dynamite,
is a secret joke for Canyon folk.

Library of Congress Cataloging-in-Publication Data

Marshall, Muriel.
  Red hole in time / Muriel Marshall. – 1st ed.
    p. cm. – (Essays on the American West ; no. 9)
  Bibliography: p.
  Includes index.
  ISBN 0-89096-316-9 (cloth) (alk. paper) : $29.50 ; 0-89096-332-0 (paper) : $12.95
  1. Escalante Canyon (Colo.)–History. 2. Escalante Canyon
(Colo.)–Description and Travel. I. Title. II. Series.
F782.E82M37 1988   87-21715
978.8'17–dc19   CIP

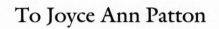
To Joyce Ann Patton

Contents

List of Illustrations

Red Hole in Time

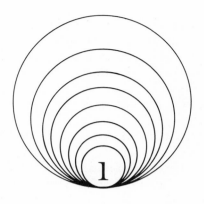

The Vortex

Flatlander Jeff Dillard was riding flank on three trainloads of long-horn cattle strung out on an Indian trail across the ragged eaves of a mountain that looked like the backside of a hundred-mile-long shed.

"After we'd unloaded in the flats down at Roubideau Switch, we just moseyed them along, letting them rest up from the ordeal in the cars and get their bellies full of fat sage and grass. They'd got dry and started walking, lined out a mile or so on the trail, when I happened to look up ahead and saw those cows disappearing into the ground.

"I wasn't trail boss any more, so it wasn't my responsibility. All the way across the plains from Texas to the foot of the Rockies, I was trail boss; but I'd never worked cattle in mountains – hardly even seen real mountains – so when they loaded that herd on the narrow-gauge for the trip over the Continental Divide I lost my authority and was just one of the cowboys. I heard talk of things I didn't understand – summer range on top, wintering on the bottoms – but I kept my mouth shut, not wanting to show my ignorance.

"While the herd grazed I had noticed mountains off to both sides, but the trail led across benches not much worse gullied than I was used to.

"Then I saw that herd disappearing. Like the cows were strung on a string that something had hold of and was pulling into the ground. I forgot about not showing my ignorance and spurred up to see what the hell was happening.

"Well, those cows were dropping into a huge hole in the earth.

"They were trailing down a mile and a half of cliff on a zigzag shelf so narrow in places that if they'd had a good fill of water their rib-sprung bellies would've bumped them off the ledge.

"I could see the lead cows lined along the creek down there. They looked like ants.

"That was my first sight of Escalante Canyon."

It was everybody's first sight of Escalante for seventy years. Later widened enough to take a wagon's wheels, it remained a descent to freeze the heart. Falling away beneath the feet, or hanging overhead, the Big Hill trail was the only feasible way from or to the Outside during the entire lifetime of those who first went down in.

If, as they say, biology is destiny—the luck of the draw, being born male or female—so is geography. The newborn opens eyes on a spot of the globe he did not choose—Africa, Siberia, a basement in Harlem, a penthouse on the Riviera. The "where" makes a difference. Willy-nilly he has to deal with what he's been dealt; he can accept and go with the flow, struggle to make something of it, struggle to get away, or sit and whine about a stacked deck.

To people who found themselves, by birth or by choice, at the bottom of Escalante Canyon, geography made all the difference. The red walls and the risky escape route affected all who lived down there whether they regarded the Canyon as paradise or prison or, indeed, ever looked up from the grindstone to wonder why or where they were.

Because of the walls, the Canyon is a cosmos, a world in a hole, as if some closed-circuit experiment were being conducted.

All that ever happened to anyone happened to those here but, magnified by the refraction of the walls, everything they did focused larger than life and put messages on the scenery, in story and artifact, that still speak to mindful explorers who in the outside world are themselves beating against, or flying over, or snuggling into, invisible-walled situations.

The Canyon exerts a force field that at times has seemed to reach out and hook people down in.

It hooked Jeff Dillard in 1883 on the wage he was paid to trail longhorns to the San Miguel River, where Johnson & Johnson Surgical Supply Co. was setting up a cattle ranch to mollify stockholders who had lost money when the company had failed at gold placering. The wage stopped when the cattle were turned over, but Dillard stayed.

It hooked John Musser on a bad debt. A businessman, he went in there merely to recover a loan on some cows. He never came back out, neither he nor his sons, for a hundred years, though errands the Canyon sent them on have ranged as far as cattle-industry congresses in the nation's capital.

It hooked city-girl Emma Roethenbach in Denver three hundred miles away on the bait of a note in a box of peaches. Once she reached the bottom of the Big Hill alive, she never risked the trip again and spent the rest of her days down there. That's how they tell it. Actually, except for seven straight years, Emma managed to get out at least once a year to go to the store in town.

To snag Jeff Dillard the Canyon had to wait; he trailed the longhorns down through it and out to the mountain-slope mesas where he put down his roots. But the Canyon entangled him eventually, after he was hostage to a family of loved ones. His son "married the enemy," Maxine Lowe, daughter of the killer of his wife's brother Cash Sampson.

As for the two men whose shoot-out made the Canyon famous in the West—flamboyant Ben Lowe and ex-lawman Cash Sampson—they might have lived to be old men if they had not been drawn into the Canyon vortex, where red walls crowded their long-sputtering quarrel into fierce explosion and a face-off over gun barrels.

But then they would not have become legend.

"That Canyon is nothing but a grave without a lid," said cowboy Bud Huffington. He was lamenting only the Canyon's distance in time and hard riding from Saturday night fun in town, but his words had prophetic weight—the Canyon's record of inexplicable deaths and disappearances is second only to that of its frayed marriages.

"Escalante Canyon is a hidden paradise, a ruby gem at the bottom of the world," wrote old Cap Smith in terms as flowery as the verses he carved on tombstones for Canyon people he outlasted.

If the Canyon seemed to pull people, it put up terrific resistance against their property. Sowbelly Barclay bought a triple-deck Studebaker wagon in town, hitched up, and set out to put it on the bottom of the Canyon.

"I don't know why Grandfather thought he had to have a wagon down there," Brown Blumberg said. "There was no kind of a road to run it on. But he plain stubborn did. When he got that wagon as far as the top of the Big Hill, he took it apart and packed the pieces down on muleback."

If it was difficult to get things into the Canyon, it was excruciating to get them out unless they had legs; consequently, most of what settlers managed to lug down is still there, witnessing to what they did and how they did it, as if they put yesterday away in a cellar to keep its flavor fresh for us to taste today.

Escalante is a crooked slot with gold at both ends, loose placer gold in gravel at the mouth, tight quartz-vein gold in granite at the head, and possibly several wagonloads of high-grade cached somewhere in the middle. Between gold and gold are strewn relics of all the other ways men have made livings, and tried to make fortunes in ventures ranging from a few setting hens, to a lot of bootleg liquor, to walking inventories of gold on the hoof, beef.

No one has ever neatened the Canyon. The leavings—ruins of buildings, antique machinery, Indian petroglyphs—are still lying around to be prowled and read like a diary in artifacts. But so powerful is the Canyon's own charisma, they are not clutter but accessories, as if a stately woman had put on a few inconspicuous ornaments.

The Canyon's walled-off wild freedom entranced whole generations of men, some to the exclusion of everything else, enslaving them. It entranced and made hostages of women (mainly through attachment to their men) and alienated others; the divorce and tacit separation record among Escalante families was high in an era when the frequency of divorce compared with the returns of Halley's Comet. As the years went on, the Canyon tended to become a world of bachelors, married or otherwise.

It has become a ghost world where almost nobody lives.

These are some of the people and places we will get to know down there. Our vehicle—whether auto or armchair—is equipped with a time machine (all books are time machines) that will unreel the story of each scene as we go. Without it you could travel from end to end of the Canyon, see the beauty and feel on your spirit the dark-bright brooding of its mood, but you could not by merely looking see the happenings that created the mood and keep it hanging there.

How, without our time-recapturing machine, could you know, seeing three remaining posts of a picket corral, that here a doctor making a house call swung down off his horse and with all goodwill, innocence, and the latest scientific breakthrough went into the house and killed a child?

Or how, without hearing the story, could you guess that one certain pinnacle of rock-capped mudstone—in this canyon bristling with pinnacles—leaning over the road like a boy in a tilted hat, is laughing at every government official who wheels by? Boy Rock is a secret joke, doing the laughing for poker-faced Canyon folks who protested in vain when forty years ago the government decreed Boy must be blasted down lest he topple and smash somebody passing along the safe, new road they were building into the Canyon.

Doing their official durndest, with diligence and dynamite, they couldn't budge him.

Carved into the lee slope of the Uncompahgre Plateau in western Colorado, Escalante Canyon is easy to find (though only recently easy to enter) and impossible to get lost in.

Nowadays you do not enter from the side, down the hanging ledges of the Big Hill, as Dillard and the longhorns did, but you still must descend almost a thousand feet to get into this hole. The graveled turnoff heads west from U.S. Highway 50 thirty miles south of Grand Junction. It is marked by a historical signboard briefly describing the 1776 expedition of the Spanish Fathers Escalante and Domínguez.

Most ghostly of all the Canyon's ghosts is the man for whom it is named. He never set foot in it. Likely some official belatedly decided something in the vicinity should be named for the famous man, but by then everything nearer his line of march had already been taken.

The next canyon to the north (inferior in size, history, scenery, and accessibility) is named for Escalante's companion and superior, Father Domínguez, leader of the year-long great circle exploratory journey now universally called the Escalante Expedition, though Father Escalante was merely journalist for the trip. This was not the first time in history that a ghostwriter took precedence over the real protagonist. Amerigo Vespucci, by writing about his travels, got the only two continents on a whole hemisphere of this globe named after him, though it was Columbus, not he, who first found the Atlantic crossing to India blocked by certain uncharted stretches of real estate.

The geological fun and games that made Escalante Canyon an underground island begin right here on the flats beside the historical marker.

To go down into Escalante Canyon you first climb uphill, from any side or any approach, even this approach via the Canyon's mouth; but in this case the rise is unimposing, a mere eighty-foot slope. Before starting up you cross an even less imposing dry wash over a small wooden bridge that is the acme of unimposingness. Take a look; nature is playing a joke on you! This dry wash in its flattish valley of scruffy sagebrush and mangy adobe clay, so small you could jump a horse across it, is the seam between two vast and very strange plateaus, the Uncompahgre and Grand Mesa, pushing the sky a mile higher on the west and on the east.

The seam parallels the highway for thirty miles, but nature has so thoroughly masked its drama in nonentity that millions of motorists have whizzed alongside it, and hundreds of cowboys have trailed cattle up and down it, never dreaming what they are looking at. Even the Gunnison River, whose course should cut along this seam line between the two mountain ranges it drains on either side, got off track and carved itself a 600-foot-deep detour swinging miles back into the Uncompahgre Plateau, and in doing so completed the isolation of the Escalante, cutting off access to the Canyon mouth.

Allowing for erosional give and take between the two formations, the dirt forming the west bank of the little dry wash is the sparkling gray-gold of disintegrated Dakota Sandstone, the stratum that tops the back slope of the Uncompahgre Plateau like tiles on a vast shed roof; and the dirt forming the east bank of the dry wash is the dull elephant-gray adobe of disintegrated Mancos Shale, bottom layer of Grand Mesa.

That's right, the top layer of the equally lofty Plateau goes under the bottom layer of Grand Mesa. Everything that is piled up to form the mile-high Mesa was once piled on top of the Plateau.

In his doctoral thesis geologist David Sinnock proposed a fabulous scenario for where all that dirt went to:

Eons ago the Uncompahgre River (including this stretch of the Gunnison), which now flows in a valley along the northeastern foot of the Plateau, once flowed in the same direction on the other side of that mountain, about where the San Miguel and Dolores rivers are now. Slowly the mountain lifted and tilted along the hundred-mile fault that forms its western edge; and without changing its northwest direction of flow, the river gradually slid sidewise down the mountain to where it is now, skinning off the mile-deep thickness of softer strata as it came, right down to Dakota Sandstone.

What geological drama!

And yet the process was so gradual that it probably was never perceptible; lift timed exactly with erosion kept climate, intricate features of stream and desert and forest, and the habitat of creatures in perfect concert all during the eons it took the river to get down here.

For all we know it may still be going on, the north-flowing river continuing its eastward slide until in the final act—still in the soft adobe-hill valley it brought with it all the way—it slams against the granite outer wall of the Black Canyon Uplift.

Beyond the rise the road turns and sags into an open palm of gulch that quickly becomes a fist of canyon, gouging down to river bottom and the mouth of Escalante Canyon beyond. It has no name.

Situated elsewhere, unsurrounded by spectacular variations of the perpendicular, such a gulch-canyon would be descriptively named and touted by chambers of commerce. Bookworm Gully?—for the way it bores down through the pages of rock formations?

The strata of the Uncompahgre Uplift slant toward you at the 4 percent grade maintained by Dakota caprock from top to bottom of the mountain; and since this is precisely the percent of tilt favored by mountain road builders, downgrade counters upgrade and you are scooting through the strata at the dizzy speed of some ten million years a second.

Below tawny sandstone is the Morrison Formation, whose colors —copper blue-greens, lavender-grays, and blood-purples—tell uranium prospectors when to get out of the pickup and start auscultating the heartbeat of the earth's bosom with their Geiger counters and scintillators. Theoretically, there should be uranium and jewel-quality opalized dinosaur bone here—elsewhere on the mountain there is plenty of both—but none so far has been found along the Escalante.

Or this gulch might be named Hanging Gardens for its desert rock-garden beauty. The sandstone ledges and dry waterfall tributaries vary from cream to ochre to gold and the purple-black of desert varnish. When the exposure is right the stones are velvet-flocked with brilliant turquoise and orange lichens—a protected species. Desert moss rock, requiring ages to develop, is under Bureau of Land Management restriction, as are the antelope that graze here.

Silhouetted along the rising skyline as the road descends, sheep-nibbled junipers strike oriental poses like bonsai trees. Significantly, there are no sheep-pruned trees in Escalante country. The war that raged throughout the West between cattlemen and sheepmen over grazing rights on public lands was fought here, too. The Night Raiders who slaughtered herds to keep sheep on this side of the river were Escalante men, among them Ben Lowe. And among the investigators of the killings was Cash Sampson.

According to when the rains come, or if they come, the desert rock garden blooms. Cacti in every shape of armored untouchableness from smug mammalian to gauche mule-ear suddenly flare into orgasms of accessibility; pink silk petals, yellow tissue and scarlet satin solicit caresses. Sego lilies flutter like pale kites on string-thin stems above the tops of sage that protects their succulence from grazers. Curving over rounded talus slopes, larkspur spills impossible convex pools of color reflecting the sky bluer than it is. If you own no cattle you can enjoy the beautiful deadly larkspur without rancor.

Or this access canyon might be named Gold Dust Gulch. The present road – last and least hazardous of five efforts to put wheels on the bottom of Escalante Canyon – is paved with gold, sort of. Its surface comes from a Highway Department gravel pit on a bench above the river, gravel that will show gold "colors" in every shovelful you pan out.

The gold was discovered even before the Utes were ousted in the fall of 1881. In those first weeks, after the Western Slope of the Rockies was opened to settlement, men went rooting and rummaging all over the landscape, trying to see what all there was in the land-grab package. Almost everything there was to discover got discovered in a matter of months.

Though the only mining ever done here was motor-powered, the gold was originally found in the good old traditional way in full formality of dirty beard, burro, shovel, and gold pan. But the early prospectors (illegal sooners) said "Giddap" in the same breath with "Eureka!" because this gold that gathers with such exciting glitter in the pan is flake gold, too light to settle behind the riffles in the water flow of the sluice box, or at least not in quantity enough to make the immense turnover of gravel pay out.

Goosefeather gold, they cussed it, and moved on to more tractable deposits.

But in the Great Depression – no jobs, no money, no welfare, and no hope – such gold-bearing gravels began to look better. It was rumored in the foodless cities that by working a ten-hour day, moving maximal tonnages of gravel to separate minimal ounces of gold, a man could make "eatin'" money, what with gold at thirty-two dollars an ounce – double what it was before government started manipulating it to make times better.

In the West, Depression-desperate men swarmed afoot out of the cities to these nonpaying goldfields—or swarmed all over any auto headed that way, pooling their pennies to buy gasoline. Using ingenuity and next to nothing else, they invented a variety of Rube Goldberg contraptions for separating gold from dirt, wet or dry.

Where there was no water, such as at Johannesburg in the desert north of Los Angeles, a kind of dry sluicing was devised to concentrate the percentage of gold to gravel before expending precious water on it.

A typical machine consisted of a naked Model T engine with one of its four piston rods somehow exposed from the motor block and rigged with levers, elbows, gears, or whatnot so that its stroke operated a slanting bellows twelve or fifteen feet long. The bellows was made of canvas over a wooden frame having cleats at spaced intervals across the top. On the downstoke of the piston the bellows filled with air, on the upstroke the air was expelled but not until after the pressure had bounced up the sags of canvas between the cleats. Each bounce lifted and jumped sand and gravel down to the next cleat. Hopefully, the gold, being heavier, would bounce less and tend to collect behind the cleats.

This was no labor-saving device. Gravel had to be dug and shovel-fed in a trickle onto the bellows at the upper end. At intervals the gravel behind the cleats was scraped into a gold pan and washed in the regular way, but in a tub of water hauled in for the purpose.

Here beside the Gunnison, water was not lacking. All you had to do was get some of the river up onto the bench where the gold is, or vice versa, and without using any nonexistent cash in the process.

Young Bert Shreeves remembers one attempt.

"It was in the early 1930's. Eight men went together on it. They couldn't raise the cash to pay the railroad to haul their equipment in, though the track runs right past the gravel points down there, so they came in over the top. There was no road down to the river from that side then, so they built their own, heaving rock off, and scraping a steep narrow shelf. You can still see the scar, too straight a slant for nature, on the far side of the gully from where the road is now.

"They had a stripped-down Star car. Put some short planks across the fenders in front, and more planks across the back behind the seat, and they hauled in pipe and three old car motors and three old pumps.

"They set the biggest motor on a pump down by the river—the

Denver & Rio Grande wouldn't let them dig under the track to lay their pipe, so they had to go upstream to the nearest trestle. That took about a quarter-mile more pipe, cutting their shoestring shorter. Even at thirteen cents a gallon, gas for the motors was hard-come money in those days.

"The gold gravel along the river here probably used to lay in a continuous bench, but gullies have come down through, cutting the bench into gravel points.

"Well, those fellows pumped the water up onto the first point, run it through their sluice box, corralled it in a pond in the flat below, where they had another pump and car motor to lift it onto the second point. They worked three points that way with the same water. Pretty ingenious.

"Only thing—the gold wouldn't settle in the riffle slots. That gold probably came all the way from lodes in the San Juan Range. A hundred miles of pounding between river rock had beat it thinner than tissue paper. It just floats right on off with the water."

Heading the project were Cy Reynolds and Bob Adams, and they did snare a little of that floating gold—$500 worth sent to the Denver mint. Reporting the results, they didn't complete the discouraging arithmetic: to get that $500 they had shoveled five thousand cubic yards of gravel.

Reynolds and Adams escaped the Canyon, getting out with all their gear, leaving not even the memory of their names in Canyon reminiscing. Gold diggers at the upper end of the Canyon, where gold hides in granite-fisted veins, didn't get away so easy; they left twenty-five summers of their lives buried in pits and tunnels.

And even the placer men had to have help to get out.

Bert Shreeves continues. "They loaded their pumps, motors, and all that pipe back onto their Star car. It didn't have the soup to pull that hill, so they hired me and my teams to drag it to the top."

After fifty years the two gravel points upstream still bear traces of the holes those men dug and curious bits of iron things they broke and discarded. The third sluice site has been swallowed in the maw of the highway gravel works.

These were not desperate men grasping at anything to feed hungry families—Escalante was no "foodless city." No one went hungry here in that or any other depression. The Escalante "hole in the earth" is also a hole in the climate, cupping summer earlier and later by nearly a month. In that climate cup they could grow almost everything they needed. What they could not provide they bartered for—a butchered pig for eyeglasses at the oculist's, a couple of chickens for getting a tooth pulled, three baskets of canning peaches for a subscription to the county paper, four bushels of wheat for a sack of flour at the flour mill.

But man does not live for bread alone—at least not since cash was invented, and pants pockets to jingle it in.

Bert Shreeves assisted a later assault on this gold.

"Upriver from the Escalante I bulldozed trail for a guy named Mallory that aimed to catch the gold on mercury-coated copper plates after he'd concentrated it in sluice boxes. I helped him get in, but I didn't help him get out, so I never did know how he fared except he didn't stay long."

The gold is still there; and when the precious metal recently reached $800 an ounce, several young prospectors (with de rigueur beards but with jeeps instead of burros) began poking around these gravel points on both sides of the river, looking for little pyramids of rock that might contain rusty old Prince Albert tobacco cans containing claim notices and poking into old records at the county courthouse for land that had been filed on so long ago it is petrified, with all its mineral rights intact.

Nothing came of it. They too drifted off and away, like goose-feather gold over the riffles.

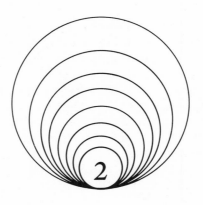

Only on Sunday

Coming down out of Gold Dust Gulch is like entering a roofless cathedral through a side transept. Beyond the great nave that is the larger Gunnison Gorge is the matching transept on the other side, Escalante Canyon.

The wide, still river dominates the Gorge floor. Wheels are rattling over crossing boards before the railroad track is noticed hidden in brush almost at water level.

It looks like a ghost track, the splintered plank crossing, the weathered X-ing sign, rabbitbrush and Mormon tea growing between the tie-ends; but this is one of the few railroads in the United States operating in black ink—black is the word; each train hauls a hundred cars of coal from Gunnison North Fork mines destined for steel mills in Utah and Japan and for power plants in California and Pennsylvania.

Even so, the coal trains are mere ghosts of the variety of life and life-stuff these rails carried when they linked ocean to ocean, yet accommodated the needs of a single settler.

One Escalante settler, Oscar Huffington, grew so many peaches the Denver & Rio Grande built siding and loading facilities here named for him, Huff Station.

Now the black trains, programmed only to origin and destination, streak by the canyon mouth oblivious. The power of their diesels, throbbing muffled and hidden, makes nothing of the difficult terrain that used to demand such a bustle of outer chuffing and clatter from steam locomotives. Engines signal the dirt-road crossing with four blasts of air-horn chords trying to imitate the long-drawn, lonely sound steam used to quaver in these echoing cliffs.

Clockwork ghosts. Each morning the trains go empty to the mines and come back filled in late afternoon. In the silence between their passings, in the heat and stillness of midday, the rails talk to themselves, iron molecules ticking as they expand, like Morse code messages from far away and long ago before telephone and wireless.

In those days a frequent passenger, watching these same cliffs-taluses slide by from coach or caboose window, was Cash Sampson. Any of a thousand flips of coin might have kept Cash Sampson and Ben Lowe from their fatal meeting in Escalante Canyon. One was a matter of inches on this very railroad, a few miles up the track.

If you stand between the rails and the faintly graded strip that is the ghost of Huff siding moled under grass, you see there would be exactly room for your body between two trains. To save right-of-way and grading costs, that strip of space is calculatedly narrow. Imagine train passing train, and you between. Throughout the clanging thunder, the earth-shuddering pound of track lifting and sinking beneath intermittent weight of the iron trucks, the dizzying flicker of cars and gaps flashing by less-than-elbow-length away, you would have to stand perfectly still to survive. Rail yard men spend their entire work lives in those inches.

The safe strip exists only as far as the two tracks are parallel; when the siding nears the switch joining it to the main line, the strip pinches off. Yardmen must know exactly how close to the end of the siding they can place freight cars and still clear a passing train.

Cash Sampson wasn't a railroad man, but as a lawman—Stock and Brand Inspector—he spent a lot of time on trains and in rail yards. His job was to discourage horse thieves and cattle rustlers by making sure animals loaded onto stockcars for shipment had matching brands and bills of sale.

On an April Sunday in Montrose, he had checked out a shipment of cattle and was looking forward to supper at the home of his pretty nieces, after a stop at the depot shoeshine stall to get the stockyard buffed off his boots. Though he worked with livestock (and consequently in manure) all his life, Cash Sampson was known as a fastidious man.

"Having finished his duties," the paper reported, "Mr. Sampson caught a passing freight car to ride to the depot, and was hanging to the ladder attached to the car. At a point near the end of the switch a freight car on the siding had been left standing too near the approach to the main line, the moving train only cleared the standing car by a foot."

The ladder cleared by less than that. Between iron ladder and boxcar, Cash Sampson was crushed the full length of his body.

They patched him up; he was a whole man when here in Escalante Canyon he took a small piece of metal in the skull.

For fifty years there were no roads down into the Gunnison Gorge. The train was the transportation in or out, or between the many points along it—mostly little homesteads on pockets of bottomland cut off from each other by cliffs thrusting sheer into the river. It was the servant of the people; anyone could flag it down. If a cow produced more butter than the farmwife needed, or if her hens laid excess eggs, she put the produce in an autographed crate beside the track; the train crew picked it up and dropped it off at the town depot. Collected by the general mercantile where she did business, its contents were credited to her annual account, and the crate returned on next day's train.

But to do this, if she lived over there in Escalante Canyon, she had to have a boat.

That the Gunnison River can now be crossed dry-wheeled without ford or ferry is not because the majority of Canyon settlers wanted a bridge.

For most of them the money crop was beef, a product that can get itself to market on its own feet (with a little prodding) over cliffs on trails originally laid out by deer and Indians. Early stockmen and the generation that came after them didn't need a bridge—nor the bothersome people that an easy road would bring.

People, cattlemen observe, contribute nothing but trouble on the range. Hunters mistake steers for deer; and hunters, sightseers, picnickers, and rockhounds seem to be innately unable to close gates they have opened.

Seeing a customarily closed gate standing open, cows do not merely settle down to eat grass on the other side but set out to explore. They can walk miles before their truancy is discovered, entailing the time cost of chasing them down and the cash cost of fines from unauthorized grass consumed on private or public lands.

Cattlemen's prejudice against people on the range was general throughout the West, tinged with schizophrenia, since they were also supposed to be the most hospitable people on earth. The bias was

Not for sixty years was there an easy-way bridge into the Canyon.

especially strong among stockmen inside the Canyon, which was obviously a kind of inverted castle created by act of God to keep cows in and people out.

The bridge is two black iron spans, one car wide, a rattling plank floor with spike heads standing up three inches to get a good look at your tires before taking a bite.

Just beyond is a legal document in the form of a tire hung on a post, stating in a circle of white letters that for the next several miles you will be traversing private property. Never mind. This road, the only passage up Escalante Canyon, has been used so long it is public thoroughfare. In this era of million-dollar law suits, the sign's chief purpose may be to clear Musser Brothers Cattle Company of charges of maintaining an attractive nuisance in case you can't resist fondling one of their cute baby calves and are mauled by its overprotective mother.

With some exceptions, the Escalante road passes through or beside Musser Brothers Cattle Company land all the way to its end. From the original Musser homestead up at the Forks, their land continues along the Spring Fork of the Escalante, and on up the mountain in a dotted line of isolated sections that give them cow-camp access to summer grazing on the vast plateau. This is the standing leg of the Musser holdings, which lie in a gigantic L upon the map. The bottom leg stretches down along the Gunnison River in a dotted line of ranches providing sheltered canyon-floor winter pasture as far as Bridgeport.

Eda Musser, 92, tiny matriarch of the family, explains the advantages of the layout and of staying with the old ways: "We can turn our cattle out onto public grazing—BLM [Bureau of Land Management] or National Forest—by merely opening gates. We can trail them to summer range on the mountain, and down to winter pasture by the river, without the expense of having them hauled back and forth in trucks twice a year, and without the risk of foot disease sometimes picked up in trucks used to haul other cattle. We don't even give rustlers the convenience of having cattle-loading chutes up there."

"Cattle rustling isn't dead, it's mechanized," explains the matriarch of another cattle family farther up the mountain. "They come in big semi-trucks by night, load up your cattle and sneak out. Our men have run onto them. So we carry guns, just like the old days, but in the pickups instead of saddle scabbards."

It has taken a hundred years and four generations for the Musser spread to reach its present size.

It began by accident and bad luck when the Canyon got its hooks into the original Musser through some lost cows he only half-owned in the first place.

A Virginian born in 1848, John W. Musser joined the Confederate Army when he was fifteen, served under General Jackson a year and a half—until the end of the war—and then began working his way westward along with other Confederate soldiers who like him found there was nothing left to go back home to. By the time he arrived in Denver he was 22, had learned how to make carriages and wagons, and how to run a business of his own.

When gold and silver were discovered in the San Juan range of southern Colorado, Musser and partner moved their smith-foundry business into boomtown Silverton and repaired ore cars for the mines. This was so profitable he was able to buy half-interest in a silver mine in nearby Howardsville. Then when Leadville mines hit an even bigger boom, he set up in business there without giving up his interests in the San Juans. By then he was thirty and had acquired a family—two children, a beautiful though fragile wife, Anna, and a lovable though feckless brother-in-law, R. S. Kelso.

Once gold and silver had been discovered in the San Juans, it was unthinkable that Ute Indians should keep that part of their immemorial domain. The treaty of 1873 took care of that. Then it was unthinkable that the broad, farmable valleys of the Colorado, Gunnison, and Uncompahgre rivers should belong to savages who were doing nothing with them but graze spare ponies. The Utes (for whom ponies, and ponies only, were wealth) refused to discuss this matter; but as luck would have it, a few hothead braves, staging a fatal demonstration at Meeker Indian Agency one mountain range north of the Escalante, provided pretext for treatying the entire tribe out of the remainder of their domain.

Campfires of the Ute exodus were still warm when adventurer R. S. Kelso came riding into the newly opened Reservation. A first-comer, he could have had his pick of level, stone-free valley farmland along any of the three great river systems. Instead he chose a cliff-girt rubbly homestead in upper Escalante Canyon. Not that the Canyon, its beauty and mood, had their hooks in R. S.—nothing ever had hooks in that quicksilver man, not even the rich widow whom he married late in life and who adored him to the end of their days together.

Immediately, while still living in a tent and cooking on a campfire, R. S. Kelso began writing glowing letters to brother-in-law John Musser about the fabulous opportunities of the open range he saw from where he was sitting. Vast, wide-open public grazing lands, hundreds of thousands of acres of free grass! All a man had to do to get rich was put a herd out to graze and stand back from the increase. No backbreaking farm labor involved, and hardly any money.

On the strength of the letter, John Musser sold his half-interest in the silver mine and staked R. S. and partner Cole to the equivalent in cows. Kelso and Cole's share in the partnership was to ride herd on the investment and brand the interest as it compounded.

Letters from R. S. ceased to glow, then ceased to come.

Finally, in response to Musser's prodding, R. S. wrote, "We can't pay you, but you can have the cattle."

That was three years later. By then there was a town thirty miles from the Canyon, a railroad through the town, and a livery stable near the boxcar that served as depot. Musser rented a horse and went to take possession of his cows. They were scattered all over the mountain and had not seen a caretaker cowpuncher in so long they fled the sight.

At thirty-five, Musser faced a life-fulcrum decision: to stay in business, writing off the money invested in cattle as total loss (there was then no income tax to make it profitable to take a loss); or sell the Leadville business and save his sideline investment by devoting himself personally to the culture of cows. Being a businessman, he opted for the latter—only the Leadville half of his assets could be liquidated for cash. Thus John W. Musser became an Escalante stockman, an occupation he disliked all his life, as he made clear when at sixty-four he laid the burden on his sons.

The Musser family arrived at the top of the Big Hill in spring of 1886. As was customary before starting down, John dismounted to tighten cinches all around, making sure saddles and packs would not slip down onto the horses' necks during the descent and frighten them into bucking or bolting on the narrow ledges. The two small children, Edith and Albert, were stuffed into panniers on either side of a trusted packhorse; month-old baby Don rode in his mother's arms on a pillow to protect him from the ramming lurch of the pommel as the horse stiff-legged it down the steep trail.

Their destination was 160 acres and a dirt-floor, dirt-roof log cabin John built for them up at the Forks.

R. S. Kelso was around somewhere. In addition to filing in the upper Canyon, he had taken up winter-graze land along the river and was improving it but not at a killing pace, as the paper noted later that same year:

"R. S. Kelso has finished hewing another log for his new house down on the Gunnison. If his health holds out and we have an open winter, he will have at least ten logs ready by spring. R. S. is a terrible worker when he gets started."

After that first homestead, the Musser family landholdings were acquired piece by piece over the years, some in bad times when the land was going for back taxes, some at such expense and hairline financial risk that the family ate and sent their children to school on life insurance loans.

The ranches were acquired principally for the public grazing rights they carried.

During the first twenty-five years of open grazing, the mountain was eaten to death because unlimited numbers of cattlemen could graze unlimited herds of cattle on it. Then to save the range the government set up ground rules: A man could graze no more cows on top in the short summers than he owned range and feed for down in the valley during the long winters. These numbers are a fixed ratio, and were all spoken for from day one. To enlarge the herd grazing on the lush spring grass of the National Forest, a stockman must buy somebody else's ranch with its concomitant grazing right.

Any improvements that came with the ranch, other than hay-fields, canals, and corrals, were useless to a buyer whose facilities were already adequate. In other regions unneeded structures were leveled to enlarge hay acreage or prettied up for dude occupants. But not here. The Musser Brothers felt no compulsion to neaten their acquired ranches by tearing down pioneer buildings and hauling ancient machinery to the dump. Anyhow, they had more work than they had hours for just keeping cows out of trouble. As a consequence, this Canyon is rich in remains of other days that like place markers in a book remind us where to turn for favorite stories.

Some of these stories are here where the road divides just beyond the small bridge over the Escalante.

On the knob between the two bridges is the present headquarters of Musser Brothers Cattle Co., moved from the original homestead at the Forks to this strategic elbow in the L of Musser holdings. To distinguish it from their other ranch sites, the Mussers call this place the Windy, ostensibly because of its position in the draft of transecting canyons, but really for a cowboy teller of tall tales known as Uncle Windy (another Canyon "in" joke that presumably Uncle Windy himself was never in on).

Added to as needed, the ranch spread—house, barns, sheds, corrals, chutes, haystackers—spills downhill and up again, culminating in a long shed dug into the crest of another barren knob along the river. Ribbed skeleton on a naked hill, it looks like the Ark stranded on Mt. Ararat, but it is actually a drive-in feed-pellet cellar that has gone into old age in an interestingly unfinished state. Like the ranch-lands and the spread, the Big House at the Windy is an accretion. All that is recognizable of the original house is one small dormer, peeping out from the piled and spreading additions like a bird's head from a swallow nest.

If you had come by last Branding Sunday you'd have seen all the Mussers—third-generation brothers Tom and Jack, Jack's wife, Bernice, and their son, Johnnie, who with his wife, Vicki, and their two small children lives in the modern ranch-style on the opposite knob.

Musser Big House and part of ranch spread at the Windy.

All the Mussers, that is, but matriarch Eda, who these days is as translucently delicate as egg-shell porcelain and lives at the family place in town.

That Sunday they were branding calves in the hay meadow below the house. They and a lot of their friends.

It used to be that ranchers gathered to exchange sweat-work at haying time, when big crews were also needed. But these days hay is harvested by one man piloting an immense high-masted craft that, careening up and down the field while he listens to rock music in air-conditioned comfort, cuts, chews, and all but predigests the hay as it goes.

But nobody has yet devised a way of getting hundreds of range-wild calves branded without a large branding crew. Nor any good substitute for the hot iron.

"We tried other ways of marking calves, chemicals that are supposed to be more humane," Bernice Musser says, "but nothing else is permanent enough."

As the cattle industry becomes mechanized, as big ranches absorb smaller ones, fewer and fewer cowboys are needed, and it becomes harder and harder to assemble enough range-trained cowmen for infrequent tasks that require this kind of skilled teamwork. "We brand only on Sunday now," Bernice says, "because it takes a lot of men, and Sunday is the only time they can get away from the office."

A retired district judge who grew up on a cattle ranch in the Escalante, a CPA who was born here, a vice-president of a city bank who spent the summers of his college years working cattle on this ranch, a college student who will be earning summer money that way this year, a college professor, an old cowboy for whom the highlight of his retirement years is these Sundays in spring. A dozen men or so.

Unpaid—they would scorn pay—they are here because they want to be, because this is the life they grew up with, love, and rarely get to experience anymore. And because they are needed: without them the job could not be done. That is the salt that makes the pleasure more than play, and savors the genuine weariness at the end of their donated day.

Branding day is a social event. Friends and relatives, after leaving cakes and pies at the Big House, congregate at the meadow edge. Young wives and children make a grandstand of the steep bank under the ditch-side cottonwoods; grandmothers watch from the upholstered comfort of the pickups. Spare mounts graze, saddled and ready, tethered only by dropped reins.

Driven by four riders, the herd of cows with calves comes trailing up from the river, through the trees and into the lower end of the meadow. A few hundred feet from the strange and obviously dangerous goings-on at this end of the meadow, the string of cattle flattens into a wall of apprehensive faces, staring and bawling at pickups, people, and branding paraphernalia.

The wall of cow faces stays just that far all day. Men and horses doing the holding need work only the far side and flanks of the bunch. Even so, holding is no job to fall asleep at. The trick, as the hours drag on, is to stay alert, not only to forestall any animal attempting to break out but to notice it as soon as the horse does, because the horse, trained to spot any critter with escape on its mind, will lunge in any direction—quick, sudden, and regardless of whether the rider is still aboard.

By turns two ropers ride into the bunch, lay loop on a calf and drag it out across the empty space between herd and branding setup —on its feet if it wants to come that way, on knees or rump if it doesn't. While the horse holds the rope taut, two men grab the calf's off-side legs, flip it onto its side; six hands and a couple of knees hold it down while one man runs the brand with a red-hot iron, another marks the ears, and a third injects blackleg vaccine. Thin blue smoke and stink of burning hair trail across the grass.

In seconds it's all over, the calf is up and running for the bunch and mama, consoling himself at the teat while she smells him over to see what the damages are. Meanwhile another calf is being dragged up at the end of another rope.

Just like old times, except that the branding irons are not heated in an open fire of cedarwood or sage, but in a barbecuelike "stove" on legs, torched from a tank of propane gas; and except that most of the men who are doing this arduous, sweaty, dung-dusty work are desk men and college graduates; and except that some of the cows were rounded up by helicopter last fall. Well, not rounded up—located. Johnnie Musser explains, "After the main roundup I hire a helicopter for one day to spot where the straggle-bunches are. Saves two weeks of horseback time."

The roped calves come yelling, no two voices alike though the word BAWH! is always the same. Given but one syllable of sound they make a language of it—outrage, terror, appeal. Right behind each calf comes the mother. Daring the fear that keeps the bunch as far away from all this as the flanking riders allow, she dashes forward alone, her nose low and close to her dragging baby, bawling something at him all the way—advice? comfort? support?

There is no coward cow. After each calf the frantically solicitous mother. This is how, throughout the history of the cattle business, punchers knew what brand to put on a calf found on open range. Any calf that got past weaning without receiving his mother's brand was anybody's property.

Most of these cows are not first-calf heifers. They've been through this before. If they have memory, they know what the ordeal is, that it is brief, and that the calf comes out OK. They do, indeed, have memory; cows know where a salt block was last year in the woods— three ridges up, two streams over. If it's not there this year they stand around and talk about it loudly. Each new calf, it seems, comes with its own personal package of blind maternal anxiety.

Behind every unwilling calf comes the anxious mama.

How much does branding hurt? Nobody knows what pain actually is for another creature, of course, but Jack Musser says, "If you can go by how they act afterward, by whether it sets them back in their growth, branding isn't all that bad. They're up and bouncing. But if it rains and the hair is wet, the hot iron makes steam and will raise blisters that become bad sores." He motions at the sky, "If those clouds start to spill, we'll stop branding.

"Dehorning, now, that does set a calf back. Droops around. Won't eat. Even when the horn is just a little button too small to see. So we don't dehorn until they are bigger and can take it better." Since the Mussers' chief product now is breeding stock, bull calves are spared the pain and indignity of castration.

The grandstand audience on the ditch bank is watching for bits of "rodeo" to applaud or razz. They get a little.

From time to time a calf breaks out of the bunch and streaks off across the meadow with a horse streaking just behind. The old rider, Judge Kelly Calhoun, floats above the saddle—not rump-high like a jockey, but tall and graceful, taking up the motion between boots and body through the shock-absorbing pistons of thigh and shank muscles. Unyoung legs that learned this skill sixty years ago. At breakneck speed the horse angles across the hard dry alfalfa furrows as surefooted as if this were a racetrack, without stumbling or breaking rhythm; the everyday marvel of how a horse knows at high speed on uneven terrain where each of his four feet will hit ground. The horses so obviously enjoy these chases that one wonders if they don't shirk their boresome holding duties now and then, letting a calf slip out on purpose.

Young John Calhoun's horse gets the rope under its tail and starts bucking toward the photographer, who takes to the bank, giving the bronc all the room he wants.

Weather and calves come out even.

The ropers have been threading the bunch for minutes on end, finding no calf unbranded, when the first shower comes squalling down over the west rim of the canyon, scuffing up dust where hooves have cut through alfalfa, and splatting it down again with dollar-size drops.

Spectators scurry for the pickups and jolt across the meadow to the corrals to put shelter and transportation ready when the men have unsaddled and shed chaps and spurs. In the Big House, crew and spectators gather around the long table for cake, coffee, and ribbing reruns of the unintentional rodeo incidents.

"Did you notice the photographer didn't stick around to get the best shot of the day, a close-up of John's horse bucking?"

And Harry Lane, waving a cup of coffee, "Been branding your calves all day, and all you give me is light beer!"

Small children dart in and out, frisking, snatching nibbles, flexing new ego muscles by pestering rises out of their mothers. Like baby calves. The fifth generation of Escalante Musser men bangs his highchair with a spoon.

The Big House at the Windy is Bernice Musser's domain. Just as ranch women did in the old days—just as her mother-in-law, Eda, did—she provides meals for nonresident Musser kin, ranch hands, and outriding cowboys who live at distant cabins but happen in at mealtime, for cattle buyers and their wives from all over the western half of the United States, for Forest Service and BLM officials passing through, and for anybody else who drops in for business or friendship.

Within a few minutes she can supply food enough for a dozen at a table previously set for herself and Jack alone—though the latter rarely happens in the kind of Grand Central Station the Windy is.

Bernice can accomplish these logistical feats with only an old wood-fired range, and does so when the men are working one of the outlying ranches, doing roundup, dehorning, or medicating chores. But here at the home ranch she has every modern convenience—electric range, microwave oven, dishwasher, and opulent refrigerator and freezer space.

She cans and freezes fruit, bakes bread, cakes, cookies, and pies for the "old batch" hands to carry back to their cabins, and takes them herself to the ones she worries about, old men who have worked Musser cattle all their lives. She is errand girl and messenger between the widespread segments of the ranch because, though the power line extends a few miles farther into the Canyon, the telephone line stops here.

Bernice's kitchen is surrounded on three sides by living and lounging space. Broadsiding the end is a hall-like room big enough to make easy seating around an almost infinitely extendable dining table. Across a working counter stretches what in most homes would be the family room, but here where "family" includes friends, employees, and clients, there are enough sofas and lounge chairs to furnish a small hotel lobby. Opening from this is the mudroom, where men coming in from corral and range shed dirt in the shower, and dirty clothes in the automatic washer. Here on winter days they repair tack, littering the floor with saddles, bridles, and chaps being patched up. Here are sheltered calves born too weak to last through their first raw spring night outside.

Just off the kitchen is a small room that was the parlor of the original house—Jack Musser's favorite place after supper, boots off and feet up, in the depths of a leather chair. "If a cowboy hasn't beat him to it," Eda says with a mother's concern for the wear and tear a cattle spread this size inflicts on the men who both manage it and work it.

At hand are the publications that keep him abreast of the cattle business, though most of his know-how has come from experience. After high school Jack went off to Ag college to learn the latest theories in large-scale ranching, but the theories proved so irrelevant to Canyon facts that he packed up and came home early in his freshman year.

"Professor pointed out a plant he said no cow would eat, or if one did it would kill her. Well, maybe so, up there on the high plateaus. But I knew our cows got fat grazing that very plant, so I figured school didn't have a lot that would be much help down in the Canyon."

The bunkhouse at this ranch is simply the second floor of the main house, a long hall with bedrooms and dorms in all directions. "Seemed homier," Bernice explains the unusual arrangement, "and easier to heat than a separate bunkhouse."

Beyond the lounge room is the ranch office. This too is Bernice's domain. Women of the Musser family began managing the financial end of Musser Brothers Cattle Co. when the brothers were second-generation Don (John II) and Kelso. Eda explains how she got the job: "Local banks were in trouble, some failing, and the Musser Brothers account came up a thousand dollars short. Don and Kel had been too busy with ranch work to keep track. Since I was living in town to put the children in school and would be there to keep an eye on the bank, they suggested I take over the checkbook."

From keeping tabs on the bank, paperwork ballooned as income tax returns, government regulations, employee withholding and work records multiplied. Eda was still managing the business into her seventies when, having taught Bernice the ropes, she retired. The work became even more complex when Musser Brothers (now third-generation brothers Jack and Tom) turned from beef production to growing breeding stock with attendant breeding records to keep. In turn, Bernice is teaching the job to *her* daughter-in-law, Vicki.

Musser women are not exceptional in this; in many cattle families it is the wife who manages the money. Eda explains: "Cattlemen are too busy on the range to make the trip to town for every little thing, so they send their women. Pretty soon the dealers, the commission houses, and the banks know the faces and signatures of the women better than the men's. So it's the women who arrange a loan, buy another truck or tractor, decide whether heifers can be held for breeding or must be sold as beef for needed cash.

"The men will have their eye on a section of land, but they'll have to ask the women if the outfit is in a financial position to borrow and buy it."

Bernice's office is small, wall-to-wall desks and files with barely swivel-chair-rolling room, but modern.

It is unreal to look across an electronic keyboard—rows of buttons ready to supplement the brain—to the cactus-talus cliffs beyond the river where nothing has changed since pre-Indian people searched out sandy pockets in the red rocks for the forked-root datura plant that supplements the brain and makes a man think like a god.

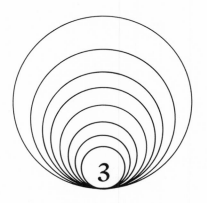

The Make-Do Trap

The man who homesteaded the cliff-walled meadowlands at the mouth of the Escalante was named Mow. Nothing is left of him except some paragraphs in the "locals" columns of 1890s newspapers, but they reveal this farmer as an expert PR man.

A gimmick of the day to get free advertising for farm or orchard produce was to take a sample to the newspaper office. If the offering was ears of corn, the editor displayed them in the window for a time then took them home to feed his chickens (everybody had chickens, even editors); if the "gift" was perishable, such as a peck of peaches, he rushed it home to be eaten or canned at once. In any case, he wrote it up. And because getting more such gifts to eke out the slim editorial livelihood of those days depended on pleasing the giver, the write-ups were flattering—but carefully short of an ultimate superlative from which the editor would have to back off the next time something nice came his way: "Some of the largest peaches we have ever seen. . . . Among the finest ears of corn ever grown in this valley." Qualifiers such as "some of" and "among" were editorial cop-outs as useful as today's "alleged."

Many growers took advantage of this free publicity, but Mow more than anyone except Old Bert Shreeves up the creek, whose region-wide reputation for raising, butchering, and curing the best pork stemmed from mouth-watering descriptions of hams and sausage he left on the editorial desk at frequent intervals. All this mutually profitable symbiosis went on under the virtuous banner of boosterism—

touting the prodigal productivity of the newly opened Indian lands in order to draw more settlers.

"Mr. Mow," the paper said in 1897, "whose ranch is at the mouth of Escalante brought to this office a sample of peaches which are as fine as anything we have ever tasted. The fruit is exceptionally large though the unthinned crop is so heavy the trees must be propped to keep them from breaking—which speaks volumes for the rich soil and benign climate in our area."

Mow had a family to help him with the decade of labor it took to make productive, level farm acreage out of the hummocky, rocky flats between creek and taluses. We don't know how many children he had or who they were, except that one of them was a child they called Lovey. Lovey was probably not her real name, but with the Canyon's proclivity for inflicting nicknames and making them stick for life, she would likely have failed to answer to anything else.

Lovey married her way out of the Canyon; she might better have stayed.

By hook, crook, or irrefutable fact Mow got undiluted superlatives out of the newspaper in 1898: "the biggest finest peaches we ever saw." And at least by 1899 he had peaches to ship: "Mr. Mow of Escalante Canyon has his orchard loaded with peaches and has begun shipment."

A peach is about as fragile as a flower; for shipping it must be chilled quickly and kept that way. To supply "icebox" cars for Mow's peaches and apricots—and those of George Palmer and other growers along the river—the D&RG built an icehouse and whistle stop named Palmer just north of the mouth of Escalante Creek. (This was so many decades before Huff siding was built that people had forgotten peaches could be a money-maker in the Canyon.) There is nothing whatever to show for Palmer now except delicate ink lettering on an ancient map, "Ferry Ice House."

The barnlike, unpainted bulk of the icehouse was situated between tracks and river beside a shallow pond that would freeze thick and refreeze quickly, providing a continuous harvest during the weeks of deepest winter. But here in the Canyon, the days of deepest winter proved too few for profitable ice harvesting, and soon the icehouse was being stocked with blocks of cold shipped down from ponds nearer the top of the ever-winter Contintental Divide.

While it lasted, the work of putting up D&RG ice brought des-

This meadow was orchard when Lovey picked peaches and planned her escape.

perately needed cash to the river-flats people. Standing on the ice in boots wedged with two or three pairs of wool socks, men worked in their shirtsleeves, and worked up a sweat, whipping long saws through fourteen to twenty inches of rock-hard crystal. Other men with teams (earning a dollar a day more) grappled and heaved the sawed blocks onto sleds and across horse-stained snow to the ice-house ramps. Inside, the large chunks were packed in enough insulating sawdust to carry a paying remainder through to midsummer fruit harvest.

   People were still "putting up ice" long after a Delta bottler named Snow in 1910 was advertising (with appropriate puns on his name) mineral and carbonated waters that were extra cold because chilled by a newfangled ice machine. If "artifical" ice had not been invented, and if we today had no other way to cool our July lemonade than by putting chunks of sawed-up January river in it, we would have to drink it warm. It is now impossible to put up a summerful of ice from the winter river. Ever since the big dams were built on the Gunnison, the river that each winter froze over so man and beast could walk across, now at winter's coldest carries only floe slush picked up from its banks and tributaries. BuRec [Bureau of Reclamation] engineers say the temperature of water coming from the bottom of Blue Mesa Dam does not vary more than four degrees winter and summer, extending the chilly habitat preferred by trout many miles down the formerly warm rivers.

Instead of freezing over in cold weather the river now fogs over as evaporation from the warmer water hits frigid air and floors Gunnison Gorge with a hover of cloud.

The cloud hugs the river, and moves with it. If on such a windless, super-cold morning you were to stand on the Dominguez Rim there overhead, you would be looking down many hundreds of feet upon a river of mist moving downstream in a slow, mysterious, and apparently causeless flow. At intervals where a rapids or gravel bar churns the current, bringing a pocket of warmer water to the surface, little spurts of cloud rise, reaching and tossing pillars of gauze into the upper air. These tall, writhing ghosts remain in place with the flow, marching one after another through the twists of the Gorge and around the bend out of sight.

Mow was an experimenter. Given a piece of ground that had never felt plow or conceived alien seed, and a hothouse pocket of climate, he tried everything—peanuts, tobacco, figs—stretching the climate to the limit.

He wasn't alone. Like kids with a new box of Tinker Toys, first settlers in the brand-new land tried to see what all they could make of what was in it, especially settlers in the Canyon, where it was so hard to bring things in from the outside. Noting that greasewood catches fire from a match, they tried extracting oil from it for their lamps. Observing that Indians used the milky juice of rabbitbrush for chewing gum, they tried making rubber of it. With deer and elk skins for the taking, and little money for buying leather, they tried tanning hides with the native plant canaigre and found it produced a surprising kind of leather. "It is impossible to burn leather that has been tanned with canaigre," reads one glowing editorial—for, of course, Mow and the others brought samples of their experiments to the newspaper.

But Mow's specialty, at the mouth of the Escalante, was being earliest: "April 23, 1899. Mr. Mow reports potato plants up and cabbage plants set out. Apricots as big as peas, peaches and pears in full bloom. Sheltered from cold winds his crops are fully two weeks earlier than elsewhere."

In full bloom.

This was the summer Lovey Mow turned seventeen. Lovey, who was to enact in person what is nowadays regarded as the most stereotypical melodrama of turn-of-the-century sentimentality: "Father, dear Father, come home to me now."

You would think she might have been consciously or unconsciously dramatizing the romantic novels of the time, but the toil devolving on all family members in making desert into farm would have left few moments for so useless a thing as reading stories. Rather, her tragedy seems to bear out the truth on which the stereotype was based—the helpless dependency of the female of those days on whatever man controlled her life—the father from birth, the husband from the marriage contract, which was her only option.

At seventeen Lovey married outside the Canyon. A few years and three children later she was living in a cattle-timbering-mining town on the other side of the mountain.

On a raw March day, following God knows what wrongs suffered, inflicted, or imagined, she went into the mine-town saloon, shawl over her head, just as in the stories. The newspaper account has the full flavor of the era:

Whiskey and Gambling Ruin Once Happy Home.

"Won't you come home to me and the children, dearie? The baby is sick, and I am tired out."

Placing her arms around her husband's neck, the young and pretty wife begged him to leave the saloon of Robert Bertie at Placerville where he was playing poker, and go home with her.

The man had been drinking, and his wife's interruption angered him. He shoved her away, and told her to go back to her children and not bother him any more.

Tears welled in her careworn eyes. She said not a word more, but slowly turned from the card table, drew a large revolver from under the faded shawl she wore to protect her from the cold, pressed the muzzle against her left breast and pulled the trigger.

She fell to the floor in a heap, with blood gushing from her breast. The bullet would have been almost instantly fatal had it not struck a rib and deflected upward.

This was her second visit to the saloon that afternoon to coax her husband to come home. He repulsed her each time. After the first visit, she returned home, took her baby to the home of her mother-in-law, secured a revolver and made her last trip to the saloon to induce her husband to come home."

Lovey did not die. Cash Sampson, who had stock to inspect in the cattle-mining town where she was hospitalized, reported to the papers that Lovey was "expected to recover from the suicide attempt."

In the course of a decade of dealing with horse thieves and rustlers, Cash Sampson doubtless saw, endured, and delivered considerable violence and mayhem. It is a clue to the man— who seemed to be all surface, so carefully did he guard whatever was beneath— that the only instance of violence he ever noted, at least in print, was in the life of a young woman.

And for once newspapers mentioned Cash Sampson without making a joke about him.

Bachelors were standard joke material for newspapers of those days, right up to and including the wedding night, after which the benedicts were off limits, editors evidently believing that outright marriage was no joke.

Cash Sampson was not only a bachelor, but a bachelor who notoriously liked women—in a ubiquitous, chivalrous sort of way. He made good copy.

"Cash Sampson, stock inspector, went up to Telluride this week, having been attracted by the schoolmarms in attendance at the teachers' institute which opened Monday."

"Cassius Clay Sampson came in on the Sunday evening train from Gunnison, accompanied by his pretty nieces Eliza and Jessie who were attending State Normal."

"Sheriff Cash Sampson was somewhere last week. Don't know where, but as usual he came home on the train with a lot of ladies. Once upon a time, it is chronicled in Holy writ, a man by the name of Sampson got into trouble though chatting with a lady."

Mow sold out to a man named Miller, about whom little is known except that he built his house too well and in the wrong place.

Like Mow he used what was at hand. We tend to think of all pioneers as living in log cabins; and they did if there were suitable trees nearby—straight trees, long on taper and slender of butt. Here at the bottom of the Gunnison Gorge the only trees were cottonwoods, crooked, big butted, contrary to the ax, and loaded with tons of water. Cut green, a cottonwood log takes a year to lose

Weighted with tons of water, cottonwoods sag as they age.

enough sap so a man can heave it around; cut dry (dead), it is rotten.

When Mow had been homesteading, the handiest building material was railroad ties, so his family dwelling was "a string of tie sheds."

At that time the D&RG was moulting railroad ties like a spring chicken. The line had been put through in such a hurry, in trying to beat the Union Pacific to the West Coast, that most of the track and all the bridges had to be rebuilt immediately. Furthermore, the Gorge itself was still in an unstable uproar over having its supporting taluses cut through by rails and at frequent intervals sent down rock and mud slides to bury the tracks, or simply pushed the whole she-bang into the river. At two cents a tie it was cheaper to haul in new than retrieve the old.

Railroad ties came already squared up. All you had to do to build a house was lay them up like extra-long bricks and toenail them together here and there. No cracks to chink; a nice flat inside wall for the wife to pretty up with wallpaper if you could afford it, with pasted sheets of newspaper if you couldn't.

But the tie house has no class. Then as now a dwelling built of railroad ties definitely has a wrong-side-of-the-tracks ambience. Scorning Mow's tie-shed dwelling, Miller set about building a real house. What he used for construction material was even more abundant and handy–rocks. He was the first of at least four men the Canyon got its hooks into through the beauty, utility, or simple ubiquity of its stone. He built his house here against the lavender-gray bluff above the branding meadow. The spill of flat rocks bulldozed away when the downriver road was put through, one corner of a doorframe held together with handwrought square nails, are all that's left of it.

By choosing this rocky slope, leaving that much more of the limited flatland for farming, Miller seems a very foresighted man, seeing a hundred years ago what developers are still blind to: that you can grow a house anywhere, but in the West crops will grow only where land is flat enough to run irrigating water. Actually, Miller wasn't looking farther than the length of his arm. He put the house where the rock was handiest–smack against the bluff.

The cliff slant that forms this part of the west Canyon wall is made of miserable stuff that can't decide whether to be rock or dried mud. With bare hands you can pry out pieces of flat rock strata from the soft dirt matrix, and that's what Miller did. For the back wall, especially, he merely had to turn, pull out a rock, turn back, and lay it up in moistened mortar made of the same sticky stuff that was holding the rock together in the hill itself.

It was a pleasant house, four rooms and loft room. Deep windows, a fireplace, and a porch out over the hill slope, providing space under its floor for saddles and gear or a playhouse where on bad days you could get the children out of the house without getting them into the weather. It was billed as the only house in the Canyon with running water. That's how Canyon folks described it to strangers, straight-faced. Come a good thunderstorm (at least twice a summer), water poured down the bluff and straight through the house, depositing a gluey layer of lavender-brown clay before sheeting in a mudfall off the front porch.

It takes a long time to build a four-room rock house single-handed, more than one summer. That mudfall must have swept through the unfinished walls and doorways several times between the laying of the first row of rocks and the capping of the window lintels. Miller, trapped by the labor already invested, went right on laying rocks and laying up trouble for himself and three-quarters of a century of future owners.

Miller himself left before long. He may have moved out of the

Canyon because he couldn't move his house—if you build a house out of rock, especially with mud mortar, you'd better put it in the right place because you don't stand much chance of changing your mind. Next to a cave, a rock house is the least portable dwelling devised by man.

Occupying the house after Miller was Bob Shreeves. This was when the Shreeves family, headquartered upcanyon, as we shall see, was homesteading and putting together its own cattle outfit and had kinfolks living in strategic cabins all up and down the Escalante and the mountainside.

Bob Shreeves was a bachelor when he first lived here, minding the family herds in winter and irrigating the orchards and hayfields in summer. He was probably not too perturbed by what the bluff intermittently did to the house. Not being indoctrinated in the feminine fetishes of mop, soap, and wax, he could do a passable job of removing the alluvium by sluicing the place out with buckets of water from the nearby irrigation ditch.

At least he kept the floor clean enough to dance on.

From time to time, to repay his social obligations, Bachelor Bob would throw a dance, issuing wholesale invitations by word of mouth and rounding up some music—fiddle, guitar, banjo, accordion, whatever was not riding herd on the mountain or serving time in jail. Refreshments other than coffee were not his concern; males who wanted anything stronger than coffee brought their own bottle to share, and females arrived with cake or pie in hand.

His dances were popular. People came not only the length of the Canyon but all the way from town by train, getting off on the far side of the river and being ferried across in Bob's rowboat. After they had danced till dawn, he rowed them back again.

It was customary to bring a bit of string and a fishhook to Bob Shreeves' dances, so you could get in some fishing while waiting to flag down the morning train. River willows supplied the poles, and an impromptu campfire took off the morning chill.

To this house Bob's nephew Young Jack Shreeves brought his bride, Velma Bowen, who, even while doing her share of woman's ranch work, found time for a hobby that was most untypically nonutilitarian and in later years brought her fame in its field—antique dolls. If she started her collection during the thirteen years they lived here in the "only house in Escalante Canyon with running water," she must have been hard put to keep the dolls—the satin-gowned Presidents' Ladies and the bare-naked Kewpies—dry and unbedraggled.

"It was terrible when that soupy water came through the house, you couldn't dam it off or stop it, just get up onto something and watch it go through. But it was worse if you weren't there. Jack and I usually spent the summers at the Shreeves' cow-camp cabin up on the Plateau, and most of the cloudbursts came while we were gone. We'd come back to find the floor deep with dried mud. Hard as brick. You'd chip and scrape at it for days to get it up."

Eventually so much of the bluff had washed down and away that the house no longer stood smack against it, and the play space under the porch had silted up to the floor joists.

After the financial stringencies of putting together the family cattle outfit slacked off (and during one of the periods when no depression was raging in the world outside), Jack Shreeves offered to build Velma another house. He asked her where she wanted it put —the Shreeves clan by that time having just about their pick of river and mountainside.

"Anywhere water can't reach!"

So the snug little wooden house with its bird's-head dormer was perched high and dry on a knob between river and creek: the Windy, the nucleus around which the Musser Brothers Cattle Co. Big House accreted.

Here at the mouth of Escalante Creek you are surrounded by weird land surveying. Look north and you are staring into a township—six miles square—that except for its northwest corner doesn't jibe with anything else on the map of North America.

It was chained specially to provide section lines for squatter homesteads down along the Gorge and Escalante bottom. But the township takes in a lot of mountain around the Canyon, just as to establish the parameters of a doughnut hole you have to include some doughnut. Land surveys square up the world six by six, strictly north and south, regardless of what's going on geographically inside the boundaries. Luckily, the Canyon angles kitty-corner across its private township, squeezing in as much bottom as possible.

Survey lines unless embodied in roads or fences are ghosts no more visible than the mapped pink and green of France and Germany seen from the air, but just as potent for kicking up trouble. That off-beat township has thrown section and township lines in a permanent tizzy on all four sides. On the grid of the map it looks as if somebody had cut out a six-mile-square piece from one map, plopped it onto another map, and pasted it fast where it fell. This is how it happened:

Early settlers in the erstwhile Ute Reservation soonered the survey crews, staking out claims in what would be the city of Grand Junction long before chains and stadia rods could step off the miles from over there (farthest west benchmark on the other side of the Continental Divide) to over here. Needing numbered corners to fasten their claims to legal descriptions, the pioneers couldn't wait for an official corner to arrive so they made their own. A committee paced out into the adobe hills north of town, drove a stake into the ground and said, "This is it."

That corner is just north of U.S. I-70 where G Road and 28th Road would intersect if they could get across the freeway.

The spot would seem an unlikely long way from First and Main, except that it was near the future Highland Canal, a reminder that these were farmers for whom determining precisely how high on the valley outskirts they could flow water from the Colorado River was more important than laying out town lots.

The Ute Principal Meridian is what they arbitrarily called a line running north and south through that stake; townships west of it would be Range 1 West, and townships on the other side, Range 1 East. The Ute Baseline is what they called a line running east and west through the stake, with Township 1 North and Township 1 South on either side of it.

When all the obviously good farmland had been taken up (this happened in about three months, as settlers poured into the vacuum left by the Indians' removal), people began staking out the obviously less good, those patches down along the Gunnison Gorge and Escalante Creek.

To accommodate them, surveyors dangled a line down off the east side of their original survey, establishing the only conforming corner that part of Escalante country would ever have with the rest of the world. Starting from there they chained off a township reaching six miles on farther south and six miles east. It hangs off the corner of the body of surveyed land, like Spain off Europe.

Some years later the nationwide survey reached this far, with the Sixth Principal Meridian from somewhere over in Kansas squaring the round earth up neatly as it came until it hit the Ute Principal Meridian, where everything fell apart like a smooth wave hitting a rock. Proper mile-square sections splintered into quarter-mile-wide sections, half-, eighth-, sixteenth-mile (but each a mile long), framing that township all around with jigsaw pieces. On the far side of the invisible rock the Sixth Principal Meridian recovered its squareness and swept on to the Utah line, where it hit another presurvey reef— Brigham Young had already laid out the entire state starting from his own Meridian and Baseline "Zero" in Temple Square in Salt Lake City.

Stalwartly, it didn't conform either.

A meridian is technically a line, and everybody knows a line has no width, so things get a little confusing when you realize that where you are sitting under this lavender-gray bluff at the mouth of the Escalante you are "in" the Sixth Principal Meridian, which extends at least as far as Kansas, and if you went south a few miles you would be "in" the New Mexico Principal Meridian, which extends to Old Mexico, and that the Musser pellet cellar, the Ark-stranded-on-Ararat on that far knob is "in" the Ute Principal Meridian.

Meridians tend to take in immense scopes of country; you are sitting, folks around here like to say, on the only spot in the United States where during coffee break you could touch base in three Principal Meridians.

In spite of the rugged terrain it covers, everything within diminutive Ute Principal Meridian township is nice and square—on the map. But homestead filing did not necessarily conform to section lines. With his eye on a nice strip of bottomland that was narrow and twisting, the settler put his fence any which way to take in as much farmland and as little worthless talus and cliff as possible, calculating the area of the crazy shapes so as not to exceed the 160 acres the government allowed.

Seabron King, who spent a lifetime confirming the match of official square sections to the zigs and zags of those old surveys, says, "Irregular as they were they were official and final. It was up to government surveyors to make their work conform to what had already been established.

"Staking out land to take in the good and leave out the bad wasn't the only thing we had to contend with in resurvey. Until 1904 the government contracted surveying to private parties, with no official personnel to check on their accuracy. Sometimes in rough terrain they'd run the township lines, all right, but leave out the section corners— except on the plat they turned in to get their money. There was one man who owned 640 acres according to the old survey; it turned out he actually owned a thousand."

The earth's surface is finite. If somebody gains 360 acres, somebody loses that much. It can get down to inches, like the one ex-cowboy Carl Smith tells:

"There was this fellow in town, had a store building and sold the next-door lot to a man who didn't think he got all that was coming to him so he had the boundary line surveyed. Sure enough the brick building was a couple of inches over the line. So he told the fellow to reimburse him for the shortage or go to court.

"Well, the fellow measured the thickness of his wall and found he had a few inches to spare so instead of paying up, he shaved off the building—this was soft brick, before they had brick kilns in town. While he was at it he shaved off an extra inch and a half. The buyer erected his building against that line, and when the last brick was laid and the roof was on he learned about that inch and a half and how much it was going to cost him."

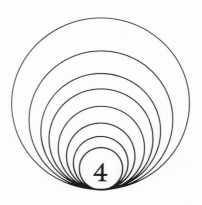

4

River-Dippers

Though no structure remains to show for Mow, there is one we know he never built—a waterwheel. He didn't have to; he had the creek flowing from dam and ditch by natural gravity onto the fields he cleared. All other farms along the Gunnison Gorge survived only by waterwheel.

In desert countries, just where water is needed most, it tends to burrow itself into deep slots where farmers can't get at it. First settlers in the arid west found plenty of farmland, millions of acres of deep-soil tablelands that were threaded through with good water systems—but straight down, in canyons like open underground pipes, out of reach.

Even more tantalizing, the river at the bottom of the slots created wonderful farmland just above the water level, but this too could not be irrigated by the usual method of raising part of the flow a few feet with a diversion dam and running water in canals onto long stretches of river bottom on both sides. Canyons have no stretches of river bottom, only patches.

Water refuses to flow straight, even in slots. Bouncing from one side of its canyon to the other and back, the river left wedges of bottomland, cut off from each other by sheer walls that made it impossible to carry river water in ditches from one patch to the next, so each patch had to have its own lift system, a waterwheel. The patches were homesteaded and named—Poverty Flat, Dad's Flat, McHugh, Palmer Bottom, Sand Flat, Gutschall, Dominguez, Bridgeport—and this one at Escalante that was Mow's Flat and is now the Windy.

First-come cattlemen, having their pick of the Territory, and with herds enough to harvest the grass of whole mountain ranges, had passed these patches by for land with wider horizons and financial promise. Spooning river water onto a few acres was beneath their notice. But for the man of little means the lure was irresistible – those lozenges of rich land and all that water flowing by! It mightily challenged a man to see what he could make of it with hard work and ingenuity; no cash, no strings to ownership except the requirement to live on the land for five years. A man and his family had to live somewhere, didn't they? Where else could five years get so much for free?

Well, most of the patches were too small to make a living on, and they were not free.

The waterwheels were huge. They had to be tall enough to lift water higher than the highest point on the farthest field. Two immense wheels on a single axle formed the machine; between them wide blades, dipping into the river current, were the "engine" taking energy from the push of the flow. Buckets fastened around the rim of the landward wheel scooped water at the bottom and dumped it at the top into an elevated trough slanting down to the irrigation ditch. Though engineering know-how was involved in construction –the ratio between size of blade and capacity of bucket, height of lift and strength of current were critical–these farmers built their own wheels. They couldn't afford to do otherwise. Even so, a wheel was expensive; a man could easily have more cash or debt in wheel lumber and hardware than in his barns, house, and fences together, which being constructed mainly of logs or posts cost little but labor.

But time and labor are also capital, the most finite capital of all –pieces of the life span. Even after a man senses he is trapped by a wrong choice, how can he, with so much of himself already invested, cut his losses, toss it all away, move on, start from scratch again? Perhaps next season the weather will be better, prices better. If the whole family works a little harder . . .

So the river-dippers, as they were called, hung on, chained to next year and their turning wheels.

Most of the patch farms barely provided room to pasture the family cow and team, to raise grain for chickens and a few pigs, and to grow "keeper" vegetables–potatoes, turnips, cabbage. Years when there was a little extra to freight to mine towns for coffee-and-sugar cash were good years; if the wheel washed away or the river changed channel, leaving it high and dry, they faced hunger. Poverty Flat says it pretty well.

The waterwheels were not very efficient. Even of water they did have power to lift, part spilled before reaching the top, creating below an unintended waste of lushness where a child, who had spent all morning hoeing red-hot earth between rows of corn, could run to quench his bare feet in drenched grass and lift his face to a perpetual slant of silver rain.

Some wheels were set to drag their buckets directly in the river current, creaking day and night from spring thaw until winter locked them fast in ice again. These didn't last long, yet one of the two surviving wheels, the wooden one at Dominguez, sits in the river, protected from the main current only by the willows that are slowly swallowing it.

Before the Bureau of Reclamation tamed the bronco Gunnison River with dams and began regulating the year-round flow by computer, spring floods crashed down through the canyon, rising ten to fifteen feet overnight. A man could lose his entire waterwheel investment while he slept, so ways were devised to keep them out of reach. Usually they operated in a channel, a loop of river ditched back into the bank far enough, it was hoped, to escape a flood.

The Big Flood, following the Big Snow of 1919, swept the waterwheels away, setting the river-dippers free. The patches gradually went back to wild, to sand and sage, and were bought for back taxes by cattlemen for winter graze.

One river-dipper held on through the Big Flood and twenty years beyond. Stubborn and ingenious, Dutch Stortz rigged his waterwheel so he could hoist it out of the water during flood stage. The Bigger Flood of 1941 got Dutch.

Exact age of the wooden wheel anchored in willows at Dominguez is unknown, but the buckets of an iron waterwheel still standing a couple of miles upstream from the Escalante bridge place it within our own era; they are old automobile gasoline tanks bolted around the wheel rim—sculpturesque example of the Escalante penchant for making-do with (or rather making-of) whatever is at hand.

The plight of river-dipper families was vaguely known, though they were so cut off—some flats were accessible only by boat in summer or ice in winter—that it was easy not to notice. After all, most children came to school barefoot at least through September.

One man noticed.

This is where we get our first glimpse of the other half of the Canyon's *crime célèbre,* the man who has been called the Escalante Robin Hood—Ben Lowe.

Ben Lowe committed philanthropy the way he did everything else, in flamboyant, thumb-nose style, with the spice of personal risk to take the cloy away.

From time to time Ben Lowe would load packhorses with beef for hungry kids on the river homesteads. What bothered more righteous citizens was that his altruism went the whole way—he also shared the virtue of generosity with other cattle owners but without their consent, butchering in blithe disregard of whose brand was on the unwitting donation.

The side road to McHugh, the first of the waterwheel patches, passes the rock spill that was once Miller's stone house and (by permission through a locked gate) continues downriver, over tippy places where cliff squeezes one side and river reaches under the other.

McHugh they call the wedge of riverland, saying McHugh the way you'd say Topeka or Houston, as if it were a town: "Pink will be late for supper, he's riding from McHugh."

James Bryan McHugh never had anything as handy as this road. In fact, until recently, when a two-wheel width was reamed through the river-cliff squeeze, access was horseback up around the gully heads and back down.

Like Escalante, McHugh is on the wrong side of the river from the railroad track, and as if that fact miffed him, James Bryan McHugh had no truck with the D&RG Western. Instead, he hauled supplies from town the hard way, out across miles of adobe barrancas along what was then already mapped as the Old Salt Lake Wagon Road, and is now U.S. Highway 50. In thaw or wet weather it took four horses to pull an empty wagon through the gray gumbo that wedged like chewing gum between wheel and wagonbox. After winding down through a side gulch, wagons forded the river at Dominguez and came back upstream to where McHugh sits between walls —the sheer Dominguez Rim overhead, and on the west a great bay of red cliffs stepping back and back into the mountain. They lost a wagon or two in high water, and more horses than anyone remembers.

Most settlers as they grew old became known as Old Man this or that—Old Man Smith, Old Man White—to distinguish them from their namesake sons. But unlike most pioneers, McHugh had money so he is remembered as the Old Gent. He came from Pennsylvania and may have had money when he came, though his grandson Jack thinks not.

"It's possible he put it all together right here in the county. The Old Gent was a pretty shrewd horsetrader. At one time he owned a couple of apartment houses in Denver, one or more in Leadville, plus buildings and land in Chicago. His headquarters was the home spread near Cedaredge. Besides that he owned pieces of land on both mountains, enough cattle to keep the grass busy, and the McHugh Investment Company."

Gift of water and wind, McHugh is made of soil finer and softer than sea sand; the Old Gent spent a lot of money and sweat on rip-rap trying to keep the river from eating his soft land away. Before river dams, floodwater tore through here like a hydraulic plow, shearing half a farm away, roiling it over the great mud-red mouldboard of current and spreading it out in silt a mile below.

Where the road barely misses the river are ghosts of old battles between water and man—a remnant of rock wall tumbling into the current, timber stubs of retaining wall no longer retaining anything.

The aforementioned sweat was not James McHugh's.

"The Old Gent didn't do much of it himself; in fact he didn't stay down there much. He had plenty of other things to see to besides baby-sitting cattle that far and that small, and you might say plenty of sons to do it for him. McHugh was just a cow camp, hay-fields, and a good warm place to winter some of the cattle he ranged on top of two mountains on free government grass during the summers."

It was a good thing the Old Gent taught his sons—and in the course of things his grandsons—the value of hard work because they didn't inherit anything from him. "He lost it all in the Depression. He'd started the McHugh Investment Company, and it was that or— well, just the Depression, like everybody else."

Because it was so nearly impossible to get in and out except on hoof, almost everything that was ever brought to McHugh is still there. The place is a museum by default. Some of it is inexplicable.

Scattered in the brush are parts of a fairly inclusive genealogy of automobiles from Model T to a sedan called a "glass car" because it had newfangled windows instead of isinglass curtains. Why cars? There was no road to, out of, or across this pocket of earth. Trapped by canyon walls, parental decree, and tons of hay to pitch into tons of cattle, did the McHugh boys just tinker and dream? Or were these old engines replacements for a waterwheel, pumping river water up onto the hayfields? If so, then why, when it was such a hassle to ford or ferry anything across the river, didn't they leave the car bodies behind?

Whether the boys prevailed on him, or the Old Gent noticed that his sons were paring down their outlook to fit the place, he got them out of this hole. While he still had the finances to do it, he got them a store to run in Cedaredge; and just before the Depression he traded McHugh for land near the home spread with a wider view on the world.

"McHugh Museum" has other fascinating pieces of time solidified into artifacts to prowl and ponder.

Relic of the Swede who first filed then forfeited this land is a name carved in sandstone: "Charles Oleson, 1883," cut with Old Country flourish, the "C" looks like an "E". A naked tractor engine is pure sculpture, four cylinders in a strange two-column block; too big and powerful for these few acres, it has stood in one spot so long it is screwed to the earth by willows growing through the boltholes. The iron handle of a well pump, high out of reach, measures how much soil has blown or washed away since someone stood over it to lever water into pail. A ruined rowboat heads inland through grass, cargoed with car parts; nearby a pair of bosom-shaped fenders breast like dolphins into wind and grass waves.

The original board-and-batten cabin is so clustered around with barrels, wheels, differentials, stoves, and other gear that it seems to be held up only by the things leaning against it. Every cookstove ever used here remains, including the propane range that fried eggs and steak for McHugh's last "old batch" resident, Pink Blumberg.

Soft pale-gold sand blows up from low-stage silt at the river's edge, blows down off the Plateau, flows down in thin orange mud when flash floods spill over the red Wingate sandstone wall on the west that stands ajar like a castle gate to let the cattle come and go through Palmer Gulch. The sand lies in dunes and hummocks, stitched down by sage and chico brush where in spring the chukars cluck to keep their young broods safely out of sight.

Until snow leaves the high country and the cattle can do their own foraging, they live on welfare here, standing around idle until the Musser truck comes and pours pellets into the troughs.

Though the Mussers only lately built the road to McHugh, they have owned it for a long time. They swapped for it.

Eda Musser had inherited a piece of land near the Old Gent's home spread at Cedaredge, and at that time the Mussers owned no river bottom property for wintering their herds. At husband Kel's suggestion, Eda made the trade, sight unseen, and in fact did not see her property for years—McHugh was accessible only by horseback, and Eda refused to ride anything but an English saddle.

"I found the western stock saddle very awkward. It bunched my riding skirt up around my knees, most uncomfortably," says Eda in the precise diction learned in elocution classes at an Eastern finishing school for young ladies. "And our stock horses disliked my saddle." Dislike was putting it mildly. That little scrap of leather, the English riding saddle, was pure insult to western horses. They kicked it off and to pieces with passion and dispatch.

"In all my years in the Canyon, a lifetime, I don't suppose I rode horseback half a dozen times." One of the times was eventually down to McHugh. "You ought to at least look at what you bought," Kel insisted.

More than the ride was an adventure.

"The only furniture in the old cabin was a set of bed springs, no mattress. We spread the blankets we'd brought rolled on our saddles and tried to sleep. Something creepy and scary in the dark kept scampering across the ceiling overhead and through the coils of the springs under us."

"Kel made a joke of it, an adventure of it, the way he always could. 'Lizard. Thinks you're nice and warm. Wants to snuggle up.'

"Next morning he cooked a cowboy breakfast over an open fire, and we began planning the house we would build there, marking out the place where it would be, deciding on the materials. It was like another honeymoon."

It is a real house they built together, not a cabin; two-story with dormer windows reaching out to bring boxes of sunlight into the upstairs bedrooms; walled with the hard yellow tile brick kilned in town of local adobe clay. Every tile, nail, board, and pane of glass was brought across the river on a basket cable.

"Kel always could do anything he set his mind to. He rigged a basket cable across the river. Well, they called it a basket cable, but it was really just a platform. Scary. You put your legs down through the two-by-fours, the weight would carry you out to the middle of the current, dipping so low your feet almost touched the water, and then you had to pull yourself the rest of the way, hand over hand up the sag of the cable. Kel could do it, I couldn't, so when I was crossing he'd pull me from the bank with a rope.

"The train crew would unload the tile along the track, and Kel would load them a few at a time, pull himself across the river, unload them and go back for more."

It is doubtful that any of the hollow tile Kel Musser heaved on and off his basket cable had been hoisted by the someday-to-be-famous muscles of Jack Dempsey. This house was built several years after teenage Dempsey had worked at the Delta Brickyard. Kel and Jack Dempsey went to Delta School together, but it was the Barker boys living at the Lowe place that Dempsey came to see when he visited the Canyon.

No trace of the basket cable remains. Sand drifts, thin-haired with grass and pewter-plated with the gray of old cottonwood leaves, slant undisturbed down to water's edge. Beyond the silent-flowing river, the railroad track makes so slight a scar under the towering cliff it is hard to realize it is still alive, that the morning coal trains came through as usual and will rumble back again this afternoon, parentheses of noise and today bracketing age and stillness.

The house is locked and empty of life, and has been ever since Pink Blumberg died. Through the windows you can see the big chair where, after he'd finished the chores, unsaddled, made his supper and washed his plate and frying pan, he would sit with his boots off watching television.

Television down in this slot in the earth?

Or, as he fell asleep, was the screen peopled with his brainbox full of Canyon memories? Pink had little else. Raised in the Canyon, he never married and had no thread of interest outside. Within the Canyon walls he allowed life to build another wall around him—his job. In spite of battling the elements, cantankerous cows, and deadly broncs, the cowboy's life has always been uniquely sheltered. His wage was low—thirty dollars a month and found in the old days—but it took care of everything on God's earth he needed or wanted. The "found" was food, shelter, and companionship in bunkhouse and ranchhouse.

What the cowboy was sheltered from was ever having to decide anything really crucial. The thirty dollars (increasing as times changed and decades passed) was as certain as sunrise; all of it could be spent in one bang-up Saturday night in town with no risk or regret.

If, as Pink did, he started working for the outfit right out of

◄ McHugh house, built of tile made at the plant where Jack Dempsey worked.

grade school, he was a permanent part of the family. They took care of him when hurt or sick, salved his rope burns, plied his head colds with camphor, put up with his moods, and respected his increasing knowledge of matters that required only minor decisions of a man — the condition of grass on Sowbelly Ridge, whether old Half-horn was good for one more calf. General life-support and insurance program, right on through old age, decrepitude, and grave marker.

"Pink's getting so he thinks he's the only one can do anything right," Bernice Musser said toward the end of his life when he was withdrawing into the third set of nested walls, the ones inside his skull. "When the men build fence, he comes right behind and builds it over, his way. We can't have that of course, it's expensive paying two men to get one job done," and even while she said it she was rolling out cookies to take down to his cabin at McHugh.

Never making a decision is decision itself. Whether Pink ever realized this or not, his brother did.

"I worked all my life for the Mussers," Brownie Blumberg said in old age, adding like an epitaph, "I started my future too late."

There's no remembrance (and of course no record) that this particular scrap of riverbend land was one of the "poverty flat" homesteads Ben Lowe packed meat to from time to time before whoever lived here first gave up, letting the preemption lapse for McHugh to seize. But it is easy to imagine Ben Lowe coming down off the mountain through those red gates in the cliff, riding tall and easy on a working cowhorse — not one of his race horses, Bonnie or Flaxie, or his trick horse, Cloud, lest their feet or delicate legs be rock-bruised on the rough trail. Behind him on a lead string is a packhorse, humped like a camel with quarters of beef in flour sacks, beef skinned clean of the telltale brand that might have been Ben's own or Mussers' or Shreeves' or anybody's he thought had enough and to spare.

A Kentucky gentleman and preacher's son, renowned for stately manners, drunk or sober, he would have presented the gift with flair and sensitivity, after sharing a bottle with the man of the house to ease him off the prod of his pride.

Perhaps it was done like an afterthought on leaving, one long leg swinging across the saddle, swung back down, "Oh, say, maybe you could do me a favor. Found one of my steers on Sowbelly Ridge hobbling along on a bum leg, and I had to dress it out. More meat than we can use at camp in this warm weather. Ruby's in town and none of the rest of us have time to brine it down. Seems too bad to let it spoil . . . "

Having fresh beef on hand without the branded hide it came wrapped in, showing whose it had been while alive, was risky business—as much as a man's freedom was worth. The law required that the hide with brand intact be displayed (it was usually draped over the corral fence) for at least thirty days after butchering. This applied even to bonded butchershop meatcutters.

Ben Lowe was a man who thrived on risk, created risk just for the hell of it whenever it was in boringly short supply. And perhaps his Robin Hood concern for poverty-flats children was as much to satisfy his needs as theirs. But he wasn't a man to force risk on others. If Stock Inspector Sampson should happen by and find a river-dipper rich with beef and no hide to show it belonged to him . . .

Or not just happen by, be following a trail. Ben Lowe's reputation had earned a special half-fond, half-exasperated surveillance of the law over his comings and goings.

"Warm as it is, might be a good idea to get that beef under brine right away."

The farthest north along the river leg of the Musser holdings L is the Bridgeport ranch. They acquired it to expand cattle-wintering quarters, after several fortunes had been made and lost in peaches by other owners there.

Bridgeport was probably Eda and Kel's last "honeymoon" place. By then they were both old, frail-looking as last year's leaves but still tough as whang leather. Their sons were running the outfit by then, and one day the old couple left their home in town to go down and visit the boys at Bridgeport. What happened demonstrates the mobility expected of an Escalante cattleman's wife, even a retired one.

"We just went for the afternoon, but our son Jack said, 'Would you mind staying here a day or two while we go put up hay?' and as Kel said afterward, 'They never came back.'

"When I saw we were going to have to hold the place down indefinitely, I said, 'Well, you better bring me some furniture.' All they had down there was camping stuff.

"Every time we moved, from one of the ranches to another—every time they moved me—they always left something I treasured behind. Like the furniture Kel made when we were first starting and had so little money.

"The boys brought my furniture from the home place, things I like to have around me, and we didn't mind the isolation. It was like old times, Kel and I doing things together. Of course, there were the cowboys to do the heavy work, the riding."

To reach Bridgeport any way but horseback, you first go back up Gold Dust Gulch to the highway, north to the Indian Rock Road, and down another nameless gulch to the Gunnison and the railroad again. It is a lovely scene, buff-rose and red cliffs, the river feather-fringed with willow and tamarisk. This, however, is all you will see unless accompanied by a cattleman with a key to the bridge, which is in such excitingly perilous shape the Bureau of Land Management has padlocked it to protect the public, giving keys only to cattlemen who run stock on the other side of the river and have no other wheeled access to that range. The rationale of this piece of bureaucratic thinking would seem to be that no bridge would dare fall down with a cattleman on it.

One wagon wide, the swinging bridge is little more than a horizontal plank ladder suspended by two cables, and having an added third cable anchored upstream to keep wind sway down to seasick level.

Morgan Hendrickson, who punched cows at Bridgeport in his twenties, describes coming home from a dance in town, carrying only the normal cargo of pre- and postdance refreshments.

"I was driving the Model T, and it didn't have any headlights so I'd hung a kerosene lantern out front to see where the road was. That bridge is narrow. This was before they put in siderails and the sway cable, and the bridge would swing like a hammock. Swing so bad you couldn't tell exactly where it was, where to aim your front wheels, even if you could see which I hardly couldn't."

Like other hard-to-get-to places, Bridgeport is rich with the artifacts of bygone ranch life and work.

Just beyond the ranch house screen porch is a cabin-size stone oven where bread was baked for the hundreds of peach pickers when the orchards were in their prime. Eda explains how the oven worked. A big log fire was built in the bottom, the coals raked out when the oven was hot enough, the loaves pushed in on wooden paddles, and left till they turned golden brown in the heat radiating from the hot walls.

Bridge at Bridgeport, so unsafe only cattlemen may set foot on it. ►

"Can you imagine how many loaves it would take to fill it? How much flour, how many hours of kneading? But then, she had Mexican women to help her."

Of course! That's why its shape looks familiar—a Mexican "*horno*" outdoor oven, but bigger and made of bricks and cement rather than stone and adobe-mud plaster. Iron doors instead of a tilt of slabrock to close it.

The oven is relic of another way of Canyon life, the hundreds of Mexican fruit pickers who at harvest season came here crammed in railroad coaches, in boxcars, even on flatbeds fringed with their dangling legs.

And Mexican trackworkers.

The story of laying and maintaining those railroad tracks is a saga of the varied streams of immigration to the New World where, anybody could tell you, boundless opportunity beckoned. Grading and laying track was mainly done by the brawn (and in spite of the brawling) of Irish and Italian immigrants. By the time the maintenance section houses had been stationed at convenient intervals up and down the line—at Escalante, Bridgeport, Whitewater—the sons of Ireland and Italy had merged into the general population, having found better jobs or lands and fortunes for themselves. When areas of hard times in Europe shifted, shifting the source of immigrants, their place was taken by Greeks who though bigger were not as belligerent, but whose fights tended to be less fun and more fatal. They too eventually blended into the population, often first getting into sheep raising then into commercial enterprises.

The first influx of Mexican railroad and field labor coincided with the dispersal of Pancho Villa's "*banditos.*"

Though Mexicans also individually merged into the general population with the passing of time, as evidenced by local Spanish-surnamed families who assumed important positions in the farming, stockraising, business, and professional community, still the ethnic shape of the crews employed to keep the railroad lines repaired remained predominantly Mexican.

Perhaps their stasis was because they came late, the free land and first expansion opportunity having tightened up a little by the time they arrived. Late for the first big boom party of the opening of the Western Slope of the Rockies, they may have felt locked in. At any rate, they seem not to have gone tearing off in all directions to greener fields, as their predecessors had done. Or perhaps the ethnic shape was only apparent and the labor force of workers who composed it was continually replenished with new immigrants from Mexico, as former track workers acquired better jobs or property, just as the shape of a riffle in a river remains the same though the water continually changes.

But even in the flow of the most rapidly interchanging riffles there are quiet places where the motion is circular, moving yet staying. So it may be that the immigrants (some of them) from south of the border brought the cause of their stasis with them—the gentle, shallow vortex of their chemical antidote for the drive and the pangs of discontent, marijuana, which they grew in little hidden patches all up and down the railroad line.

For some time no one seems to have been much concerned about this imported means of achieving coziness with the status quo, but by the late 1920's local newspapers were reporting official raids on marijuana patches almost as frequently as on bootleg liquor stills. Except for the spelling of the word, accounts such as the following might have been written yesterday.

"Sheriff's deputies discovered another plot of Mexican mariguana growing along the railroad Monday. The officers cut and confiscated the entire crop of 190 plants."

The penalty for growing marijuana was considerably less than that for bootlegging, even for a man arrested several times in the same August for his several patches: "Gabino, Mexican arrested for growing a large quantity of mariguana, pleaded guilty and was given six months in jail."

Since marijuana seeds itself with almost the abandon of tumbleweeds, it sprang up wild downwind or downwater from the little hidden plots tucked into arroyo niches. And since marijuana hangs onto life with as much enthusiasm as it imparts it, waif plants are occasionally still found flourishing in such places.

Eliminating bastard crops unintentionally fathered was not a part of the penalty of being arrested for growing marijuana, nor was anybody paid to seek out and discover the wild weeds, as was done in the Midwest when the government, after paying farmers to produce marijuana for hemp rope and cordage during World War II, paid the same farmers to grub it out of the fence rows upon the conclusion of that governmental venture in growing pot.

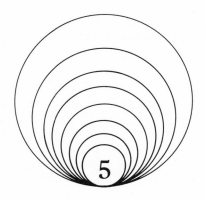

Shoog the Bootlegger

Up Escalante Creek from the Windy the Canyon squeezes in, becoming so narrow, so high-walled, that in deep winter the sun shines for only an hour and a half each day, rising after eleven, rolling along the south rim and setting before one o'clock. It is a dark, forbidding place to build a house and raise a family, but a man did it.

In his later years he was called Shoog, for sugar, because of the quantities of that commodity he bought for purposes well known but not openly discussed. Shoog grew up in town and came of "good family," according to the *Denver Post* when he became news. The local paper, reporting in great detail otherwise, was noncommital about that.

When Shoog was eighteen and his brother sixteen, they got into an argument with a Kentuckian on Main Street in front of the Remington-Elliot Store, concerning who actually did what in the town's last baseball game.

This was before national and college teams, manipulating all shapes and sizes of ball, had taken over sports completely, making mere spectators out of the rest of the population. Even the smallest town had its own ball team composed of men who all week were earnestly engaged in getting ahead in their various trades, businesses, and professions, and who on Sundays played ball just as earnestly, aware that the town's honor and place in the world rested upon them. Whether the town team won, or how it got cheated out of winning, was a dead serious item of conversation. Shoog played first base on the town team.

The Kentuckian took exception to a disparaging brag made by the younger boy, pushed him off the boardwalk into the street dirt, and came down on him in a whirl of feet, fists, and elbows. Seeing his brother getting the worst of the fight, Shoog took his part. With a knife.

Badly slashed—one stab pierced his heart—the Kentuckian drew a revolver and fired one shot that went into the dirt. He stumbled up the street as far as the Oasis Saloon, fell and died.

Young Shoog was sentenced to the state penitentiary. The experience soured him, or he was born that way. "Shoog and all his kinfolks was tough. Even their women was tough, good-looking but big and tough," a contemporary remembered.

Perhaps prison left him with an affinity for such another walled-in place as this spot where nothing and nobody could slip up behind him.

The slot had barely land enough to support a cow, two pigs for winter butchering, chickens, and a few rows of garden truck. Not enough sun for fruit trees or corn, which was probably why Shoog bought all that sugar. There was so little room that the chicken houses were shallow caves, still to be seen in the north cliff wall. At least that is what they say now was in those caves.

Dour man that he was, Shoog built in this dour place what has been described as the prettiest house in the Canyon. It too was a stone house, but Shoog wasn't content to take whatever rock happened to be near to hand, nor use it the way he found it. He went up on top and quarried golden-tan Dakota Sandstone, squared it up, brought the stones down off the rim by rope and stoneboat, and fitted the shapes together with loving care. The golden-beige house, softly gleaming like a cube of muted sunlight in the dark narrows of the Canyon, was two stories high with tall windows and a fireplace deep enough to cook in.

People returning to places where they have lived refurnish them with memories, laying upon the changed space the unchanging vignettes behind their eyes. So, hanging upon the Canyon walls of this now empty slot, every time Velma Shreeves rides by, is a picture of a small child's happy morning.

"We were visiting whoever owned the house then, and had come into the Canyon down the Big Hill, the fire felt so good. My uncle Jack Austin, who was a handsome young bachelor at the time, was frying pancakes in the fireplace, tossing them in the air and catching them to make us laugh."

That beautiful, welcoming house was totally out of character with the man Shoog was known to be. It was as if the big, sullenly belligerent, often lawless man, by erecting that glowing building in this glowering place, tried to make a statement about an inner self he was unable to express otherwise. Making it right, making it beautiful, making it permanent in stone, to speak well of him for all time against the things that were known and said about him.

Up on the bench north of the Canyon slot you can still find the pit where he quarried the rock, but not a stone of Shoog's house remains.

When the WPA put in the present road and bridge, Shoog's house was standing empty; he and the several families it sheltered after him had come and gone unable to make it in a spot of so little earth and sun. Ownership had fallen into the limbo of unpaid taxes. So they used Shoog's cut stone for culvert abutments at gully crossings. You can see his work in culvert facings in the desert stretches of the Twenty-Five Mesa Road to the Plateau, hauled there and laid up by CCC boys. The yard of a professional man in town is said to be walled with Shoog's stone.

The cut stone was not stolen. Government bureaus—Forest Service and BLM—then engaged in cleaning up public domain by destroying every pioneer cabin on it, "turned their back," as the saying was, when people began hauling away Shoog's house—his statement in stone—rock by rock.

As his nickname implied, Shoog made his living by bootlegging. He was not alone in the industry; the nooks and crannies of Escalante side canyons provided a number of Canyon "businessmen" with fastnesses proof against prying sheriff and revenuer. Eda Musser says, "On nearly every one of the ranches we bought we found the remains of a still."

The market was nearby towns which in the decades on both sides of the turn of the century experimented with pre-Volstead prohibition, voting themselves dry by local option.

These extreme measures were taken because the constabulary could not cope with the frequency and range of racket and outrage of "shooting-up-Main" events. It wasn't always harmless fun, people got hurt and killed. Cutting even closer to the quick, property got damaged—windows, lights, horses, and back-bar mirrors got shot to hell. Ladies dared not come home alone from Shakespeare Reading. Sources of charity, public and private, were sick and tired of supporting the families of men whose "take home pay" was the amount left after an evening in the saloon on payday.

When a town went dry and saloons closed, drugstores filled the gap, receiving wholesale and dispensing retail, both operations at the back door after dark.

Competition between drugstores for the limited bootleg supply was fierce if secret. Until just a few years ago there was a small billboard in Escalante Canyon, startlingly out of place in the sage beside the sandy trail, advertising the "Delta Drugstore." Few people who saw it realized it was directed at Canyon suppliers, not customers.

Drugstores in those days were usually owned by doctors. Before this means of raking in a double profit was made illegal, the doctor could write prescriptions with calculated abandon, knowing he would get another cut when they were filled at his drugstore. This doctor-drugstore symbiosis is of durable tradition; only recently have physicians been "discouraged" from doing this same thing on a larger and less overt scale by owning stock in pharmaceutical firms.

If you didn't know this about doctors and drugstores it would be hard to understand why Delta doctors kept getting arrested and convicted on charges of violating liquor laws, as reported in the newspapers. And you might wonder, on reading that Dr. and Mrs. MacComber pled guilty to eleven counts of liquor violation, how a physician could consume that much booze and still see only two tonsils when the patient said "Ah." Actually Dr. Mac probably didn't drink at all since he made his house calls riding a monocycle.

Why the doctor's wife was also arrested the papers did not explain. Perhaps the gentleman shared liability as well as income by owning the drugstore jointly with his lady.

For Shoog, stilling wasn't profitable enough, or it wasn't exciting enough. From time to time he branched into other varieties of petty crime.

"Whenever there was a piddly holdup, especially along the railroad, you could be sure Shoog or one of his kin was in on it," the old-timer continued.

Holding up the railroad was a way of life. The D&RG was robbed so often along its twisty route (every sharp twist slowed the train to a boardable crawl) that it hired its own detectives to supplement Pinkerton men and the local law and offered thousands in rewards for train robbers alive or dead.

A few train robberies with some flair to them happened here in Gunnison Gorge. The bullion safe that lies gutted and rusting under an Uncompahgre cliff was torn out by its boltroots from a car floor in this canyon. And a would-be train robber got so carried away with his work one night along here that he shot the length of the Pullman car with marksmanship so poor, or so good, that he missed everybody.

But, as the man said, most of the holdups were piddly. For rail robbers of small ambition and smaller courage, the D&RG target was generally the pumpman, not because he had a lot of money but because he was handy and vulnerable.

It was the pumpman's job to ride the train from one pump station to another, fire up the steam pump engine with coal, and pump river water into the tank from which the locomotives replenished their boilers. In winter it was a terrible job, unfreezing the pipes, breaking the ice in the river, digging the coal pile out of the snow. Before a train came along to take him to the next pump he was a long time alone.

Pumpman H. H. Ingersoll knew better than to carry much money, and anyhow he didn't have much. He had three daughters none of whom wanted to get married, all of whom wanted to go to college and be schoolteachers. He moonlighted, serving as commissioner in charge of the county poor farm.

The man who held him up wore the conventional kerchief over his face, but in the moment of confrontation a gust of wind blew it aside and the pumpman recognized Shoog. H. H. Ingersoll had more than the eight dollars in his pocket to lose—there was the D&RG reward. . . .

Shoog had been out of the country many years before Ingersoll felt it safe to tell anyone whose face he had seen.

Old Shoog's escapades are not to be taken as an exceptional small rotten spot in an otherwise sound apple.

Escalante has its *crime célèbre,* the Sampson-Lowe shoot-out which has been written about so much—and so romantically because of its Old West flavor—that you'd think nothing like it happened within a hundred miles or years. To put things into perspective with that shoot-out when we come to it, and with today as compared to yesterday in matters of general wickedness, it is only necessary to lift head over the Canyon rim and take a look at the outside world through back issues of local newspapers.

People who write sentimentally about the "good old days," cleaning up history to suit preconceived ideas, and to give children a proper respect for their forebears—and incidentally an impossible scale against which they can only measure their own times pessimistically—such writers give the impression that by comparison the world today is worse, and worsening at a rate just two jumps from damnation; that we can do nothing to save it except chuck progress and get back to simpler, harder-working, more innocent and moral times when everything and everybody was natural and good.

The bad old facts are much more optimistic for us.

If crime, as reported in newspapers of those days, is balanced against the per capita ratio of people engaging in and suffering from it, the times were more violent then than now, the violence as mean, as nasty, and just as inventive.

Within the scope of what the Indian calls "one sleep" of Escalante Canyon there was an average of two fatal shoot-outs a year, scores of rape cases in which the accused were often businessmen and ranchers, kidnappings (in one a rape victim was kidnapped to keep her from testifying). Stockmen were tried for performing abortions on ladies who were not their wives. Several mothers deserted small children, several times as many as many fathers did the same thing. A Negro was shot to death for throwing rocks at a pursuing officer. A Chinaman barely escaped lynching for daring to move into town. A mob emasculated a man. The illegitimate baby of a schoolteacher was drowned in the Gunnison to protect the family honor and her job, and her younger brother was railroaded to the insane asylum lest he credibly tell what he saw. Men had their toes cut off by shovels in quarrels over whose turn it was to open the irrigating headgate. Banks failed because bankers were crooked; depositors lost their money for good, no recourse, no insurance.

Some crimes were so modern we think our generation invented them. Mexican gandydancers grew marijuana along the railroad, Japanese farmhands made sake out of rice and prunes, and somebody came up with the idea of steeping the one in the other to make a tea that in that era's synonym for "mind-blowing" had the kick of a government mule.

Two ladies were driving from town in a light buggy when a couple of men stepped out in front of the rig, opening their coats. The term "flashing" hadn't been coined yet so the weekly paper had to word its way around the bare facts: "the ladies' delicate sensibilities were subjected to an obscene and disgusting sight." The ladies were outraged, of course, but apparently the sight was even more shocking to the horses. They bolted, tearing off across country, bouncing the buggy to pieces.

All this in a few years in a thinly populated area, a good community where one town of less than a thousand souls had nineteen churches. To come up with a comparable menu of juicy news, today's newspapers draw on the entire world.

On a statewide scale, here on the last frontier, the good upstanding settlers were finishing off the job of stealing this continent from the Indian—it wasn't the government that broke the treaties, it was ordinary men and their wives and their children slipping over into treaty lands, building cabins and digging gold mines there, and then demanding that the government give them armed protection from the savages. "The Ute Must Go" was the slogan in Eastern Slope headlines that opened up the Western Slope of Colorado and, coincidentally, Escalante Canyon.

(The joke is that when the Indian had been shoved onto worthless land, land nobody wanted, it turned out to be enormously valuable for oil, uranium, coal, and other goodies, but that wasn't until after the world had become so much better that it is unthinkable to simply move in and take it away by force, as would have happened in the good old days.)

Nor was the West a small rotten spot on the sound apple of world affairs. Elsewhere terrorist-type crimes were committed by both sides in the battle between laborer and employer; workers used dynamite bombs in their struggle to reduce the workday from twelve to eight hours, and employers hired men to shoot into encampments of workers' wives and children. Twenty blacks were lynched in one June in one state; a president of the United States was assassinated by a tourist concealing the weapon in his bandaged hand.

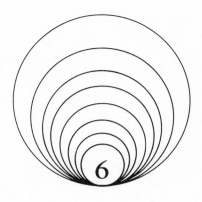

Mail-Order Bride

The crooked slant of Escalante Canyon cuts into the Uncompahgre Uplift a little faster than the lift, and in its length exposes the geological serial story right down to chapter one—granite. But first, after leaving Shoog's slot, we scan back through some rock pages we read on our way down Gold Dust Gulch. The reds, purples, and grays of the Morrison again promise uranium but don't deliver—though Eda Musser recalls a near miss:

"We had a uranium scare in the Canyon years ago when Charlie Steen was becoming a uranium millionaire over at Moab. Men crawled all over Escalante with Geiger counters, but nothing came of it, thank goodness! Geologists pretty much leave the Canyon alone because, unless they see it, they think the Morrison can't possibly be this close to granite."

Scare is the word. For cattlemen who make their living off the top eight inches of ground, wealth found underneath means nothing but trouble. Alex Calhoun ran cattle all over the west side of the mountain; by working himself and crew twelve hours a day in saddle and hayfield, he was just beginning to see over the top of his debt when the boom hit. His home spread took in most of that rare-earths treasure chest, Naturita Valley. When uranium, vanadium, gold, and other minerals were discovered on all sides of his property, and money poured into pockets as far away as England, did Alex sell cattle, buy mine machinery, and get out of debt and rich? He did not. He sold Naturita Valley along with everything under it, and moved to Escalante Canyon.

"All that ruckus, people digging all over the range, mine hoist boilers huffing and tooting, kept the cows so upset they wouldn't stand still long enough to eat grass or let the calves suck."

Through all the uranium booms and busts, that one flurry was the only attempt to find it in Escalante. Whatever they failed to discover is still here. Also unexplored are blue-green strata that, cut through by canyons farther north, yield copper and amethysts.

In the last of Shoog's Narrows, just before the Canyon widens into hayfields again, the native cottonwoods have been left to grow as old and big as they want to be. Crowded along the creek, they lean far out over the water on both sides as if giving the lie to know-it-alls who say there's nothing to the folk myth that cottonwoods always lean toward water, disclosing its flow even when invisible underground. Taller, straighter cottonwoods stand apart in dandelion-starred grassy parks, their magnificent spread inviting picnics and cameras.

Beyond the meadow is the beginning of what was headquarters ranch for three generations of the Shreeves' cattle outfit. The stages of its waxing and waning are marked in barns, sheds, and dwellings, now easing groundward like old cottonwoods that have lived long enough. The nearest of them, that ghost-white, ghost-empty cottage at the meadow's end, was built to be the honeymoon home for third-generation Bert and Virgie Shreeves. Glassless blind windows look toward the river gap; high in the yard cottonwood a child's treehouse creaks a lonesome door in the wind.

At the upper end of the ranch spread the main house still stands sound and firm because Musser employee John Cunningham (a cattle breeder in his own right) lives there with his family. Between these houses, as between parentheses, are the acres of corrals where each spring and fall Musser men work Musser cattle, doing the sorting chores of the cow business.

Original homesteader here was not Shreeves, but Justin McCarthy, a man who is remembered mainly for the way history played hob with his name. The cliff-top flats to the north are named for him. A trail that starts in his backyard and follows the ridges to the very top of the mountain is named for him. But by coincidence the three men who robbed the Delta Farmers and Merchants Bank in 1893 were named McCarty—the McCarty Gang. The one McCarty not killed in the holdup was thought to have escaped on some trail headed this way over the mountain. As time went on people assumed

Cottonwood spreads picnic shade where the Canyon briefly opens out.

that trail and bench were named for the desperado—the meek may inherit the earth but the unmeek get their names on it.

In mapping the mountain, the Forest Service either didn't research Escalante history or didn't think it made one "h" of a lot of difference. So there it is on the map, McCarty Bench and McCarty Trail. Even Justin McCarthy's homestead is called the McCarty.

He ran into other coincidental problems with his name. About twenty miles south of Escalante another McCarthy with the same initials was tarred and feathered for beating his son with a singletree; and there was that contemporary overseas with exactly the same name—Justin McCarthy fighting the English in Ireland, getting his

Honeymoon house lasted past Bert and Virgie's fiftieth anniversary.

Working equipment at the new Musser corrals on the old Shreeves ranch. ►

name and his uproar in all the papers, even the one in the town where our Justin McCarthy went to buy saltside, coffee, and nails.

Justin McCarthy was a gold prospector who supported his chancy life-style by running a vacation dude ranch for mules.

At this time when there were still no laws about how many hours you could work a man per day, or how young you could put a boy to doing man's work, there were labor laws for mules (and horses, burros, or any other four-legged creatures working in the eternal dark of the mines). The law stipulated that mine animals must spend a certain number of weeks of each year out in the sunshine.

McCarthy saw a hole in the economy and filled it.

The marvelous faculty of man and nature (one man or one living cell) for seeing a niche and filling it to advantage is seldom glimpsed in this age of intermeshing big business, feasibility studies, and bosses to assign every task. But wherever we can stop the action at the pioneer stage—as in the records, memories, and artifacts of Escalante Canyon—we can watch this faculty operating on a one-to-one level. Pioneers came west randomly bringing whatever skills they happened to have, and it always happened that whatever needed to be done when in the wilds of the undeveloped land, there would be somebody who could do it. If wooden wagon wheels shrank in the unaccustomed dry air, somebody turned up with the know-how to shrink iron tire down to fit shrunken wheel. If a valley was long on clay and short on houselogs, somebody turned up who knew how to fire brick.

So McCarthy boarded mules, bringing them a hundred miles by trail or rail, feeding in deep of winter the wild-grass hay he had grown in his summer meadows, scythed by hand, and ricked to cure sweet and fragrant in the Canyon sun.

McCarthy built three log cabins on his claim, two close together composing a single dwelling as was customary because logs tended to come in one-room lengths, or at least they were easiest handled in that length when the usual method of "lumbering" was to snake a log to the site at the end of a lariat tied to the saddlehorn. For a two-room house you built two one-room cabins close together. A "Batch" would live in one and store stuff—horse feed, stock salt, a quarter of venison—in the other. Families cooked and ate in one and slept in the other. Later the space between the cabins would be roofed and called a breezeway, though it was usually just a place to keep rain off saddles, firewood, stock salt, etc. Still later the breezeway was walled and became a real room. Often the original cabin accreted so many lean-tos it was hard to find the starting unit.

When McCarthy sold his homestead to Old Jack Shreeves he moved into the third cabin. No matter that it was on the piece of land he had just sold, people preferred company to property-line niceties in those sparsely settled places and times—the Shreeveses just planted their family orchard all around Justin. Actually, Old Jack Shreeves didn't buy the place directly from McCarthy, but from a brief and untitled owner with the fabulous name of Heinie Brightfield. Justin just kept right on living there.

Pioneer Jack Shreeves (called Old Jack to distinguish him from his grandson Young Jack, now retired) came originally from England. His midway point was a farm in Iowa.

What brought him from England to Iowa is misted in time, but there is little doubt what made him leave Iowa for the recently opened Ute Indian Reservation—D&RG Railroad propaganda. Pushing rails into new territory was done on speculation, and railroads covered their bets by plastering Eastern newspapers with glowing advertisements to lure fare-and-freight producing settlers to each new area their rails opened up. Each in turn was touted as the best yet, land of instant riches. Source material for these flowery ads was published brags such as Mow's superlative peaches.

Jack Shreeves is remembered as a soft-spoken little Englishman with lamentable luck in wives. He was two (maybe three) times a widower, and once divorced. Widowers were numerous in those times when hard work, poor nutrition, frequent and ill-attended childbirth killed off women early. The saying "Every baby costs a tooth" cited only the prenatal calcium deficiency. Most widowers arranged child care for their motherless children by remarrying, and since this was not the most romantic basis for marriage, it often resulted in frustrated wives and a bad reputation for stepmotherhood. Jack opted to place his five children in an Iowa orphanage.

It was a terrible place. The baby and a two-year-old girl died of hunger and neglect. Bert Shreeves, who had been seven years old when his mother died, was in little better condition when Old Jack discovered the situation and got his son and two remaining daughters out of there.

Bert Shreeves (called Old Bert to distinguish him from his son Young Bert, now retired) carried bitter memories of that orphanage all his life, and because of it felt all the more tenderness for his step-mother when Jack remarried.

The Shreeves family arrived in the fall of 1899. By this time "Old Bert" was 20 years old, and his sisters, Nell and Bess, were grown women. He had two stepbrothers, Bob and Bill Shreeves, ages nine and eleven.

During the month they stayed in a Delta boardinghouse while Old Jack was locating and filing on Justin McCarthy's place, Old Bert turned 21, old enough to take up a homestead on his own, which he immediately did, selecting land joining the McCarty on the west. His stepmother also filed a claim. That is why there have always been several dwellings in this one farmyard. They sit on separate home-steads. To "prove up" a homestead you had to put a house on it and live there, even if it was a shack just over the fence from papa's place, where you ate all your meals.

Finding ways to enjoy the advantages of government programs without meeting the requirements exactly as intended is another crea-tive device not invented by our generation. In many instances a man quite legally proved up on four times the acreage the law meant to allow a household by having his wife and two older children file in their own names on adjacent land and then putting the four "proof" cabins within arm's reach of each other where the four pieces of land shared a corner. Three of the cabins were merely bedrooms, at least for the nights (ninety or so per year) the law required residence on the specified piece of land.

What Bert built on his claim wasn't the two-story house that stands there now; that came later. His token dwelling seldom saw him; like his father and young brothers he spent most of his time riding, build-ing fence, grubbing brush, and pushing cows or irrigation water this way or that.

During the second summer the Canyon put the Shreeves' staying-power to test – drought. When the creek dried up, the nearest mouth-ful of water was in the river two miles away. Livestock could be led to it, but water for house, chickens, pigs, vegetable garden, and newly planted fruit trees was hauled in kegs on packhorses.

As they became old enough, stepbrothers Bob and Bill took up homesteads, in fact every member of that generation of Shreeves, men and women, filed claims. Eventually the outfit included the en-tire lower end of the Escalante for winter range, four quarter-section tracts on top of the mountain for summer range cow camps, and a midway spring-and-fall holding ranch on Escalante Spring Fork—the XVX.

Under the firm hand of Old Jack, the outfit was run as a unit, as was usual with family cattle outfits. Family members, pooling work, pooling losses, pooling profits if any, lived where assigned in cabins strung from river to mountaintop, moving up or down as work changed with seasons.

The dilemma of an enterprise based on real estate that a man puts together with the help of his sons is that if it is divided among them either as they come of age or on his death, the fractions of land will none of them support the enterprise alone. And when the sons have sons, further dividing the property . . .

In America the usual way to avoid this kind of dissolution is to form a family corporation. Working heirs are the managers, non-working heirs draw a commensurate share of the profits and have only that much say in how it is run. This idea looked scary to British-born pioneer Jack Shreeves. He held fast to lessons learned in the Old Country where, until primogeniture laws were passed, land became so fragmented that a man's inheritance might be barely enough land to plant three rows of cabbages. The way to keep an estate intact, of useful size, was to pass it on intact to the oldest son. Which is what he did.

Old Bert was in his early thirties when his father retired, turning control of the entire outfit over to his firstborn son. The two younger sons had just come of age. There were older daughters, but according to British tradition females had no inheritance rights in real property. They were supposed to get out and marry some.

Under the English system, estates were indeed kept intact, but younger sons often fell apart for lack of responsibility. If the estate was large enough they were provided a quarterly remittance that enabled them to live well without effort on their part. As a consequence, they tended to fill idle time with mischievous adventures embarrassing to their families, who encouraged them to live elsewhere, preferably in America.

British "remittance men" were common in the pioneer West, and several visited the Escalante—one is remembered for the number of bear killed one after another by the hunting party he hired merely to get one bear foot larger than any his friends had bagged and mounted.

Britisher Jack Shreeves would seem to have created the Canyon's own version of remittance men. After he turned the outfit over to his firstborn, his younger sons stayed on, working under direction and drawing a livelihood from their work. But not sharing management decisions and problems, they tended to take on the happy-go-lucky attitude of the cowboy; since their income was someone else's responsibility, it was for spending like pay for Saturday night fun in town. Black Bill, one of them was nicknamed. His escapades are recalled as just short of Ben Lowe's in frequency and flair.

When tragedy struck the two of them in the black diphtheria year and they left the Canyon because they could no longer stand the sight of it, they had no roots in Shreeves family lands, cattle, horses, houses, and range rights. The two pieces of homestead land they did hold in their own names they left to whoever wanted them, dust under their horses' hooves when they rode away.

The year Old Bert was 33 he lost his beloved stepmother.

"After his stepmother died," Young Bert says, "Dad decided he'd better start looking for a wife."

Apparently, he saw no suitable candidates in the Canyon at the time. It took a special kind of woman to make an Escalante Canyon rancher's wife. She had to be hardworking, willing to do without luxuries, at peace with isolation, and ready to set up housekeeping wherever the work was. She might be called on to pull stakes at least twice a year to follow the cattle from canyon to mountaintop and back.

It's not true, Canyon folks say, that Bert got his wife from Montgomery Ward, putting his age, dimensions, and prospects at the bottom of an order for watermelon seed. What Bert did, they say, was put a marriage proposal note in one of the boxes of peaches he was shipping to Denver, a girl working in the fruit read it and accepted. The next time he had a shipment of cattle to Denver he looked her up and married her. Bert's "Heart in Hand" bride, they call her, a quaint term stemming from the opening phrase in proper love letters of the time, "With heart in hand . . . "

If that's how Bert got his bride, he wasn't out of line with current ways of evening up the distribution of the sexes, which got out of kilter when single men went West leaving beauless maids in the East. In the town paper that same year a Miss Bessie Smith of Atlanta, Georgia, ran the following ad:

"It is getting to be a fad to advertise for a husband, and I being in the market would like you to help me. Business girl, 28, can cook, drive, keep house. 154 lbs, 5′4″. People say I am pretty." (Just to keep our thumb in the right page of history, the driving Miss Smith mentioned was horses hitched to buggies.)

Though naturally none of Bert's children was around for some time, and their account is therefore hearsay, they tell the mail-order-bride story differently.

"Otto Smith, Cap Smith's son, was quite a guy for the girls, he put a note in a box of peaches being shipped to Denver, and the girl who found it answered back, sending her picture. Otto showed the picture to Dad, and Dad said, 'I like her looks,' and wrote to her. They corresponded, and became engaged by mail. Then in the fall when he was shipping beef to Denver, he went to see her. In December he went back and married her."

When Old Bert Shreeves (age 34) brought Emma Roethenbach to Escalante Canyon, it was the first time she had ever been outside Denver city limits.

In 1913 access into Escalante was the same as when Dillard and the longhorns came in 1883. From town the rocky, dusty ruts scrambled over the mesa benches, struggled in and out of Roubideau Canyon, headed up around Negro and Club gulches and back to the Escalante rim, where that sliver of ledge-hung road dived and shimmied down the face of the 600-foot Big Hill. The shelf had been widened—just enough that two horses hitched to wagon or buggy could walk side by side without falling over the edge. If the rig was very long somebody had to pry-pole the rear end around the hairpin switchbacks.

Folklore has it that once Emma found herself safely down that cliff she never went back up it, never once left the Canyon. That isn't quite true, though her son Jack says: "I know of seven years she never left the ranch, much less the Canyon. It was a terrible problem to go to town any way but horseback. Took four horses just to pull a buggy up the Big Hill, and to spare the teams people used to get out and walk all the way up. She seemed happy. . . . "

If she wasn't, nobody knew about it. Actually, she didn't have many adjustments to make; she was used to hard work and primitive living—houses of working-class people in Denver had backhouses on the alleys and chamberpots under the beds. As for the change from city crowds to Canyon isolation, Emma herself took care of that.

". . . and she soon had a herd of babies to tie her down." Ten babies, all born on this ranch, with or without a doctor—doctors made horseback housecalls to deliver Canyon babies if called in time to arrive before the baby did, the call also going out on horseback. If no doctor appeared, a neighbor woman served as midwife.

Cap Smith's diary notes such an emergency.

"Mrs Rogers has a baby girl. Dr. Jim Burgin came from Delta, but his car got stuck six miles off and he walked on in, arriving way too late. Dolly and I were called by Rogers who sent a boy on horse. But the baby was born before we got there. Dolly washed and dressed her. We didn't get to bed till four o'clock in the morning."

Cowboy Don Musser gave up tallying Shreeveses by name and started nicknaming by number—Nina and Antenna for the ninth and tenth—nicknames that, luckily for the one christened George, didn't stick.

Few people could keep track of just how many Shreeveses there were. Esther Stephens remembers fondly, "They didn't come to town often, and they came scared. They'd dart and hide in Emma's skirts like a skittery brood of baby quail, and just as hard to count."

When, in about the sixth year of marriage, Bert began to suspect there would be an awful lot of Shreeveses, he built a house to fit the prospects—two stories, dormered in the style of the times, a parlor, and big front porch. That is the dark green house topping the bend at the McCarty.

They had barely got the roof on, planning to finish the inside during the winter, when on Thanksgiving Eve the 1919 "Big Snow" fell.

In town store roofs caved under three feet of sodden snow. Snow lay deeper on the mountain where cattle, lingering in Indian summer, were trapped halfway down and starved to death. Trampling trails on horses slogging breast-deep through snow, cattlemen saved what they could. Men worked their hearts out, and still went broke that year.

Jack Shreeves recalls a smaller, but to a child more poignant, tragedy of that Thanksgiving morning.

"I was only a little kid, but I remember bundling up and going out with Dad to help find the chickens. All summer they had roosted where they wanted to, little secret places they liked. Nights hadn't been chill enough to make them take to the shelter of the chicken house.

"Snow was over my head. We had to dig to find them—under a slanting post, squirmed into a bush, in the lee of a rock. We didn't find many alive."

The big house wasn't finished that winter. Nobody remembers just when the housewarming was held. What they do remember is that the Canyon's fatal epidemic of black diphtheria started at a dance in this house.

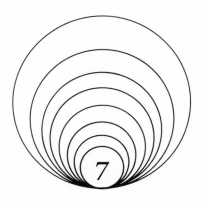

Diphtheria Dance

At Escalante dances people waltzed, schottisched, and two-stepped from dusk to dawn because the fun had to last long enough to be worth the trouble of getting there, and because it was safer to travel the crooked, rocky, steep roads and negotiate creek crossings by light of day. This was true both before and after the advent of the automobile.

Horses are supposed to be able to see in the dark and always know the way home, and so they can and do, but only bachelor cowboys rode horseback to dances. Families with females came in buggies or wagons, wearing their prettiest dresses and least-practical shoes. Horses pulling wagon or buggy at night pick careful course and footing for themselves regardless of what holes or humps the wheels shortcut into.

And automobile headlights aren't always where they do the most good on roads with twists so sharp the beam illuminates cliff while ruts make a blind left, possibly into a fallen boulder or a sleeping cow; or with humps so steep the headlights seek the stars while the driver wonders whether the road down there goes straight, right, left, or at all—if there had been a gully washer since last trip.

Because Escalante folks enjoyed the reputation of having a special capacity for fun, their dances were popular; people came from so far away they had to start out in the morning to get there by nightfall. Those arriving by train were boated across the Gunnison and taken upcanyon by hay wagon. Those coming on foot wore walking boots and carried dancing shoes.

Ben Lowe came to Escalante dances even before moving to the Canyon. Any dance he attended was special. Whether because of his reputation or his personality, the atmosphere changed when he walked in the door, even when he rode up.

While the women in the schoolhouse laid off their things, lit the wall-bracket oil lamps, and pushed school desks against the walls, the men lingered at the dusk-lit corral waiting for the first strains of music calling them in. Careful of their best clothes, they'd unsaddled or unharnessed and pitched hay from the stack provided for schoolchildren's mounts and stood leaning on the fence, passing the predance priming bottle, talking, idly watching the animals roll in the corral dust to scratch backs made itchy with sweat and hair turned the wrong way by straps and pads; idly watching the status maneuvers among the horses that, though well acquainted with one another, must reestablish by laid-back ears or nip who was to be boss of this particular get-together.

If Ben Lowe rode up the air changed. Bodies straightened slightly, even though still elbow-propped along the rails; faces lit slightly with a warmer look than had greeted other arrivals, or chilled slightly, according to whether or not the mouth in the face had recently called Ben Lowe (not in his presence) a horse-stealing outlaw.

He would take a sociable drink from the passed bottle but seldom more. Notorious for drinking sprees, he confined them to saloons, needing no priming to enjoy the dance, and apparently considering it unchivalrous to get drunk in the presence of ladies.

When the men came in from the corral, if Ben Lowe was among them the dance at once became special. Not that he looked different or dressed better—the youngster Cap Smith, called Silk Hat Harry, wore flashier clothes, and the striped silk shirts Tom Fiore imported from his native Italy on his $35-a-month cowboy's wage didn't get him any extra notice.

For one thing, Ben Lowe, this Kentucky preacher's son, was the best dancer anywhere around—tall, smooth-moving, and courtly on the floor.

One little great-grandmother said in a voice still bemused, "He was a show-off dancer, but who he showed off was his partner. He could make you look and feel like the best dancer in the world. Dance steps in those days were pretty rigid, you learned them in dancing school, but Ben Lowe invented steps—as if the music and holding a girl came out joy in his feet. He'd lead you so smooth and sure through complicated steps you hardly knew how you did it."

Escalante dances were held every two weeks during winter slack-work time, alternating between the Upper and Lower Canyon schools, and refreshments were potlock—each lady bringing a tea towel–covered basket of goodies. But ranchers with the means and room enjoyed hosting their own. Each March Bert and Emma Shreeves celebrated Old Jack's birthday with a dance in their nice big house.

Their daughter Marie remembers, "They'd push back the furniture, open living room and dining room together, and line the walls with benches. Dad would have fixed a quarter of beef for sandwiches."

"Fixing" a quarter of beef meant corning it, explains Nelson Huffington, next neighbor up the creek. "In the winter, you'd fatten a cow that was too old to calve, too tough for steaks and roasts, but was more flavorful than young beef. And you'd put the meat in a barrel of brine to pickle and get tender and tasty."

Bert Shreeves, whose cured hams and sausage were famous (justly, and because he got them praised in the paper), was also expert at making dried beef for "chipping."

From an old recipe, this is how it was done: "Take one very thin old cow (fat gets rancid and has to be stripped off when making dried chip beef), kill her, hang the carcass on your meat scaffold, clean and skin it."

There she is, drawn and quartered on a bench table in the back-yard with one of the kids waving a leafy branch to keep off the last flies of fall. Using the butcher knife as little as possible, starting at the hocks and working up, you pull the muscles apart along their natural divisions leaving the meat in large smooth chunks that, when dried, would slice paper thin across the grain. Women could, and did, butcher and saw up any size animal into roasts and steaks, but it took manpower to separate beef muscle with bare hands.

After weighing the meat on the granary scales you measure the cure mixture—5 pounds salt, 3 pounds sugar, 2 ounces saltpeter for every 100 pounds of meat, divided into thirds. Saltpeter, of course, is pure dirty-word nitrate, but people ate lots of it, survived, and even managed to procreate, which is matter for wonderment since the U.S. Army of those days put saltpeter in the soldierboys' rations expressly to inhibit their natural inclinations along those lines.

After one-third of the curing mixture has been rubbed into all surfaces, you pack the chunks of meat into a wooden barrel to os-mose in their extracted juices for three days.

Then again you are up to your elbows, rubbing in another third of the cure mixture, keeping careful track of which pieces were formerly where, because the last out is last into the barrel. This process is repeated one more time. After the final three days, the meat is spread to drain for one day and is then ready to be hung in the smokehouse to dry.

Not your microwave–TV dinner quickie. But then once you finished, the job was done for the year, and you always had something nice on hand for company. Delicious and beautiful–tissue-thin slices with iridescent sheen.

Home Cured Dried Beef, the recipe concludes, will keep indefinitely with no sealing or covering other than a piece of flour sack to keep off dirt. The reason it wouldn't spoil is because no bacteria could live in it, as back-to-raw-nature people remind us with horrified glee.

"Refreshment wasn't just a snack. It was a feast," Marie Shreeves continues. "People ate hearty. Dancing all night was strenuous the way those cowboys danced."

Emma Shreeves would bake all day, ovensful of bread and pies and cakes. At midnight the food would be set out on the big table with all the leaves in–thick slices of fresh crusty bread and new butter; platters of dark juicy corned beef, of dried beef slices delicate as petals, of rose-gray iridescent ham Bert had cured; sweet pickles and dill, green tomato relish, piccalilli Emma had put up in summer; sometimes kraut; coffee poured from a big granite-enamel pot on the woodstove, served with hand-skimmed cream; chocolate or angel cake, slabs of pie–pumpkin, apple, and venison mincemeat.

Dance preparations included getting out all the spare bedding because families brought their small children along–babysitters were unheard of (grandmothers or otherwise), it being unthinkable to ask anyone to stay home from a dance for any such frivolous reason as minding the kids.

In fact, the dances were a part of small-fry social life. As long as they could stay awake they enjoyed the festivities–papas inviting tiny daughters to polka, pretty aunts teaching small nephews how to do-si-do–and on falling asleep were carried to the beds upstairs. When beds were full they were tucked into heaped piece quilts on bedroom floors. The music and noise didn't faze their slumber, though the dancing could get exuberant. A cryptic note in Cap Smith's diary says of one such dance, "Pearl fell through the floor," without specifying whether this was Pearl Walker (male) or Pearl Anderson (female).

Music was provided by local groups–combinations of fiddle, banjo, harmonica, guitar, saxophone, or accordion–content to be paid in the fun, the feast, and whatever turned up in the hat passed during the evening.

Liquor was on the side—outside, among the wagons.

On a Saturday in March, 1923, Bert and Emma Shreeves hosted the dance no one who attended will ever forget.

Oscar Huffington wrote in his diary: "About all the Canyon people came, and some outsiders including a new family named Street. Marion Wells was beauing his sweetheart, Miss Simineo, the teacher at the Upper School. But Miss Simineo didn't dance much because she didn't feel well."

Miss Millie Simineo, of Kannah Creek down the Gunnison, had recently returned to the Canyon from visiting outside, it was remembered later. She boarded near her school with Bob and Teet Shreeves, whose assignment with the Shreeves spread at that time was to hold down the outfit's XVX ranch in the Upper Escalante. Bob and Teet attended the dance with their five-year-old boy, Sonny. Sonny wasn't feeling well, either, and was put to bed early in the evening.

Also bedded early was the little Street boy, Willdean. His big sister Gertha remembers:

"Along in the night my four-year-old brother Willdean got sleepy. I picked him up, cuddled him—he was our family pet—and snuggled him into the quilts with little Sonny Shreeves. I'll never forget. . . . Willdean was singing his own lullaby, kind of sleepy-soft, 'Watching and waiting and ready to go,' but I didn't think anything of the words of that old hymn at the time, he was always happy and singing."

When daylight came, the dance broke off, men hitched up their teams, women gathered up the children, and they all pulled out for home, rig after rig.

Gertha Street Austin, just out of her teens and mother of two small sons of her own, drove with her little family behind her parents' rig down to the tall stone house Shoog built in the narrows of the Canyon, where they all planned to prepare and eat Sunday dinner together.

Oscar's record fills in what was happening in the Upper Canyon: "On Monday Miss Simineo wasn't able to open her school. Bob Shreeves went to fetch Dr. Cleland, and after the doctor parked his car on the rim of the Big Hill, brought him the rest of the way with team and spring-wagon. By the time they came, Bob Shreeves' little boy was sick also. Cleland treated the sick ones the best he could, and stayed the night so he could doctor them next morning. He was tired from the trip, and did not sit up with the patients.

"Sometime after midnight Mrs. Shreeves got up to see how Miss Simineo was, and found her dead. As soon as the doctor stepped into her room he knew by the smell she'd died of diphtheria."

Eda Musser remembers, "Marion Wells, who was working for us then, took his sweetheart's body out of the Canyon to Delta in the back of his wagon. Kel wanted to do it for him, to spare him, but he wouldn't have it that way. All we could do was give him a mattress to lay her on, and a quilt to cover her . . . and try to get through the day, thinking of him driving those long miles."

Huffington's diary goes on, "When the doctor found out it was diphtheria, he said he must have vaccine for the Canyon children, so Bob Shreeves saddled and raced the word to Ray Lockhart who rode down the Canyon as fast as the horse could stand. When he got to my place I gave him a fresh horse. He made the quickest horseback trip to town and back that ever was made." But it was too late for Sonny Shreeves. He died that afternoon, the fourth day after the dance.

"Bob and Teet Shreeves brought the doctor and the little boy's body down the Canyon with team and spring-wagon. I had just started up the road on horseback when I met them. The doctor said he had to get back to town as soon as he could, so he walked up the Big Hill out of the Canyon to his car.

"Bob and his wife just wanted to be at their own home place at the mouth of the Escalante, so I tied my horse behind their wagon, and drove their team down to their place to stay with them through that night."

Oscar's diary records his activities, not his thoughts, but it must have been a night of sorrowful memories for him. When he was a boy at home a diphtheria epidemic had stricken five of his brothers and sisters. One did not survive the choking death, twelve-year-old Della Huffington, the first white child born in the settlement, and almost the first to be buried in the new cemetery.

"About eleven, Bert Shreeves came down, saying the little Street boy was sick and they needed someone to sit up with him. So I went and sat with the sick boy. At daylight I went back and had a little breakfast with Bob and his wife, and helped them get started out for town with Sonny's body."

In that sad journey, Bob and Teet Shreeves turned their faces from the Canyon forever. Leaving their homestead to Bert, they rode away before summer's end, never to return.

"I went back to the Street place," Oscar wrote, "and sat with the little boy until the doctor sent by Cleland came."

To "sit up" with the critically ill was about all anyone could do in the days before antibiotics and other medical miracles. It was powerful medicine, however, especially powerful if the watcher was a grown man, a man not a relative whose undermining weaknesses were known. Escalante men were accustomed to take on the duty of sitting up with the sick. They did it to give the family a rest, but there was more to it than that. The patient opened eyes to see the massive male body still there, still leaning attentively but without fussing anxiety, too big for the chair, too big for the room, his strength all one piece like a block, invincible. His very presence was medication, a continuous-drip infusion of support. Thus supported, death-taut nerves relaxed and terror abated, freeing the body to do its work of healing itself if it could.

"I sat up with the little Street boy all night. Toward morning he seemed to be breathing easier, I began to feel sure he was going to make it.

"When I saw the doctor ride up and get off his horse, I went out to the corrals and stayed there talking with Bill Shreeves who was to spell me off, sitting up with the boy during the day. After a while the doctor came out and told us he'd given Willdean a good dose of that medicine, and thought the boy would be all right.

"So I left. Went on up the Canyon to my lower ranch. That evening I heard the boy had died about four o'clock. I was surprised to hear it, the way he was doing when I left his bedside."

Gertha retraces the days following the dance:
"After dinner at my folks' place that Sunday, my husband and I and our baby went to our home on Tongue Creek, leaving our two-and-a-half-year-old boy, Uhlan, because he begged to stay and play with Willdean, whom he dearly loved."

As soon as Gertha heard diphtheria had struck the Street family, she rushed back, but the house was quarantined.

"Until the doctor could get me inoculated he wouldn't let me in. My little Uhlan tried to talk to me through the window, but the doctor wouldn't let me any nearer than the corral, so I bedded down there, spreading quilts on the powdery dry manure for my baby and me. People feel differently about barnyards now than we did then; it was the softest place outside the house.

"I'll always think the doctor, not diphtheria, killed little Willdean. He didn't choke to death like the other children did. The doctor gave him an injection, and he was getting better. Maybe the treatment was new, maybe the doctor thought if one shot would make him better, two might cure him. He gave him another shot, and little Willdean just died, right then.

"I don't think the doctor even realized what did it. He was trying to comfort my mother, 'You're fortunate to have eight others. It's not as if you had only one to lose, as I have.' That drove my mother wild. I guess he couldn't know that every baby just makes love and loss that much bigger.

"Uhlan got diphtheria lightly, but Theo, my teen-age sister, almost died.

"Only three came to little Willdean's funeral. Walter Hellman gave the money to bury him. Times were very hard."

Times were terribly hard. People concentrated what they had of strength and means on saving victims still living; many were terrified to go near the dead. During the swath of that epidemic in county and Canyon, a number of unclaimed bodies were buried in unmarked potter's-field graves.

A mere fluke of timing had put the Street family in the reach of the epidemic.

Henry and Mollie Street of Missouri had been living in the stone house in that sunless Canyon bottleneck for only a few weeks when they attended the Shreeves dance. Mollie hadn't wanted to move to the Canyon in the first place, and after Willdean's death she refused to remain a moment longer.

"When the quarantine was lifted, they just cleared out," Gertha remembers, "leaving all Willdean's things and a lot of their own. Whoever tore the house down for the cut-stone probably carried off their things. Makes you wonder who else might have got diphtheria from handling them—the doctor said the germs could live for ten years.

"And there was the woman who borrowed the buggy Willdean rode home in from the dance that night. I don't remember her name, somebody from the Upper Canyon, her twelve-year-old girl caught diphtheria from the buggy cushions and died."

Rumor and panic riddled the Canyon community. Nellie Walker recalls, "One woman had some of the diphtheria medicine, but refused to give any of it to another whose child was dying, though her own children weren't sick and never did get sick."

People did what they could to stave it off. After attending children sick and dead of the disease, Oscar Huffington went home, took a hot bath, and burned sulphur to fumigate house and clothes. "Dr. Burgin, the Health Officer, came out to investigate, and said it would be all right."

The Mesa County School District had no faith in fumigants. It ordered that the Upper Canyon schoolhouse—where Miss Simineo had taught—be burned to the ground, with all its contents untouched to the last book and eraser.

This, Kel Musser did.

In at least one case fumigating was not effective. Marie Shreeves recalls what happened in Bert and Emma's house after the dance.

"My brother and I got diphtheria, he so bad he almost died, and they put us upstairs away from the family. To keep the membrane from closing and choking him to death, the doctor told him to cough and spit. I wasn't very old, and I wasn't very sick, and I couldn't get out of there. I thought his hacking and spitting would drive me crazy, but he got well." Indians, they say, prevent the death-choke by thrusting a cocklebur stem into the throat, and twisting it to tangle and pull out the deadly diphtheria membrane.

"Afterward Dad fumigated. Burned tins of poison formaldehyde in every room."

The formaldehyde was ineffective or did not penetrate bedding folded away in trunks and chests after the dance. Nellie Walker, who was then Mrs. Bill Shreeves says: "That summer we moved to Shreeves cow camp on the mountain. Bert had supplied camp bedding from his house, and our little girl Wilma slept in it. That was in August. She was six, her new dresses ready for first day of school, when she got sick the same way Sonny did. We were just sitting down to dinner when we saw it. We left everything, put her in the wagon, and tore down off the mountain."

Details of that trip are misted in Nellie's memory. "We must have pushed the horses too hard; they gave out partway down and we had to leave the wagon. I don't remember how we got to my folks' place near the Big Hill. Somebody raced horseback to get a doctor."

What happened then is etched on her mind. "When the doctor came he was drunk. He'd stopped off where some Japanese were making sake and bought a gallon. He gave Wilma an injection, and while waiting for it to take effect, kept nipping the bottle. Pretty soon he roused, looked at Wilma as if he'd never seen her before, 'This child is very ill,' he said. 'I must give her an injection.'

"I told him he already had, but he argued. 'I know better than that. If I gave her two, she'd die of heart attack.' He gave her another, and she died. Just turned her head and died."

Nellie herself took diphtheria, and was quarantined in a house in town, without help or nursing. "A boy from across the alley would set food outside my door, and a doctor put medicine on my doorstep."

Bill Shreeves did not come to see her, perhaps did not know she was ill. After the death of his child, he simply rode away, taking little but his gun and the clothes he was wearing. Nellie also had had her fill of the Canyon; upon recovery she sold the homestead to Oscar Huffington.

After resurgence of the disease on the mountain, rumors rampaged again; anyone too late from work or errand was wildly reported to have died in the woods somewhere alone.

When Nellie and Bill Shreeves had discovered Wilma couldn't swallow, they had rushed off leaving food on their plates half eaten, and the door wide open. Someone had come in and eaten that food; cleaned the plates, it was said; and for a while no one knew who.

It was Nelson Huffington and Frank Ward.

"I'd been helping Wards build fence, but it was Sunday, so we were just out riding. When we reached Shreeves' camp the door was open but nobody answered our yell, so we went in. The table was set, meat still warm, canned peaches, cream. Beat us what took them away so fast. But we were teenage boys and hungry, so we made a hearty meal. Then after folks found out we'd eaten where the diphtheria victim ate, they wouldn't let us near."

People were terrified. The wagon Nellie and Bill abandoned when the team gave out stayed where they left it. Brush grew up through it and the road went out around.

Nelson Huffington didn't get diphtheria, but his father did. Oscar had escaped the epidemic that killed his sister, and untold exposures through the years afterward including nursing Willdean through two nights. Then when this epidemic was over he came down with it. Well, not actually down.

"Dad never missed a day's work," Nelson remembers. "He tied a bottle of coal oil to the saddle and gargled it every little while. Took him about a month, but he beat it."

Hard times as well as sickness and death took the heart out of Canyon people. But Bert and Emma Shreeves weathered through, and continued to expand in acres and cattle. All ten of their children are alive today.

Old Jack Shreeves retired to a home in Delta, and Old Bert became the family patriarch. He ran the outfit until 1960, retiring in favor of his four sons, who operated it until 1965, when it was sold to the Musser family.

Reviewing the mysterious circumstances of the Canyon deaths, a physician now surmises: "That Dr. Cleland didn't diagnose Miss Simineo's diphtheria at once is understandable; in early stages it is hard to distinguish from other throat infections. But later it has a characteristic bad odor that he recognized when he stepped into the dead girl's room.

"As for the two nonchoking deaths, they were probably due to anaphylactic shock, a fatal allergic reaction to the horse serum used in preparing antitoxin. The first injection would have triggered the allergy, making the second one fatal. Treatment has since changed, but at that time several injections were advised in acute cases."

Before his own death Dr. Cleland brought the terror of the quick-killing disease into the modern era, speaking to Marie Shreeves, who was by then a nurse:

"Diphtheria is now so nearly wiped out by preventive immunization that a doctor can go completely through medical school without ever seeing a diphtheria throat. It is doubtful he would recognize it in time. We'd damned well better make sure no child misses the protection."

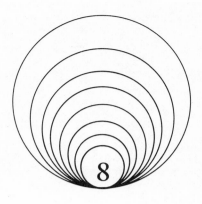

Escape Hatch

About four miles into the Canyon, the Dry Fork turnoff swings left down to the creek and a little natural park beside a low-water ford across the Escalante. In the deep shade of cottonwoods, sky shine reflected from the water fills the park with cool light. Tire tracks come up out of the water on the far bank and disappear around the first bend of Dry Fork Canyon. That road is the Escalante Canyon's present-day backdoor. With fortitude and four-wheel drive, and after detouring miles just to climb the grade, it would take you out on the rim and there lay decision upon you at a fork—the left heads crosswise of the gully canyons toward town, the right takes a hog-back to the mountaintop.

As a means of getting to either destination, that fairly recent jeep road is not the best option, but it does have a point of interest—beyond the ford and around the bend is an Indian billboard, a cliff inscribed with petroglyphs. Being low, handy, and named on Forest Service maps, the pictographs have been so badly vandalized it is hard to tell which figures were made by Indians, and which by copy-cats. Archeologists say, however, that the horse-and-rider figures are genuine, indicating comparative recentness—carved after the Spanish introduced the horse on this continent.

The smooth, sheer walls of the Canyon invite doodling. Whether the base color is red or the purple-black of desert varnish, a sharp instrument scratches through to lighter material, making every mark stand out in bold relief.

Non-Indian writing on Indian Cliff, if it was done long enough

Depleted by irrigation ditches, the creek is a mere trickle at Dry Fork ford.

ago (and did not obliterate older inscriptions) is considered not van-
dalism but part of history. Almost as prized as the Indian writing
are pioneer names: "Fred and Elizabeth Blumberg 1894" and "Ben
and Ruby Lowe," supposed to have been carved on their wedding day.

High on the rim above Escalante Ford is a small notch with a
faint scar sidling down from it – the place where Dillard and the longhorns disappeared into the earth. The scar is what is left of the "road"
city girl Emma Shreeves survived in getting down to what would be
her lifelong home.

For half a century that was the only way to get wheels down into
the Canyon. Firstcomers had nothing as good as that scratched-out
shelf. They hairpinned straight down, with all their stuff. If they
couldn't put it on the back of horse or mule, they left it up on top.
All except one outfit. Before the Indians left, before cattlemen and
homesteaders came, freighters put wagons down that cliff.

Tradition has it they were Germans, freighting gold ore between
territories that would become Utah and Colorado.

Starting late in the season, faced with the likelihood of arriving
on the Continental Divide just in time to die of starvation in deep

Indian petroglyphs and pioneer autographs on Dry Fork red wall.

snow, they elected to take a shortcut over the Uncompahgre Plateau. They were driving ox teams, surest and stoutest haulers in the world, and the slowest, inching along at the rate of five or six miles a day. The big bend the Old Salt Lake Wagon Road took around the north end of the Plateau represented about the number of extra days that would put them on a timberline pass in midblizzard.

The Uncompahgre horizon looks as smooth as a pencil mark, the mountain is so long it looks low; but it is two miles high, and the innocent-looking skyline conceals a welter of terrible going, all of it then unmapped. If the Germans consulted any Indians about the difficulties and time involved in taking the shortcut, they paid no attention or were talking to Indians who had no experience with ox trains and were thinking in terms of pony distances per day.

How they got up the west face of the Plateau, which is like the front of a great surf roller, God only knows. By the time they had struggled down the backslope of the mountain, with its immense intersecting canyons streaming from the crest, winter was upon them.

Scouting a place to hole up till spring, they came to that spot

up there on the rim, looked down and saw the three necessities—
wood, water, and grass—the last still autumn-green in the shelter of
the cliffs. Had they gone half a pony-day or two ox-days farther they
could have trailed their wagon wheels down a gentle slope into the
wide, grassy valley of the Uncompahgre River.

Instead they felled trees for drag brakes and eased the wagons
down one after another to the bottom. Then when spring came they
disovered they couldn't get the wagons back up.

Abandoning everything but the skeleton of half a wagon, they
tied bedrolls and remaining grub onto one pair of wheels, hitched
one ox team to it, and hauled it out. At least it is assumed they
made it out, since no unaccounted-for bones have been found on
that side of the Canyon.

Why didn't they leave the wagons up on the rim while the oxen
wintered below? Well, the story has it, the wagons were loaded with
high-grade gold ore, and the men were afraid somebody might come
along and pack it off. That high-grade is supposed to have been
cached down here in the crannies of the cliffs. If so, no one has announced discovery of it.

No bits of those wagons, iron tires, hubs, spokes, or running
gear, remain to verify the story, but perhaps the Utes, who were then
in the iron-arrowhead stage of transition between bow and gun, made
weapons of the metal and fire with the wood. Nevertheless, the story
about the Germans was substantiated by some strictly un-Indian
artifacts—when the Blumberg brothers came to the Canyon in 1881
they found several head of castrated oxen grazing in the creek bottoms.

"At the time my father and uncles arrived," Brown Blumberg
says, "the flats along Escalante Creek were choked with wild hay, so
thick and tall you could hardly walk through it. As soon as they
could afford it, they bought a mowing machine and rake in Delta,
hauled them as far as the rim in a wagon, took them apart and packed
the pieces down that hill on muleback. The same way my Granddad
Barclay did that wagon he thought he had to have down there."

Five years later when the first Musser, John W., brought his family to the Canyon, the pack trail was still so narrow it barely cleared
the panniers carrying his children.

"Eventually three men—Musser, Wilson and Barclay—took the
trail on and moved enough rock so you could inch a wagon down
without tipping over," Brownie said. "Even so, for as long as we had
to use it, it was a fight every time you went up that road."

Two places on the Hill were named milestones of survival—the

Elbow and the Frog. "Once you had squeezed around the Elbow without falling off, you started breathing again. And when the pinnacle called the Frog came in sight, you knew you'd made it down alive one more time."

The Big Hill wasn't much safer when, decades later, Musser's son Kel brought his bride, Eda Baker, to the Canyon.

"When we got to the Elbow," Eda remembers, "Kel suggested I get off and walk down behind the wagon."

"I asked him, 'Are you going to walk down?'

"'I have to drive the team.' The road around the Elbow was so narrow a man had no room to set his feet between the wheel and the edge."

Eda stayed beside him on the wagon seat. "I told him if he went over, I'd go with him."

Nelson Huffington says of his Grandfather Burton: "He once came down the Big Hill from a trip to the mines, four horses, wagon and trailer wagon. The horses got to running, he couldn't stop them, and the whole thing went over, wagons, horses, and all. Grandfather jumped clear. He lost a horse and had to do some patching on the wagon when he got it back onto the road and home." It makes a terrifying vision up there—the galloping horses, panicked, trying to outrun the loaded wagons careening down upon them, wheels braked solid as sled runners, iron tires striking fire from the rocks. . . .

How a story can change, reverberating from person to person in a closed community, as sound changes in echoing from canyon wall to wall, is shown by the way one cowboy tells this same story now:

"Old fellow, I don't remember his name, came home from Saturday night in town, drunk as a lord. Came to the top of the rim about three in the morning of a moonless night. Took his outfit down that cliff grade, standing up in the wagon, whipping and yelling the horses on. The rig went over. Drunk as he was, he jumped clear, but it made kindling of the wagon and killed the horses. They laid down over the edge there for ages, the bones still in harness."

In the 1920s the road was improved, but to such little effect that the "improvement" was called Suicide Grade.

The Hill was as fatal to motorized horsepower as to the flesh-and-blood model. One spring day Frank O'Brien, driving a cloth-top touring car, was bringing his wife and two babies to the Canyon, where he was batching at Cap Smith's place while she lived in town so the four older children could attend school. He eased his car down onto the freeze-thaw ledge of the Big Hill, but in rounding the turn along the shelf road the car slipped off and rolled down the steep declivity.

Mrs. O'Brien with baby Ramona in her arms was thrown out, receiving minor scratches; Dorothy, two-and-a-half, was found hanging by her clothes from a barbed wire fence, howling but unhurt. O'Brien himself rode the tumbling wreckage all the way down, and escaped injury of any kind—only to be killed nine months later by a bucking horse.

So far as is known, the Big Hill never did kill anyone, but only because it awed people into extreme caution.

The Hill took a whack at every sort of vehicle devised by man. When the bicycle craze touched cattle country and cowboys felt compelled to break one to ride, Arthur Ward, 15, of Escalante Forks got a bike and of course had to ride it to town—half carrying it up the Big Hill—just to prove he could ride it back down in one living, breathing piece.

He almost didn't. In a report that might well have been his obituary the paper noted, "Arthur, who has ridden bucking broncos, wildest of them all, was outnumbered by two wheels, flying out over the rim of the grade, and picking himself up at the bottom with a gash in his thigh, shredded clothing, and unnumerable rock bruises and cactus punctures."

The Big Hill posed a formidable problem for the Model T Ford in which the gas tank was situated under the front seat, gas reaching the carburetor by simple gravity flow. It worked fine on fairly level ground or nearly full tank, but given a steep hill and low tank, the carburetor would be higher than the gasoline and the motor would die of malnutrition.

Smart drivers measured the gas (no gauge) before tackling a steep hill. This was done by removing the seat cushion—along with whoever was sitting on it—and the gas cap, sticking a piece of wooden yardstick into the tank, yanking it out fast and taking a quick reading of the wetline. The reading had to be quick because gasoline "creeps" up a wooden yardstick lightning fast. The yardstick was wood because only a fool would go banging around an open gas tank with ungrounded, spark-prone metal ruler, and anyhow metal doesn't register much of a wetline.

If the inches-of-gas-to-feet-of-climb ratio was unfavorable, the driver was not necessarily stumped. He could turn the car around and back uphill, a position that put his carburetor well below the gas level no matter what.

This took some doing (no rearview mirror) because the driver couldn't twist far enough around for a really full view up ahead (backwards), being anchored frontwards to the controls by all four extremities—one foot on the reverse (middle) pedal, one poised over the brake pedal, one hand gripping the steering wheel, and the other on the gas lever (accelerator) below it.

Or he could drive by watching his wake—peering backward through the windshield, concentrating on keeping his tracks as straight as possible while being piloted by a passenger (or by all of them at once if they hadn't chickened out, electing to walk) yelling gee-haw directions above the racket of the car, which was considerable—the Model T resented having to back up and protested with chattering, shaking, and jerking. Furthermore, the back-up maneuver could not be executed slowly and cautiosly because a certain speed had to be maintained in order to make the grade at all.

Such a procedure was barely feasible when the car had a good straight run at a hill; it was unthinkable on the narrow, crooked, cliff-hung Big Hill, but people did it.

"On the steepest part of the shelf, from the Frog to the Elbow," says Brown Blumberg, "if it was icy they would stop and put small rocks in the road ahead, and drive up backwards over them." Obviously young men in those days didn't need to think up artificial stimulants, such as jumping motorbikes over eleven buses, to keep the old adrenalin spurting.

Emma Shreeves, according to her daughter Marie, survived another experience on the Big Hill that helps explain her disinclination to go to town.

"My cousin Joe Fisher was taking mother and the baby up Suicide Grade in a Model T. That model was famous for not feeding gas on a steep hill. Up near the top it stalled out, he had no brakes and it started back down the curving grade. "Joe yelled 'Jump!' and did so, leaving mother with the baby in her lap still in the car. Fortunately, it headed for the bank, not the rim."

With such perils hanging literally over their heads, Escalante Model T owners tended to keep careful track of how many miles (no speedometer) they could buzz around on Canyon bottom errands and still have enough gas to get up the Hill to town for refill. How much "dead" fuel must be in the tank for a frontal attack on the Big

Hill is now unknown, but Walter Marshall said it took at least seven and a half gallons (in a ten-gallon tank) to go frontwards up Ford Hump, a famous Model T nemesis on the transcontinental road (then dirt) between Illinois and California.

To avoid driving only on the top third of the tank, Canyon Model T owners invented transplants and tricks.

"I myself," says Brownie, "took a vacuum fuel system off some other make of junked car and grafted it on my Model T."

Another trick, invented by Wilfred Edwards, was to drill a hole in the gas cap and insert a tire valve. The lucky passenger with a tire pump clamped between his thighs, pumped furiously to keep enough air pressure in the tank to force gasoline, and the car, uphill. Henry Ford eventually solved the gravity-feed problem by putting the gas tank in front of the dash, smack on top of the carburetor.

The Model T clutch gave Canyon folks even more trouble.

Precisely how the Model T transmission worked few knew but God and Henry. Fortunately, you didn't have to psyche it out to drive and do your own overhaul. It consisted of three webbing bands, like saddle cinches, around three spinning drums activated by tromping three pedals. (Tromp is the word; you tromped hard to reduce slippage and early burnout.) Tromping left pedal put you in low gear, tromping middle pedal put you in reverse, tromping right pedal got you stopped, hopefully. If it didn't, you could tromp reverse, or low, or both, or all three, at the same time yanking full back on the neutral lever (farm implement squeeze-handle type) on the floor to your left, which was the only part of the four-way back-up brake system that dealt directly with the wheels. If there was anything the Model T had a surplus of it was brake. When Joe Fisher was out of brakes on the Big Hill with Emma and the baby he was out of a lot.

In climbing, the car remained in low gear only as long as the low pedal was held down. If it took two hours to climb a mountain, that's how long you pushed down on the pedal, leg rigid, body braced against the seat back. But the wear and tear on the driver was nothing compared to the wear and tear on the clutch, especially if the car was put up grades so steep (like the Big Hill) they could only be climbed by slipping the clutch a little to keep up momentum.

Brownie says, "When we lived at Sawtell in the far end of the Canyon, we could go to town maybe twice before we had to put new bands in the transmission."

If the clutch played out, you took up the floorboards (real wood), unbolted a plate on the transmission housing, and tightened the bands by screwing the flange-fingers closer together. When take-up room was nil, you replaced the bands. The trick was to ease the new bands down, around the drum and back up, working blind, and get them bolted together without dropping a nut into the transmission, a misfortune that could cause hours, days, of fishing with a crooked wire. One man, it is said, gave up fishing and with a little help from his friends turned the car upside down and shook the nut out.

Preventing the dropped-nut syndrome by stuffing the operating opening with waste had its own hazards. Waste (shredded rag sold by the barrel) was used by mechanics to wipe their hands on (besides their pants) before the invention of today's sanitized, reusable wipe cloths. A piece of waste could loosen unnoticed and become a part of the engine's splash lube system. This didn't necessarily damage anything—there was very little that could mortally wound a Model T—but beyond chewing it up there was nothing the motor could do (no filter) to keep the stuff from glomming around drums, gears, magneto flywheel, crank shaft, and other items splashing in and out of their common oil pool in the bottom of the engine housing. If the car's sluggish performance indicated this kind of constipation, the remedy was radical—everything was taken to pieces, washed in a dishpanful of gasoline, and put back together again.

Eventually the clutch problem was solved by an add-on, the Ruxtel axle. It was operated by a lever on the floor which the driver pulled back when the hill was too much for the standard clutch. This backward yank on the lever produced a long-repeated Canyon joke.

Joe Rogers, renowned for an impressive stutter, acquired the Canyon's first Ruxtel and got so excited at how it took the Big Hill frontwards he could hardly get his brag out. "I j-j-just throwed it in r-r-reverse and up we went!"

Unless otherwise manipulated, the Model T, living or dead, was always in high gear. To get into neutral—disassociate motor from wheels—you either held the low pedal halfway down, or pulled the neutral lever halfway back. The lever enabled the driver to get out of the car while it was running without having it go on without him. It also enabled him to stand in front of it and crank without getting run over. People who forgot to set the lever before cranking discovered the Model T could not be held off by straight-arming, a fact that probably postponed garages, with their dangerous back wall and scanty jump-room, for several years.

Escalante had one hazard that didn't single out the Model T—Hub Cap Draw above Cap Smith's place. Hubcaps on all cars then were not dispensable decorations, they were the wheel grease cups, about the size of coffee mugs sticking out four or so inches farther than anything else on the car. At Hub Cap Draw the road made a sharp twist into a narrow cleft where a rock protruded just right to knock hubs off wheels. They were made of pure enduring brass, and unless their loss was noted before the next gully washer they joined Indian arrowheads as artifacts of man's sojourn on this planet.

Such tight corners were frequent. Before the upcanyon road was straightened, it zigged up every talus draw almost to the cliff and zagged back around the points. These tight corners did single out trouble for the Model T, whose lights—powered by the magneto flywheel—were bright only at cruising speed. When the car slowed to take a sharp corner they dimmed to candles. To see at all, you had to race the motor without racing the wheels by slipping the clutch (there goes that clutch again) while pulling down the gas lever. But delicately! If too big a shot of voltage hit those lights the bulbs burnt out. (You always carried spare bulbs, of course. In fact, the number of spare things carried on a Model T almost amounted to complete replacement.)

Canyon rocks cut tires to pieces. Rubber was fragile; tires were skinny and carried very high pressure. Trips you made without a flat were the ones you talked about.

"Once I fixed eleven flats between Delta and the Forks," Morgan says. No demountable rims; to fix a flat tire you pulled it off the wheel (still on the car) and patched the tube with a kit that included a nutmeg grater and little pan for setting a vulcanizing fire, tucked the tube in the tire (carefully because folds caused pinch blowouts), shoehorned the tire back onto rim, and replaced the air with a hand pump, counting the strokes to estimate how much you had squeezed in. For the last thirty strokes the air inside fought back.

The jeep road across Dry Creek Ford and past Indian Writing Wall was the third attempt to scrape a road down into the Canyon. It angles up Dry Fork to the rim, continues around Negro and Club gulches to Cactus Park, where it joins the State Honorcamp road to town.

That you can now come into Escalante Canyon over a road that is merely dusty, crossing the Gunnison bridge instead of going up around it, is owing to the Huffington peach orchards that begin just beyond the Dry Fork turnoff.

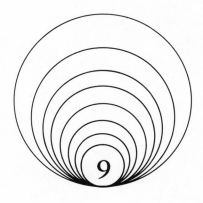

9

The Canyon Is My Mistress

Smothered in a froth of peach blossom like a lumpy pudding in a nest of pink whipped cream, the houses, cabins, bunkhouses, cookhouse, corrals, barns, blacksmith, implement and packing sheds of the Huffington Lower Ranch emerge as you drive on a spring day up past the orchards from the Dry Fork. Most of these buildings are now unused, but not empty, crammed with the tools and gear of almost a hundred years of this ranch's waxing and waning.

The layout sits in a wide place in the Canyon, a deep bowl with gaps in the walls on either side like pouring spouts. The spouts pour in not out. Dry Creek in red flood seems to be scouring half the mountain down into the Escalante just below Huffington. And on this side that terrible flood funnel, Boyce Gulch (also usually dry), is aimed down a cloudburst-cut chute directly at the house.

After Boyce Gulch swept away most of the Lower Ranch, a breakwater was built to nudge it aside, but gully washers are undercutting the concrete wall, banging it to pieces with boulders and banking silt passage around it.

Something like that is happening to the ranch itself.

Interspacing with Shreeves and Musser spreads, this outfit once strung out in holdings along the ladder of Canyon climate from winter warmth along the Gunnison to cow camps a mile higher on summer-lush mountain grass. But unlike their outfits, which in the case of the Mussers had the start of Old John's mine money, and in the case of the Shreeveses had the advantage of a large family of work-

Huffington orchard and butte form composition in triangles.

ers, this spread is the creation of one man—starting from scratch and slaving with dogged, single-minded labor—Oscar Huffington.

With his full and eager consent, the Canyon ate him alive. We see it happen in the diary he kept for forty years. His story is pure pioneer classic.

He started west when he was still merely the genes of his Ken-

tucky-born father and Illinois-born mother. Traveling westward sepa-
rately by saddle and wagon, Sylvester Huffington and Sarah Harrison
met and married in Cherokee, Kansas. Sylvester was a surveyor; Sarah
was a Harrison of the family line that produced two United States
presidents.

When Oscar was two, a small band of Utes in faraway north-
western Colorado rebelled against an Indian agent who was trying
to starve them into becoming "civilized" farmers by withholding rations which were government reparations for lands already taken
from them. For this rebellion, the Meeker Massacre, the entire Ute
nation was ousted from all but a fraction of its homeland in what
was to be Colorado, opening millions of acres to homestead.

Two years before the date, September 3, 1881, when the last Ute
was to be off the Reservation and the first settler allowed in, Sylvester sold his property down to two wagonloads, rounded up his tribe,
and headed west again. To get your pick of new-opened lands you
had to "sooner the boomers," and the first surveyor on the spot stood
best chance of getting the job of laying out the unsurveyed land.

Final camp was made at new mine town Gunnison, last town
before the Reservation boundary. The Huffington outfit joined a
growing colony of white-tops standing with dropped wagon tongues
pointed west, waiting for the Utes to go.

While he waited, Sylvester and teams worked on grading track
for the railroad that was advancing toward town at the rate of about
a mile a day.

Next spring, months before the new land legally opened, Sylvester with five other men saddled and slipped into the Reservation
to locate choice valley land. Beyond Whiskey Road they were stopped
by soldiers garrisoned at the Uncompahgre Indian Agency to prevent bloodshed—ostensibly by subduing Indians, actually by keeping aggressive whites out until the Indians were gone.

The six sooners slipped past and staked out claims at what they
were sure (rightly) would be a town some day—the delta of bottomland created by the juncture of the Uncompahgre and Gunnison
rivers. Cutting young cottonwoods, Sylvester built the standard
homestead dwelling—a one-room, dirt-roof, dirt-floor cabin—then
slipped back to Gunnison to wait for the official opening.

On that day, wagons loaded, family aboard, Sylvester was hitching the teams, bending to fasten trace to singletree when a man rode
up, shouting news relayed from the newly arrived telegraph wire.

"President Garfield died last night! Never came to after that gunshot last spring!" If the news had a special poignancy for Sarah, with her family connections, she didn't express it. Sylvester hitched the other trace.

That last part of the family's covered-wagon trek is the only part Oscar Huffington, then four, was old enough to remember. His sole memories were lying on heaped bedding in the back of the wagon, face to face with the family cow ambling behind at the end of a short rope, and gathering squawbrush berries for camp-cooked sauce. Cattle and fruit were to be his whole life.

Finding himself one of four surveyors in the new settlement, Sylvester diversified, setting up a dairy where townfolk sent children with pails to get warm milk straight from the cow. Oscar's preschool contribution to the family economy was to keep the cows on public grass and out of fields, gardens, and especially alfalfa. "If a cow unused to alfalfa wolfs down much of the sweet stuff, it forms a sudden pressure of gas that stops the heart in minutes or seconds."

One day the cows slipped past their small herder and he couldn't drive them out. They began to drop.

"Dad whipped out his knife and stabbed their paunch. Gas shot the stuff about ten feet high, but he saved the cows." Guilt and horror branded Oscar's child brain with a fact that was to rule his life—only single-minded vigilance could prevent disaster in the cattle business.

As for fruit, during childhood there was only the native squawbush, so called because Indian women cooked with the red berries, wove baskets of the pliant stems, and used strips of its thin bark for cord.

"We'd break off branches and beat them on bedsheets to knock the berries off, pour them into buckets and go down to the river to fill the buckets and float the leaves away. Our mother made jelly, jam, and sauce with them, sometimes pie and 'lemonade.'"

Oscar Huffington was in his late teens when he came to Escalante Canyon. Not yet of age, he couldn't take up a homestead, but his father had traded for squatter rights to land at the mouth of the gulch named for the first settler, Al Boyce. It was no gift, father giving son a start in life—Sylvester had ten other children—so Oscar lacked even that much help in conquering the Canyon. But he had been cowboying since he was thirteen, saving toward his start.

"I bought the squatter rights from Father and managed to hold it until I came of age and could file on the 160 acres under the Pre-emption Act."

The first thing Oscar did with his land was plant fruit on it and go in debt for cattle. He cleared and scraped off a few acres for or-chard—three of the apple trees he planted in 1896 are still bearing. In partnership with his brother-in-law Herb Wells (he had to have someone old enough to sign papers), he borrowed money to buy ninety-two cows and three bulls.

He borrowed again to prove up his pre-emption; borrowed to prove up a homestead at the upper end of the Canyon; borrowed to prove up land down on the river at Negro Gulch; borrowed to buy out his partner; borrowed to buy more cattle, more land. He bought Cap Smith's place, the Bill Shreeves homestead, the Walker place, the Moss place, and eventually Dillard's place at Roubideau, along with Dillard cattle.

In fact, owing to recurring hard times, to his own relentless drive, and to the fact that if you sell she-stuff to meet payments you thereby reduce next year's calf crop, he operated on ten percent money most of his working life.

"March 30, 1901 I proved up on my 160-acre ranch in the Esca-lante Canyon. I had to mortgage it to William Helmke for $600, drawing interest at ten percent to make proof of my ranch. In the summer I built fence for Jeff Dillard. Cattle was so cheap I had to work out to keep my outfit going."

He rode for the Club outfit with Ben Lowe's prank partner Char-ley Sewell. He rode for Jeff Dillard with Cash Sampson when Cash was just another cowboy. He rode for E. J. Mathews "drawing $1.50 a day, boarding myself and furnishing my own horses."

"During the winter grubbed brush across from my house. Thick skunkbrush, willows and cottonwoods. The ground was frozen so hard, just grubbed off on top of the ground. For two or three years harrowed in grass seed until the roots rotted enough to plow.

"Started building a summercamp log cabin on top of Love Mesa where there was a good spring of water. Cut quakenasp, peeled and split logs to make a trough roof. It was a good roof for a long time."

A trough roof is a kind of organic tile roof, the "tiles" being split aspen poles. The first eaves-to-comb layer of poles is placed flat side up, and the second layer is nailed with the flat sides down over the cracks. Good for a long time it was, but eventually it warped, letting in whatever was coming from the sky—sun, rain, or snow—this at a stage of his affairs when Oscar had neither money nor time to rebuild. Banker's son Harry Stockham, happening by, said of Oscar's expedient to stay out of the drips, "First time I ever saw a tent pitched inside a cabin."

On January 1, 1903, Oscar noted that he visited the Burtons three miles up the creek. Though it turns out this was a courting call on Mary Emma, the entry is all about work:

"Herb and I are hauling rock off the weaning lot. We have built corrals, a long shed, and granary down by the creek. We are feeding the cattle by hand. I went to town with team and wagon to help my father put up his ice, hauling it off the river."

It was about this time that Old Sylvester Huffington decided to do something about Ben Lowe.

Ben Lowe's favorite escape route, after a glorious "shooting up Main" escapade, was up a draw through the bluff west of town. Sylvester's new brick house sat in the mouth of the draw, and he was tired of late-night racket and ricochet as bullets zinged backward and forward between Lowe and the pursuing Law. So one night he put a bullet of his own up that draw.

"Granddad must have aimed pretty close," his grandson Nelson says. "Next morning they found Ben's hat up there with a bullet hole through the crown."

Ten days after that visit to the Burtons, Oscar and Mary Emma were married at his parents' home. Next day he wrote: "We went to the Canyon with team and wagon. That was our honeymoon trip."

Oscar plunged back into work, harder and longer hours than before because now he was feeding cattle for his mother-in-law, Mrs. Burton, as well as riding fence for Dillard, working cattle for Mathews on 25 Mesa, IX cattle in Tabeguache Basin and E cattle on Middle Point, working alone much of the time. "Cash Sampson is in town sick in bed."

Cash Sampson was frequently sick, suffering tonsillitis, pneumonia, an abscessed jaw, and later the lingering bone-pain from being crushed between two railroad cars.

Sometimes Mary Emma rode with Oscar on cattle-moving chores; then, after a day in the saddle, made supper, frying meat and potatoes on the tin campstove. "We didn't have much of anything for the cabin. I made a bedstead out of some little quakenasp peeled poles. Made two tables. Had to use blocks of log to sit on."

When the work site changed, he moved her to the nearest cow camp—down to the Roubideau cabin, up to 25 Mesa camp, over to Love Mesa—in each place making do with what could be packed in on a horse. But she might as well have stayed in the Canyon or with her mother, as indeed she often did, for Oscar had projects going in a dozen places, cutting trails on top, cutting hay in the bottoms, cutting cattle almost anywhere. Like other Escalante cowmen, he was oftener out on the range than home for supper, or even home for Sunday. He wrote what he was to write over and over again: "Mary Emma says she is tired of being alone."

"Jan. 12, 1905. Mary Emma [in the last days of pregnancy] is in town with her mother. Mrs. Burton has a nice little house rented to school her children. I ride out about every day to see how Mary Emma is.

"22nd. Mary Emma and I moved out to Roubideau. We have a little squawling brat to take care of, Nelson."

By this time the Escalante ranch would bear their economic weight, so they moved there, tiny Nelson snuggled in a baby buggy in front of the wagon seat. "We just had a log cabin with flat roof and dirt on it. Didn't have much of a cooking outfit, but we got by."

A dirt-roof cabin is made by laying a ridge log across the end walls, bending poles over it from side to side as close together as possible, padding it with a foot or so of shredded cedar bark, and piling enough dirt on top to turn rain. It doesn't always turn rain, snow seeps through, creatures set up housekeeping in the bark, and when they scurry overhead roof dirt showers down. Plates were covered with tea towels until the moment of dishing food. Some women stretched sheets or wagon umbrellas over cookstove and table.

Oscar had been living in this cabin, what little time he was indoors, for nine years. Evidently he had never really looked at it until Mary Emma returned with a new baby in her arms. If she opened his eyes by complaining, there is no hint of it.

"My wife goes with me to feed my cattle at the Burton place. Nelson is too little to help us," he noted, "only two and a half months old." Feeding cattle meant pitching enough hay to fill 200 bellies — first sawing a wagon-size slab through the stack, pitching it from stack to wagon then off again in a continuous string across the frozen pasture. Every morning.

The rancher being his own boss, does not punch a time clock. So he is free? Does what he wants, when he wants?

The Canyon punches the time clock. Cracks the whip. Time to plant or the corn won't make. Time to irrigate the oats, the potatoes, the orchard — one shovel, one ditch of water, a hundred furrows all dust-thirsty at once. Time to bring the cattle down off the mountain before it snows them in and they starve. Time to trail the cattle fifteen or twenty miles up the Canyon to spring grass on the mountain.

The cows finishing off Mrs. Burton's haystacks in early spring, lifting noses to sniff for new grass, are sprung with calves. The idea is to move them up on the range while they are still in that condition, the calves inside, riding.

"I got up to Wards with the cows and springer heifers. Getting them up before they calve will save driving the little calves so far. They are hard to drive. Sometimes they get so tired we have to carry them across our saddles."

Then it's time, tight-wedged between first and second haycutting, to brand those calves. Before the June branding "calf ride," Oscar moved Mary Emma and the baby by wagon up through the forest to the 25 Mesa camp on the mountain.

The calf ride starts at the south end of the hundred-mile-long mountain and works along the crest past the individual stockmen's grazing allotments. As each allotment is reached, its cowboys join the crew then drop out again at their far boundary—except a few like Oscar, who rode for hire for all outfits and stayed until the job was done.

The job consisted of riding down off the crest on both sides, flushing cattle out of gullies, breaks, points, scrub oak, pine and juniper, driving them up to "gather grounds" spaced along the crest, and there roping and branding every calf with the owner's mark worn by its mother.

It took a month and about thirty men.

Each rancher had a cabin on his allotment just below the crest and, though a chuckwagon accompanied the ride, it was a matter of pride for his wife to put on big feeds for the crew working his stock. Of this particular ride, Oscar wrote:

"9th. Roundup time is on. About 30 riders met at the Cross Camp, Ida Ray and Mrs. Will Ray are doing the cooking. Were there three days and gathered a lot of strays and branded a lot of calves for the Rays.

"13th. We moved to Ed Healey's camp on 7N Mesa. Were there three days, got a number of strays and branded a lot of calves, On the 17th we moved to 25 Mesa camp, Mary Emma is cooking. Were there two days, branded mostly IX calves.

"20th. Moved over to Jeff Dillard's camp. Were there three days and rode Maupin, Obergfell and Love Mesa ranges. We still have between 25 and 30 riders.

"24th. Moved to the Club Camp on the other side of the range. We rode four days.

"July 2nd. I went over to 25 Mesa and found Mary Emma and Nelson all right, but she said she was tired of staying alone so much. Also Nelson keeps running away.

"4th. Went over to Noah White's sawmill for lumber to fence the yard so Nelson couldn't get away.

"9th. Packed my bed on a horse and met the Roundup at Sheep Creek. We went from Sheep Creek to Ray's camp, to Hilkeys camp, Hackworths, to 25 Camp, Dillards, Club and 47 Camp. The ride ended on the 31st and all the cowboys went to their camps. We had a great ride, handled lots of wild cattle. I finished fencing the yard at 25 Camp. Got Nelson fenced in."

The "beef gather" started each year in September, and it also took a month or more.

"3rd. I got Mary Emma's horse named Johnnie ready and she went to the Canyon to Mrs. Burton's ranch while I gather my beef cattle on Love Mesa. I went down more than half way to help pack Nelson in front of us. She made it through all right to her mother's place.

"5th. We started riding Maupin's and Obergfell's range and putting their beef cattle in pastures. We rode three days on the other side of the Divide, then went to Love Mesa and rode a week.

"27th. We are rounding up the holding pastures and getting the beef all in one pasture . . . drove them to Fall Cabin for holding over night. We left next morning as soon as light enough to see, and drove to Roubideau stockyard. Rested the cattle one day, and loaded them out for Denver."

Then he was saddling Johnnie for another move.

"29th   Mary Emma and Nelson and I moved out to Roubideau. It was a long way to pack our baby."

Less than a year later there was another baby to pack.

The Canyon was punching the time clock, cracking the whip those final days before the arrival of their second child, Rosa. It was haying time, critical days, make-or-break days for the feed that will keep the cattle alive through next winter. A delay reduces the next cutting by that many tons; worse, it widens chance of cloudburst or long rains that mat hay to the ground.

Oscar took his wife to his father's home in town for the birth, arranged for a doctor, and returned to the hayfields. Working fourteen hours a day, he was racing to get the hay safely up before June rains, racing to finish before the baby came.

Sarah Harrison Huffington delivered her son's baby.

"June 1, 1907 I had Dr. Burgin engaged, but he didn't get there in time. It was all over when the doctor arrived. I failed to get out there when Rosa was born. Bert Shreeves and I were stacking hay. 27th. Done haying. Cut and shocked most of it myself. 28th. Went to town with team and wagon to bring my family back to the Canyon."

The Canyon kept tempting Oscar with new seductions; just when a project was almost secure, almost paying out, some new enticing opportunity flirted him into pursuit.

Far upstream, above the last cabin claim, was a walled grassy valley grazed by several stockmen but never filed on. Buying a preemption had not used up Oscar's homestead right, so he filed on another 160 acres at Picket Corral, and having filed must then build the required improvements and live there the specified portions of three years.

He first built a tent house. Mary Emma and the children came from her mother's place to spend the summer. It was a beautiful spot, deer drinking from the creek at dawn just beyond the leather-hinged tent door, wild turkeys sailing down off Love Mesa to their creekside roost at twilight. But lonesome. No one came by, Oscar was always elsewhere, on the Hill working cattle, in the Canyon irrigating hay. Nelson at seven was riding with the men, counted a man.

Camp-keeping duties were slight and soon over, a pan or two to wash up, lightbread to set. To fill the hours Mary Emma began sketching—the outline of a fire-warped cedar tree, emphasizing the agony, a view out through the gap in the Canyon walls to an empty meadow, using heavy colors that stressed the crush and pressure of isolation.

When the creek went summer-dry Oscar packed horses and moved her and Rosa to cow camp, a cabin and corral at a spring in a forest clearing.

Then after the fall rides it was time to close the cow camp. Taking canned goods that would freeze and burst they left life-saving food for any winter-stranded cowman. Inside the mouse-tight lids of syrup and lard pails they stored matches, flour, sugar, coffee, baking powder, beans, bacon drippings, and salt. The last chore was to put prop-poles in the center of the room to keep the roof from caving under heavy snows.

The Canyon tantalized Oscar with water that he couldn't touch —water actually flowing through his land.

Diversion rights on Spring Fork—Escalante Creek's only source of perennial water—had been taken by decree years before he arrived. All he could divert from the creek was the brief snowmelt runoff. Though in hottest summer the creek continued to flow through his land, he could not divert it onto his parched fields. Any water not used by earlier comers upstream, Blumbergs and Barclay, was decreed to earlier filers downstream, Mow and McCarthy.

So Oscar went up the mountainside and, with team and scraper, built a dam to store snowmelt and bring summer-long water to his acres of Canyon floor.

With more water he could add more land. When Bill Shreeves left after his daughter died in the diphtheria epidemic, and Nellie cut ties to the Canyon by selling her land there, Oscar borrowed again and bought it, converting it into what he always called his Upper Ranch, and which he eventually planted to thousands of peach trees.

After the Desert Homestead Act was passed, a man who had already used his rights could file again, on even more acreage. Oscar filed on 640 acres on the river at the mouth of Negro gulch. Once more he built the required improvements—four miles of fence and a dwelling—and batched there alone three winters to meet the residence stipulation.

His string of holdings from foot to crest of the mountain was now complete, but one by one he added others, going in debt to fatten the string.

This far-reaching domain required endless riding. He was always trailing cattle somewhere—onto the mountain, off the mountain, crosswise of it, into and out of holding or feeding pastures. He was always riding to get cows out of trouble—out of grazed-off range, out of bogs, out of poison larkspur, out of some cliff-hung predicament, out of snow. If early snow trapped cattle in high country, he searched out the last critter, on skis (Norwegian snowshoes) whenever snow-depth exceeded the belly clearance of a horse.

"On the third day, found the five bulls I was out, almost starved," he wrote. "Packed in some feed till I can break a trail."

He distributed salt on packhorses, a ton and a half a season—almost twice as much as his cows could lick. To make sure his own stock had any salt, he had to provide the wild creatures with plenty.

"That ought to keep the deer happy," he wrote one night in

camp, after pan-fried steak and before exhaustion sledgehammered him into bedroll and unconsciousness.

"Went down last week to see my family at Mrs. Burton's."

Dovetailed between range-riding chores, he was clearing land and building on it. With the help of one hired man ($35 a month and "found," the found being food he himself cooked), Oscar grubbed out brush, pulled out cedar and cottonwoods, lugged rocks and boulders, filled gullies and leveled humps with no heavier or speedier equipment than muscle, plow, scraper, and the sled they called a stoneboat.

The land didn't stay clear. Fields were sprouting saplings, skunkbush, and rocks at one of his homesteads while he was clearing another. Frost pushed new crops of rocks from underground; flash floods spewed rocks from canyon-wall gulches, swept away bridges he laid across the creek, took diversion dams he beaver-built of brush and mud, and filled irrigation ditches he dug to fields and meadows he had cleared.

Besides dwellings, at each of his "places" he built a cellar of peeled logs chinked with lime plaster, and a screen-wire meat house where quarters of beef and venison chilled at night out of reach of blowflies by day. At the Upper and Lower ranches, midway of the Canyon, he built bunkhouses, barns, shops, sheds, and corrals. He built fences, fences, fences. Oscar Huffington was instigator of the Poison Fence drifting laterally for miles along the mountainside to keep his and other stockmen's herds from larkspur until after the deadly blooming passed.

Nothing stayed built. While he was erecting something new at Picket Corral, something old at the home place was falling down.

He was always going off somewhere to plow, plant, harvest, or winter-prune something at the Lower Ranch, the Upper Ranch, or Picket Corral. Even before he took on those thousands of peach trees, the amount and variety of things Oscar grew is incredible. He planted, irrigated, and harvested fields of hay, sudan grass, oats, millet, barley, corn, sorghum, potatoes, garden truck, and a general orchard including apples, pears, apricots, plums, grapes, and berries.

"Cradled my oats in front of my house, bound them in bundles and shocked them." The cradle scythe has a rack of curved slender

Mortise and tenon gate made when wire and iron were scarce. ▶

oak tines, like a comb, on the back of the blade to catch the stalks as they are cut. Holding the scythe by its two spaced handles so that the blade is horizontal close to the ground, a man swings it in great sweeps, his whole body turning a half-circle to put power behind the cutting edge and swathe a full-size bundle with each swing. The man repeats this great powerful sweep all day long to harvest a mere two acres. Grain-harvest time is midsummer; heat beating down from the blazing sky is trapped by the Canyon and reverberates like a furnace from red walls and red ground. Sweat flows in rivulets confirming the curse of Eden. For a rest break he drops scythe and goes back to tie the bundles with wisps of straw and stack them grain-end up in little "stooks" to turn the weather.

Oscar's cradle scythe, burnished silken smooth by decades of grain harvests, now rests among towers of old splint peach baskets in Nelson Huffington's packing shed. The summer Oscar was finally able to afford a horse-powered mowing machine, it was swept away in a Boyce Gulch flood before ever he got to use it. Ten years passed before he could buy another.

Oats were sown broadcast with sweeping arm just as in paintings of the sower's graceful task, a fairly quick job. But potatoes were planted one eye at a time—an acre and a half of them to last Oscar's family and hired help through the year.

After the land had been cleared of brush and rock, plowed and harrowed, there was the indoors job of cutting potato eye sprouts with a knife—dishpans and buckets full of coat button–size eyes each with enough potato flesh to provide nourishment until new roots could form. Then the planting: for each a hole is opened with a gouge of the hoe, the potato eye dropped in place, carefully "looking at you" to speed the sprout by pointing it toward light, and then a second stroke of the hoe to cover the eye, and a third to pat the earth down firm. Another half stride, another hole.

To plant an acre and a half, these operations were repeated something like sixty thousand times.

Oscar Huffington's diary is mainly a record of work. "April 1, 1934, We will start turning out some of the cattle on Dry Mesa. 16th, J. B. [Thompson, the current hired man] and I branded 21 spring calves here at Picket Corral. 27th, We started marking out some of the fields. 28th, I went down to the peach orchard [15 miles horseback] to get ready to irrigate. 30th, I set water on over half my peach orchard. Nov 24, Moved 102 cows to railyard. Snowing, couldn't get them to cross the bridge. Had to bring them back.

"Dec 1, J. B. and I rode Love Mesa. Didn't find a cow. Cold wind blowing all day. Awfully cold. Nearly froze. Dec. 20, A bunch of us fellows have been riding Dry Mesa getting the cattle off. I have my cattle in pretty good shape for winter, but am out some of them yet."

When he shipped his cattle to Denver he went along, riding in the caboose and returning next day on his pass, oblivious to the city's bright lights. "I never had time to play and get drunk," he noted wistfully in his diary. And when, his herds having increased beyond his own land to feed, he drove his cattle to the valley for leased winter feed and stayed the night with friends there, he was only an early evening spectator as Art Starr and Harry Stockham played poker until dawn.

As his outfit grew there were always crews of men to line up, to line out, and be part of—calf-branding crews, haying crews, pruning crews, peach-thinning crews, picking and packing crews, beef-gather crews.

His operation spanned two world wars, during which it was impossible to get hired men or male crews. "I worked a female haying crew this week, the first time in my life," he wrote with mingled admiration for the job they did, and chagrin at having to set them at it.

It spanned two world depressions during which the feed he put into his cows exceeded the value of their carcasses whether for meat or breeding; and debt grinned over his shoulder as he watched other men's lifework being wiped out—Shoog's place changed hands for $40 back taxes.

He traveled thousands of miles up and down the slot of this Canyon. Most of his life he did his own cooking, washing, and housecleaning. "Rained. Spent the day cleaning up the cabin. Baked light bread."

His humor, his awareness of his own work drive as compared with other men's, appear in a story he told.

"Joe Fisher came to work for me. I showed him where the ditch survey stakes are. We walked up the line and Joe said, 'You might get this ditch done in 1925, but you won't get it done in 1924.'

"There was lots of big scrub oak where the ditch was to start. Joe said, 'How're you going to get these oaks out?' I said, 'We are going to dig them out. That is what we brought these grubbing hoes, axes and shovels for.'

"We got the ditch down to a deep gulch by the time Joe's month was up. He quit. Thought he had a girl down in the Canyon to watch. That morning he washed his shirt.

"When we went in for noon, he pulled the shirt off the line, said, 'It's terribly wrinkled.' I said, 'Well, you go find a smooth rock, put it on the stove, and iron it.'

"I let Joe monkey around with his hot rock for a while and then showed him where the flatirons were. Joe pulled out that evening, left me to finish the ditch." Which Oscar did. In time to water the 1924 crop.

Oscar suffered his share of range-work injuries—a broken arm, a broken collarbone, broken ribs (and the agony of riding off the mountain with them gouging at his lung), an axe-cut knee, a bronc-damaged spine, and a dynamite blast that cost him one eye and clear vision in the other. He scarcely slowed down for any of these things.

The picture you get from Oscar's diary is not that of a man with his nose to the grindstone, but of a man with a dozen china plates spinning on teetering poles, dashing from one to another to deep them all spinning, the entire structure balanced on a tightrope over a pit of debt, fickle weather, and erratic prices.

For fifty years.

The little building listing like a boat on a surf of boulders brought down by Boyce Gulch, foredeck of porch and portholelike windows lined along the side, is the second Lower Escalante schoolhouse. The first was log, and was bulldozed by the government in that aforementioned spasm of housecleaning. Nelson Huffington rescued this one, jacking it up and towing it home.

More than one generation of memories is embodied in the building. Nelson's son Bonsal describes the dwindling of the school as people moved out of the Canyon leaving the houses empty of children, one by one.

"There were five kids when I was in first grade, four when I was in second, three when I was in third and fourth. When I was in the fifth there would have been just me and another kid. I guess they thought we weren't worth it; they closed the school and started busing us to town."

The Canyon never had a high school. Those families who could

Lower School, abandoned when student body got down to two. ▶

afford it, and thought it important, bought or rented houses in town where wives made wintertime homes for their teenage children, taking along the younger ones, thus further diminishing Canyon grammar school attendance.

This situation prevailed as long as it took a full day to go to town behind a trudging team, and very little less by saddle. It ended only when the Gunnison was bridged and a school bus could make quick passage in and out. By that time there were hardly any teenagers left in the Canyon. For fathers and husbands whose range work kept them away from home days at a time, the absences became weeks after the family moved to town and another thirty miles of riding was added to the homecoming. But this Canyon-inflicted wedge of absence did not seem to increase the hazards to family unity; the high rate of divorce and separation was even higher in families where the women seldom left the Canyon, and felt little hope of ever getting out.

Oscar rented a house in town for his family the school term Nelson was nine and Rosa seven. Like other cattlemen, he visited his family there when work and the Canyon, its whims of weather and opportunities and disasters, allowed. Once a month . . . Once in two months . . .

Mary Emma, whom the Canyon had never wholly claimed, began to swing free of it.

As if sensing this, Oscar began a beautiful house at Picket Corral; squared logs, hand-hewn with the adz; roomy, wide windows and a veranda looking down over the slope of meadow and the creek. No batch cabin this, a woman's house. He made it so painstakingly well, so beautifully, and took such joy in the building that it completely engrossed him and, ironically, she saw less of him than ever.

For a long time she had been filling the loneliness by painting Canyon scenes; now she began to range farther, to art schools and friends and work in Idaho and California, taking Rosa with her.

Eventually her visits to the Canyon were rare enough to be noted in Oscar's diary with the case reversed. Instead of writing, as he so often had, "I visited my wife and family in town last Sunday," he was writing "My wife came to visit me in May. She helped me lay linoleum in the bunkhouse."

"Got back from the upper Canyon and found that Nelson's mother and my little daughter Rosa were here with Nelson in the rock house Cap Smith built for me, so we are all together again. Rosa started going to school here in the Canyon."

Mary Emma worked hard during the weeks of these visits, can-

Huffington Big House; peach crew cookhouse at left.

ning up the produce of orchard and garden, trailing packhorse-loads of food to the cow camp, cooking for Oscar and his cowpunchers there.

Whether to please her and make Canyon life easier for her, hoping to keep her, it was at this time that Oscar built the two-story house here at the home place – the building that is for this outfit the Big House. A real house, built by a town carpenter in city style – white clapboard siding, a parlor with carpets, a kitchen with built-in cupboards and sink, a bath with running water from a huge cistern Oscar dug to supply the house and fruit packing sheds.

Mary Emma never lived in it, nor actually did Oscar. Divorce proceedings began before the house was done; he turned it over to his hired man, Joe Rogers, who had family enough to fill it. Oscar and Nelson continued to batch in the cut-stone cabin Cap Smith built, there across the drive where Nelson's wife, Annie, keeps her setting hens now.

Nelson worked with his father during vacations through high school, and full time afterward. In 1925 Oscar noted:

"Nelson isn't here. He is busy watching one of the Rudolph girls at Roubideau."

After Nelson and Annie Rudolph married they moved into the big house, renting the Lower Ranch from Oscar on a business basis. Nelson began independent of his father, just as Oscar had begun without help from Sylvester. Oscar wrote, "Nelson thinks they can make money on the place."

They did, producing vegetables, cream, eggs, chickens, turkeys, and fruit, which they sold to towns up and down the railroad track in both directions. Unlike cowpunching, this livelihood allowed them to be together, work together.

Oscar Huffington was 54 years old when he surrendered to the blandishments of the Canyon's hothouse climate and went into peaches big, planting 810 trees on the old Tom Brent place, which he called the Upper Ranch.

People said he was crazy. A peach bruises if you give it a good hard look; it wasn't as if his orchards were down on the river like Mow's and Bridgeport's where all you had to do was ease them into iced cars. What Oscar'd put on the cars, after jolting up the Big Hill and across the gullies to town, would be peach jam. Oscar just planted more peach trees.

The Dust Bowl drought struck; irrigation water dried up. He borrowed a couple of wagon tanks in Delta, bailed water from creek pools, and put half a barrel of water around each of about two thousand trees—twice. Unfazed, he planted a second peach orchard on the Lower Ranch.

It was peaches that finally got him out of debt.

"In one good year, when peaches froze everywhere but here," Nelson remembers, "he made $63,000. He didn't have to sell any breed cows that year, and that's what got him out on top. With cattle your holdings can get so big you have to sell off so much breeding stock every year for cash to meet the interest and pay the hired help that you never build up the herd enough to come out."

It was Oscar's peaches that got the Gunnison bridged.

"Dad and Bert Shreeves and I attended every county commissioners' meeting for two years, and finally convinced them that with WPA labor and by moving the old, unused State Bridge down here from the mouth of Black Canyon, they could get the job done without breaking the county. Well, the county was already broke, that was at the end of the Depression, so the job had to be done without cash."

The bridge and the new access road directly to the highway opened the Canyon to the outside, putting the farthest ranches within an hour of an ice cream sundae in town. The tyranny of the Big Hill, controlling the quality of Escalante Canyon life for more than half a century, was over instantly; it took a little longer for the steep road to slough and narrow to a trail for deer and rabbits.

For Oscar, the bridge merely meant less time spent on errands, more on work—"Shod Baldy Horse and Paint Horse today. Shod them all around without any help, if I am 65 years old!"—and more trouble: "Six of us pruned nine hours. I should have more help. If they would close those pool halls in Delta I could get help."

On December 5, 1947, at 70, he wrote:

"I am selling my outfit, all my stock and ranches to Nelson and Annie. We got the papers all signed up this afternoon. Now I am retired.

"I have built up a fine outfit from nearly nothing since I went into the Escalante Canyon in 1896. I run my cattle for 48 years and had them up to 500 head.

"But I have seen a lot of terrible hard times, and I have rode a lot of cold days, gathering my cattle, getting them to feed. Many a time I would have to get off my horse and walk to keep warm. Now I think I will start traveling and see some of this world besides Escalante Canyon."

Nelson and Annie Huffington came to terms with the Canyon—their terms. Seeing it could easily eat them alive, as it had consumed Oscar, they sold most of the land to the State Fish and Game Commission, and most of the cows, keeping only the Upper Ranch and the Lower Ranch, the home place.

Still a thousand trees too much. The pruning crews, thinning crews, picking crews, packing crews, truckers for Nelson to ramrod, for Annie to cook for. The terrible pressure of the brief days between the moment when the peach is too green to pick and the moment when it is too ripe to sell.

"Unless you've been there you can't imagine the pressure of detail," Nelson says. "Little things that are vital because everything has to come together. Crates came knocked down, somebody had to nail them, somebody had to paste the labels on. Maybe the crates or labels won't arrive on time. Or some of the crew get sick or drunk. Or it rains. Or the market drops. Or there's trouble with the cattle just when peaches are working you night and day."

In 1963 the Upper Orchard froze, setting them free. "We didn't

Ghost survivors of thousands of peach trees killed in the 1963 freeze.

know the trees were gone until the new leaves failed to come. It was terrible!"

And yet not terrible. Now they merely irrigate and prune the orchards that are left. They deal with just two customers who, trucking in from the East, bring their own crews to harvest and haul the fruit away. Annie cooks only for Nelson; Nelson never misses the weekly lodge meeting in town.

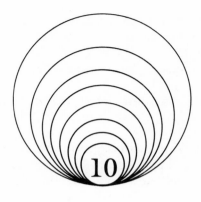

Picture Postcard Cabin

Walled in a sunken world (whether considered prison or paradise), escaping to town only once or twice a year unless sent away to school, what did children and teenagers do for recreation before radio and television?

Well, for one thing, teenagers as a term or class did not exist. By thirteen a person was adult in all but size, license to vote and drink liquor (with some exceptions to the latter restriction). Though wisdom and judgment took longer, life skills had been mastered by then—a boy of thirteen counted as a man in riding roundup, and with pride and confidence knew it; a girl of thirteen (if the mother was ill, having a baby, or dead) could cook for the family and contribute her share of show-off delicacies when women pooled dishes for the big spread that was de rigueur when the labor-exchange haying or roundup crew was working her home place.

Childhood also was not a class, but a condition of anticipation. Kids did play, but the play imitated adulthood and the lifework it prepared them for, whether good or bad. An Englishwoman, Isabella Bird, touring Colorado before the turn of the century wrote:

"One of the most painful things in the Western States and Territories is the extinction of childhood. I have never seen any children, only debased imitations of men and women, cankered by greed and selfishness and asserting and gaining complete independence of their parents at ten years old. The atmosphere in which they are brought up is one of greed, godlessness, and frequently of profanity."

Though one's defensive reaction is that Miss Bird might have taken a look at children in English coal mines before denouncing those in America, there is evidence of truth in her statement: children of pioneers *were* exploited—worked to the detriment of their education—and some children *did* copy the crimes they saw their elders committing.

Cap Smith, after a small-fry guest had been hosted with dignity and no questions asked, wrote in his diary, "Harry the Calf Thief nooned here today."

Girls played "cooking" with clay mud and lemonita-berry ingredients until they were old enough to handle a hot biscuit pan safely, at about four and a half, and from then on eased into the real routine, except for kneading bread, which takes woman-size weight and muscle.

Boys practiced roping, riding, and shooting; hunted and fished. While fun, honing these skills was not really play, being oriented toward usefulness—especially the hunting and fishing, which were serious sources of family food. After game laws were passed, hunting became the responsibility of boys as young as seven in many families, it being thought that a little boy would get off lighter than a grown man if caught with an illegal deer carcass.

Such precautions were hardly necessary—the Canyon had such a formidable reputation for being its own law that officials avoided going down into its fastnesses; even that indomitable super-sleuth Game Warden Ott Peterson.

Infants of both sexes were "saddle broke about the same time they were house broke"—riding while still so little their legs stuck straight out across the breadth of the horse. Many a child at four, on a trained cutting horse, was the indispensable other half of a team doing the pesky job of separating weaner calves from mother cows.

For pure recreation untainted by usefulness or profit, Escalante has one spectacular sport—gully washer watching.

After rapid snowmelt or a general hard rain, every cove in the cliffs spills a waterfall. Even in dry weather, if a cloudburst dumps its load into a distant drainage, any rim cove may suddenly shoot water out into the air and fill the gully below with a roaring flood.

None of these places is map-named, but the children who rushed off to see them in action had names for them all.

"Peek-a-boo, is what my little sisters called the side canyon across from the Shreeves' home place," Jack Shreeves remembers. "When there'd been a cloudburst up on McCarty Bench they would tear in, yelling, 'Peek-a-boo is running!' and tear off to their favorite lookout rock to watch the water rip-snort down that gulch."

Boyce Gulch, across from Huffington Big House, has no water-fall. No mere bench-drainer, Boyce gathers runoff clear to the mountaintop; floods that roar through its lower slot long ago gouged down to creek level.

The children who stood on a grandstand talus to watch Boyce in rampage were Joe Rogers' five kids, but to see Boyce's biggest run, they didn't have to leave the house.

"Luckily, the rain was so heavy it kept the Roger children in the house," Oscar wrote later. "If they'd gone to watch the flood come down the gulch as they usually do, they would have been swept away and drowned."

A rolling mountain of water with trees and rocks tumbling along its face burst out of the gulch filling Escalante Canyon cliff to cliff. Water, boulders, and debris swept through yard, farm lot, and orchard, filled the basement of the new house, and wrenched at the foundations. It ripped out corrals, sheds, barns, cabins; carried away a hay wagon and the mowing machine Oscar had just bought; left timbers and twisted remnants of ironwork miles downstream.

The flood scoured away Joe Rogers' truck garden—roots, dirt, and all. In minutes the family lost what was to have been their groceries for the year. Children, even children who are practicing adults, are still children—while the big folks despaired over ruined property and crops destroyed too late in the year for replanting, the children mourned watermelons they had not tasted and would not taste for another eternity of seasons.

"Escalante Creek carries huge boulders," Annie Huffington says. "You can hear them thundering and grinding along the bottom, making the ground tremble. It's scary listening to it at night in your bed only a few yards away."

Water runs high in Escalante Creek at spring runoff, but the flood's timing, height, and duration are only roughly predictable by snow depth on the mountain. If spring comes slow, with cold nights refreezing the day's melt, runoff is low and long. Hot days and warm nights bring it down all at once. Winds from Utah deserts, whether blowing hot or cold, sublimate the snow, evaporate it where it lies before it can turn to water. In flood, Dry Fork ford and other crossings are impassable to wheels or hooves because of the depth, force of current, and the boulders and trees swept along in it. When the only road up the Canyon cut across the zig-zag stream from one bottom to another, floods islanded people from each other and from help weeks at a time.

Floods take out irrigation diversion dams with such regularity that Canyon people learned to make only expendable ones—brush and mud dams copied from beaver engineering.

In damming a stream, man's instinct is to think crosswise to the flow of water. So he lays logs or rows of stone from bank to bank across the current, which exposes the longest surface to the power of moving water. Beaver instinct is to think with the current. He places pieces of sapling butt-end upstream; the trailing branch stubs dig in and serve as bracing. Water presses only against ends, not sides, and any force less than flood or cloudburst merely wedges the dam tighter, filling crevices with debris and sediment.

Snow depth gives some inkling of what runoff will be, but as for cloudburst there's no way to outguess the hour or swath. It may not be raining within miles of where you are, but suddenly water will be pouring in sheets from canyon cliff rims, funneling down through side gulches, piling up faster than the creekbed can carry it off. Slowed by ground friction, by the rocks and brush and trees it picks up, the leading edge of the flood can build to a twenty-foot wall of water faced with rolling masses of debris. It bulldozes new scenery as it goes, scraping channels down to bedrock through flats that had been fertile meadows.

Eda Musser says, "Those summer floods are terrible. You can hear one coming long before it reaches you, rumbling and roaring. You can smell it coming. It pushes a wave of air ahead of it . . . a bad, awful smell." The Escalante, in flood or normal flow, has killed people, even some who had known its power all their lives. As for outlanders, every summer or so it drowns a swimmer unacquainted with the danger hidden beneath even the low-water clarity of its pools.

Where the sand road crosses Boyce you look creekward between two fences down a ghost lane that was the access to the "improved" Big Hill road known as Suicide Grade.

Even ghostlier nonpresences inhabit Dry Mesa benches beyond Suicide—the Bighorn sheep that wintered there. A sentinel ram, statuelike on lofty rock, nose lifted to test the air for trouble, spiral horns laid back in regal curves, was a common sight from cabin door. They were killed off, prey to disease brought by imported domestic sheep, and prey to "remittance men" and other dilettantes who hunted their heads to decorate game rooms in the East and England where, horns still regal and nostrils still lifted to sense trouble, their glass gaze overlooked poker and pool.

Later, the mesa benches were populated with runaway or laid-off mine burros. They had gone wild and, as old mining men noted, "there is no cantankerouser wild than burro wild." Nelson Huffington recalls, "A young fellow—a 'remit' with nothing better to do—threw his rope on a wild burro and then couldn't figure how to take it off without getting himself hurt, so he shot it."

Beyond a push of cliff the Canyon opens out again to frame an empty stone cabin so perfect in rustic proportions, so perfectly situated under parklike cottonwoods, that it seems to be posing for a greeting card. And it may be—so many artists paint it, so many photographers film it that the yard looks faintly incomplete without easel or tripod.

Cabin and setting are public property acquired by the State Fish and Game Commission from Nelson Huffington, who irrigates and pastures the state's meadows. That the house still exists is owing to Nelson's quiet resistance. The Commission set up a small-game habitat here, stocked it with chukar partridge, and in keeping with the then-governmental policy of returning public lands "to the wild" by burning all structures on them, arranged to have the buildings razed. After a nearby log cabin—the first Lower Canyon schoolhouse—was bulldozed, Nelson was requested to do the same for the Walker stone house. He managed to stall until personnel and policy changed.

The stone house was built in 1911 by Harry Walker and his sons. They came in two covered wagons, long after pioneering by prairie schooner was passé, railroads being as ubiquitous as highways are now. By then all the good homestead land was taken. This spot, though short on acres and irrigating water, was long on rocks, which is perhaps why they filed on it. All the Walkers were masons by trade.

Harry Walker has been described as a rough man but with a sophistication Canyon people did not understand. He had large, liquid eyes in an era when the fashion in eyes was slits narrowed under Stetson brims; they called him "Old Onion Eye," but considering his reputation for pride and the guts to support it, probably never to his face.

Son Frank describes the construction of this beautiful stone cottage: "The walls are eighteen inches think, stone mortared with mud dug from a hole in the yard. Later, when Dad got more money, he

Walker stone cabins, still sound though held together with mud.

'pointed' the joints on the outside with cement mortar, more to give it a finished look than for support. The whole thing is built pretty solid."

Solid it is. Square of corner, straight of roof comb after seventy-five years. Vandals have carried away windows and doors; cattle have hoof-punched holes in the floor, butted and rubbed holes in the pink-, blue-, and green-tinted plaster, exposing lathwork like skeletal ribs, but the structure itself is unweakened.

Vandals are not to blame for the crack in the huge slab of stone that forms the mantelpiece. Hilda Walker, widow of another son, Roy, explains: "That happened before the Walkers moved in. Harry and his boys found that huge stone up on the hillside, backed a wagon up to it, heaved and pried it aboard, then slid it into place on log skids. When the house was all done the Walker young folks [Harry and Nellie Walker had seven children] threw a housewarming dance and built a nice big fire in the fireplace. It was early spring, and evidently the frost hadn't completely gone out of that mantel slab. It split. Sounded like a rifle shot."

Mrs. Harry Walker is spoken of as "a delicately raised gentlelady" who never seemed to know how to cope with primitive living, her husband's absences, or the rambunctious sons growing up around her.

Finding herself mistress of that stone cabin, she tinted the plaster walls with pastel calsomine to a hairline of the dark rugged fireplace stones—baby pink, pale blue, lilac—colors she mixed from powders that came in paper boxes, colors so fragile they had to be redone every year or so. Whether she prettied the fireplace itself with saved lace valentines and urns of dyed pampas plumes, as the fashion was outside the Canyon, is not remembered, but her grandchildren think of the fireplace fondly for its very roughness—on its jagged projections they hung their Christmas stockings.

The cabin's perfection, its strength and beauty of line were a trap, and everything she did to make it better tightened the trap. Why should a man build another house elsewhere when he had such as this to come home to after weeks of batching or boarding at a brick-laying job outside?

"Mother was too tender for Canyon ways," her namesake daughter, Nellie Walker Shreeves, says. "On a knoll west of the house are two little unmarked graves. It grieved Mother that no one ever came to tend them, so every spring she gathered wild flowers to decorate them."

These graves, and another at the Canyon mouth, are thought to hold children lost in the diphtheria epidemic. Velma Shreeves says, "No, by that time burials could only be in official graveyards. Earlier, though, people did bury their loved ones on the home place, wanting them near."

The stone cottage is not large—four small rooms, living room, kitchen, two bedrooms and a stairs, two more rooms under the roof —yet, until the older boys built rock cabins of their own, as many as eleven Walkers, children and grandchildren, lived in five of the six rooms. The sixth was usually occupied by the schoolteacher.

Whoever lived nearest either Canyon schoolhouse was expected to board the teacher. The Walkers, having the schoolhouse in their yard, usually had the teacher. Boarding the schoolmarm was a tricky responsibility: her salary was small (about the same as cowboy wages but with no "and found"); she couldn't afford to pay much, yet she must be so well fed and bedded she wouldn't want to leave. It was hard to get and keep young schoolteachers that far from town-type fun. And they were all young; schoolboards in those days regarded the married state as unfitting a woman to teach children and fired them the moment they became brides.

Everybody strove to keep them happy in the Canyon, especially at the Upper School, twice as far from town. "We had no luck with teachers up there, even when we hired one that'd been married and had children. The Walker boys, Roy or Pearl, would come up with team and spring wagon and take her to town every Friday evening and go get her Sunday afternoon. Still she wasn't satisfied." Cash Sampson, attracted to schoolteachers in the aggregate, sometimes risked his bachelor status for the public good by driving to the Canyon to squire one of them to town and back by buggy.

To homegrown food, Mrs. Walker added the store-bought delicacies requested by her boarder, eking pennies from cash Old Onion Eye brought from some job outside, and with gentlelady tact keeping the teacher unaware than the family did not share these dainties. The Walker children were old enough to understand, but grandson Billy Shreeves didn't, and doesn't to this day: "That old teacher had to have an orange every morning! I used to hate her sitting there peeling it, juice squirting. Biting, chewing, and I didn't have any!"

Miss Pearl Anderson, the Canyon's most fondly remembered teacher, boarded with the Joe Rogerses in the Huffington Big House. When in late spring of her second year she said she would be teaching in town next term, Mrs. Joe threw a bribe party so elaborate the menu was published in the paper:

"Mashed potatoes, chicken pie, cabbage slaw, parsnips, cheese and macaroni, bread and butter, fried salad, coffee, jello with whipped country cream, almonds, peanuts, after-dinner mints, cake, bananas, oranges, apples, candies, nuts and Maraschino cherries. Games, music and dancing."

If the supper had the flavor of a bribe, it didn't change Miss Pearl's mind.

Perhaps she was frightened of the Canyon, or felt unable to cope with it. During the summer between her two terms the Lowe-Sampson shoot-out had occurred; when school took up that fall, there were the Lowe children sitting at their desks as if nothing had happened—except that their faces were too still, their play too silent.

She set them to making contour maps, mixing salt and flour with water to shape a sparkling world as far away from the Canyon as imagination could go: the sixth grade, Robert Lowe, Frank and B. J.

Walker, made the British Isles; fifth grade, Joe Fisher, Nelson Huffington, Thelma and Charles Rogers, shaped the cordillera of the North American continent. Billie Lowe, along with Joe Rogers, Jr., was in fourth grade that year, not wearing his gun to school, of course, but his small hip sagged as with the weight of the .45 that he had worn and had been unable to use to save his father's life. Elaine Lowe, starting second grade, had had no other teacher.

Perhaps Miss Pearl missed the world-famous singers and drama companies that gold mine–wealthy Frank Sanders and Andy Meldrum brought to the Anna-Dora Opera House in Delta.

Perhaps she missed regular church services. There never was a church building in the Escalante, and only briefly was there what every other pioneer community had – religious services in the schoolhouse. This happened midway of the Canyon's history and had shattering results.

At that time there was a nationwide surge of competitive proselytizing; Delta newspapers were listing on page one the names of converts scored by rival revivalists in town. Fire-and-brimstone lay preachers, with a firm date for the End of the World, came out to scare the Canyon into salvation at a series of "protracted" meetings. Most Canyon residents ignored them, or attended a time or two out of politeness – after all, if they'd wanted church they would have built one. But a few got religion. One of Cap Smith's sons turned from sin to Sunday School superintending, a change folks found no fault with since (as he rose to confess) he'd hitherto been generally known for laziness, inebriation, and mischief.

But one hitherto jolly matron took the doomsaying so grimly to heart that she became permanently joyless. Nothing ever again was funny or fun, everything prompted a moral or a don't. Her husband, feeling his life not worth the living – at least that is how Canyon folks explained what he did – drowned himself in Escalante Creek.

And a 14-year-old girl was scared or ecstasized into hysteria, a state not uncommon when teenage females are systematically worked up by revivalists or rock singers. This child lost control at a time and place when local officials responsible for getting people declared insane – for life and without recourse – were trigger-happy. It was only a few years later that Delta librarian Evaline Nutter received an inquiry from her sister, who was in New York doing sociological research: "Why does our county have the highest insanity commitment per capita in the nation?"

The young girl "suddenly lost her mental faculty Sunday night, and was a raving maniac," the paper diagnosed.

Luckily she "came to" before action was taken.

"I never liked the Canyon," Frank Walker says. "You'd only get to town once or twice a year. All summer you slaved, just to save up enough to live through the winter.

"People talk about the good old days when prices were low, but if flour costs only four bits a sack it doesn't do you much good if you haven't got the four bits."

The Walker boys—Roy, Pearl, Frank, and B. J.—had early responsibilities, but little restraint. "The day a spring wagon came by the house, bringing word of the Sampson-Lowe shoot-out, nobody stopped me and my 9-year-old brother from saddling and riding up for a look-see."

By the time he was 14 Frank was doing man's work in the saddle, on hay lift, and with irrigation shovel. The last was a precision skill that some men never did get the hang of—what size cuts to make in the grassy ditch bank to turn water into each of twelve to twenty laterals. The cuts must be large enough to carry a head of water the full length of the field, and yet not so large as to wash out. Each cut must be so precisely sized in relation to the others that the rows carry equal flows of water, and stay equal for twelve or twenty-four hours, depending on the length of the field.

Aside from having to know a little bit about how to do everything (and fix everything and make everything, because getting anything done by experts from outside took too long) the Canyon had two recognized fields of expertise—the cowboy and the farmer. The cowboy did the riding and ramrodding range chores, up and down the Canyon and the mountain; the farmer, tied to the irrigation shovel, stayed put and grew things to sell or put up for winter. The crop raised by cattle-outfit farmhands was hay for winter feed.

Eda Musser says, "Don was the cowboy of Musser Brothers when I came, Kel was the farmer. With the Hendrickson brothers who worked for us, Henry was the cowboy, Frank was the farmer in charge of growing feed at the Lowe."

Like the divergence in prehistoric cultures between hunter-gatherer and corn grower, the two occupations left their mark on Canyon men—or drew their kind: it was the cowboy Musser, Don, who is remembered for his Saturday night ruckuses in town and for being one of the Sheep War raiders. The Musser farmer, Kel, tended to business when in town. When the farmer Hendrickson, Henry, got himself jailed on suspicion of theft, it was the cowboy Hendrickson, Frank, who flamboyantly sprang him in the mode of his idol, Ben Lowe.

Frank Walker at 14 showed no special aptitude for either of these occupations; he was on his way to being a bricklayer like his Dad, who at this time was moonlighting by running the Canyon mail stage once a week, a job that teenager Frank was deemed man enough to take on when Walker Sr. was off laying bricks somewhere outside.

Running the mail stage was a man-size job. A fellow had to be able to negotiate the Big Hill, going and coming, with whatever freight or passengers happened along, able to size up each addition to decide whether the teams could drag that much more up the Hill, or whether the haul to the top must be made in two trips. A fellow had to know how to handle all kinds of things—an order of setting eggs from some fancy breed like Buff Orpingtons that wouldn't hatch if addled by too much jouncing, or rolls of tarpaper roofing that might shift and turn the wagon over coming down.

There was the awesome responsibility of carrying the United States Government Mail with its pension certificates for Civil War Vets in the Canyon, and the letters addressed to Sears or Wards that usually enclosed cash bills and quarters folded in paper.

The mailman was expected to have good judgment on just about everything: a man waiting at his mailbox, harrow tooth in hand, "Get this straightened at Bowen's blacksmith, and watch the color before he dunks it. Once that old geezer gets to talking . . . The color should creep back to here, if the temper's to be any match for the rocks in my field."

A woman counting coins out of a cup, "Bring me three yards of calico. It's for Sistie's first day of school, so pick out a pretty print."

"Running the mail stage wasn't a job you got bored at," Frank remembers. "On one stage trip I met about a hundred cows trailing up the road. Nothing unusual about that in the Canyon, but this time the cowboy was out front leading, not behind driving. It was Don Musser, and those cows were following him like a pack of dogs, sashaying back and forth across the road in his crazy crooked tracks.

"He'd been wintering down at Dominguez, had made himself some whiskey, and was bringing some of it with him, inside and out. He stopped and handed me his bottle. Made me feel ten feet tall, being offered a drink like a man."

During childhood prowling, two of the Walker boys made a gruesome discovery.

"When Frank and B. J. were little boys," their sister Nellie recalls, "they found a skeleton of a man up at the spring above Tatum Gulch; it had two bullet holes in the back of the skull. Mr. Burton who lived down at the mouth of the gulch had disappeared, and folks figured it was him. But the sheriff said the timing was wrong to be Burton. The bones were too old, the skull had weathered thin as paper."

Life in the Walker stone cabin wasn't easy, especially when the adult males were away for months, laying brick.

"Our cabin was so close to the road we could hear droves of horses thundering by in the night, and men yelling at them. We knew they were horse thieves, driving stock out of the Canyon, and we knew some of the horses might be Father's, but we were afraid to do anything or show ourselves. We knew they would shoot us if we tried.

"People said it was Ben Lowe and the men he ran with, Lance and Sewell. We never tried to find out. One night thieves stole forty head of our mares. Father tracked them all the way to Sinbad Basin, the outlaw hole-up in the La Sals. Rounded them up and brought them back, too, with God knows how many gun muzzles looking at him from the brush."

Ben Lowe was selling what seemed an unreasonable quantity of horses. According to newspaper items, he was shipping by the carload to Kansas, Nebraska, Texas, and a couple of Indian reservations. Ben Lowe, people said, played it both ways with the Indians. Cap Smith noted in his diary, "Some Utes came through looking for Ben Lowe. Said he'd stolen some of their horses."

But the Walker mares that made the round trip to Sinbad Basin, that weird thumbhole on the map, were kidnapped by somebody else. Ben Lowe was no outlaw, at least not the caliber of the bank robbers and murderers holed up in Sinbad. As far as is known, in all his escapades he never harmed another human until the afternoon of his death. Like Cash Sampson he used the law, not as a tool to be wielded, but as a gauge—to see what he was when matched against it, what he could get by with just half an inch beyond.

Old Onion Eye had a lot of horses to lose. During depressions when people had no money for building with brick, he raised horses to eke out a living, starting with fifty head dickered from a man at Payne's Siding. He didn't have pasture or hay for them and their get, and no range rights whatever, being a latecomer, but he turned them out on public range anyhow. "He built the herd up to about a hundred mares. The cattlemen didn't like that. They said a horse eats more than a cow, and eats it closer."

Walker horses eventually went completely wild. Later, after their masonry business prospered and the family had moved from Escalante, the government and stockmen put a bounty on wild horses with no owners to pay grazing fees.

"Those horses were running free on Dry Mesa and Negro Gulch," Nelson Huffington remembers. "Two of Noan White's boys built brush corrals with barbed wire wings. Caught and sold a bunch of them. The United States was fighting a war then, and like always in a war, buying up all the good horses and mules for the Army. Farmers and draymen had to take what was left, so even broncs brought a pretty fair price.

It wasn't just horse thieves in the night that unnerved the women and children living in this rock house.

"Cowpunchers driving cattle up to summer range or down to winter pasture would push over our fences and trail maybe a hundred cows through our crops and garden patch," Nellie says. "On purpose. When Dad and the bigger boys'd be away working. What the cows didn't eat off, was trampled into the mud. Stockmen didn't like somebody taking up land they'd always thought was theirs whether they owned it or not."

Bert Shreeves describes the cattlemen's dilemma: "That canyon is mighty narrow. Dad was always worried some squatter would fence him off, keep him from moving his cattle up and down the Canyon, or that he'd have to move his irrigation ditch up on the hillside, just about impossible."

That's why the Shreeves family members did so much homesteading of their own along the Creek. Other stockmen felt justified in using any tactic that would discourage what they regarded as blackmail homesteading. They believed squatters who filed on marginal land (land too short on acres, water, and range rights to be profitable) did so only because its strategic location would command a hold-up price from the cattlemen inconvenienced by it.

On one occasion a herd was started through the Walker truck garden when Old Onion Eye happened to be home. "Father was boiling mad. He grabbed his gun and stood in the middle of the road. Wouldn't let them past. Word got around, and they trailed their stuff out by way of Dry Mesa for a while, but they began again. It was as if they thought because we came later than they did we didn't have a right to come at all. They scorned us, like we were immigrants."

All people in the Western Hemisphere are immigrants by deed or by descent. Settlement is by successive layers in time like the stratification of rocks. When people find a pleasant place on the earth's crust, they tend to want to "lock the door behind them" and keep it to themselves, discouraging newer newcomers by a closed-club attitude if by no more aggressive means. The Puritans scorned the Irish, Irishmen the waves of Italians. Such clannishess applied in spades to the original immigrants, the Indians.

It applied in double spades to early stockmen throughout the West. History books abound with instances where cattlemen protected their range by harassing "nesters," flattening their fences, burning their houses, stealing their stock, whipping, clubbing, and even shooting them, either fatally as good riddance or off-center as good examples.

Cattlemen and sheepmen got there first, they "owned" the public range by virtue of having established prior use of it—the kind of prior right that applied, and still applies, to irrigating water. Homesteaders, by fencing pieces of land in strategic places, blocked access to vast areas of range and to springs that stockmen had always used —even had the gall to file on those springs! Homesteaders, coming in weevilly hordes, threatened to destroy an entire industry—the industry that was then the main economic support of the western half of the nation. A man felt a duty to discourage them in any way necessary.

Even the United States government, when it initiated range management to save the range grass the stock industry was overgrazing to extinction, handled these prior rights gingerly. It first issued free permits, to get the stockmen used to the idea, then began charging a few cents, adding a bit more each year until at the end of a decade or so the stockmen were broken to the permit halter and would go along with a fee that had some relation to the weight a steer or wether put on while grazing public grass.

Escalante was not immune to an attitude that prevailed all over the West, its men were not less rough-and-ready; moreover its situation was more vulnerable than most—access between winter and summer range was along the bottom of a walled slot.

The Walker family's memories of cut fences and a hundred head of cattle charging through the vegetable garden, destroying next year's food supply, are not unique.

Small Escalante outfits just starting up, pasturing a few score cows on forest grazing permits that came with the land they'd taken up or were buying, were "encouraged to quit" by having their cows run off.

"It was usually heifers," one resident remembers. "They'd drive them clear over the mountain, or down into Unaweep Canyon. You'd have to hunt for them, and if you didn't find them before the Forest Service did, you'd be fined for violating your range permit. And the heifers would be in bad shape from being driven so far on the run.

"A man operating small had to spend so much time riding to see that stock was where it should be and all right, that he couldn't get his other ranch work done like he should. After he'd had all he could take he would sell out—usually to one of 'them' at their price because that'd probably be the only offer he'd get. That was the whole idea."

In one such instance of cow-nap farther up the Canyon, a lad was riding in search of the family herd, his father being away either at work or at war—wars, of which Canyon history spans three, were favorite times for "discouraging" mom-and-pop ranch operations, since only women and children were left to hold down the home place. The boy had found the cattle and was driving them home when he was jumped by riders and beaten up. When he returned without the cows, his mother sent him back after them and, with rifle across the saddle, she followed at a distance. When the men jumped the boy again she began shooting.

In another instance a widow lady, old and frail and rather fearful anyhow (as was pointed out afterward), lived upcanyon with her grown son, who spent most of his time in the saddle to see that his stock wasn't run off. Nobody bothered the stock; instead they concentrated on the widow. When she was alone she would hear scratching on the outside wall, the windowless wall next to the cliff. Just scratching. Slow, purposeful, measured, but at irregular intervals— days when it didn't happen were as harrowing as days when it did, taut with strained listening and dread.

It wasn't neurotic imagination, as was suggested afterward. Her son examined the scratches; they were not made by bear claws or a tree branch rubbing. Straight grooves cut down across the logs by a hard, rounded object—a gun muzzle? From the window sides of the house she could see nothing, only the jumble of talus boulders where a man could come and go unseen. She never went outside to investigate; she was too terrified to move.

One day the son slipped back and was in the house when the scratching began. He shot through the wall just slightly above where a man's head might be. The scratching stopped, was never resumed.

But the widow died. Whether from terror at the shooting, from the long stress, or perhaps nothing more than her natural frailty, she suffered a heart attack.

Upstream from the Walker stone masterpiece, the creek and road detour around a strange geological bottleneck, Brent Hill. Here two Walker boys strung claims along the creek—just why, is not clear now. There is almost no farmland in the pinch of canyon within canyon down there, and the water that flows through it already belonged to others.

Perhaps the cattlemen were right and, taking a cue from the geological bottleneck, the Walker claims were designed to threaten another bottleneck, fences, making useless land worth about as much as a man cared to ask.

More likely the Walker boys just wanted an excuse to lay rock. The Walkers leave the impression they laid rocks for fun, that seeing two nice flat rocks they were irresistibly drawn to put them together and make something.

Laid up with mud mortar between uncut flagstones, the two rock "shacks" a quarter of a mile apart still stand. Sagging roof boards, a one-hinge door, a washtub with bullet holes are homesteader artifacts that browsers have so far mused over and left for the conjectures of the next prowler.

"My brother B. J. lived in that first cabin all one winter on seven rifle bullets," Nellie says. "Times were hard. He made sure he didn't pull the trigger until he knew he could kill the deer in the sights."

Frank and Pearl Walker built a more elaborate cabin a thousand feet higher at a spring on the Canyon rim at the head of Tatum Gulch. Frank described its construction at a site where the handiest material was trees rather than stone.

"It was big for a log cabin, twelve by thirty feet, which shows you the kind of trees that grew there in those days. It had a poured cement floor and a big fireplace. It's a six-hour walk up to that place, and we packed everything but the logs, every grain of cement, on muleback. Never was any kind of road up there.

"The fireplace was large enough to take four-foot logs, and had two hooks in the back where we would hang our dutch ovens to cook and bake over a cedar fire. It was a peaceful, comfortable place to live."

Peaceful, comfortable, and wholly male. It became a random kind of club frequented by young and old batches from both sides of the mountain, dropping in and staying over. The idyllic life was brief—Frank and the other Walker boys left the Canyon for the fierce competition of contract construction outside and succeeded outstandingly.

Fireplace, floor, and slabs of wall remain. It is still a six-hour hike to get a look at it, but it's a beautiful walk, most of the miles curve scenically along the clean red sandstone of the Canyon rim.

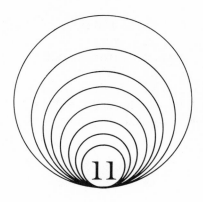

The Lovely, Tragic Lowe

Just above the Walker stone cabin the first outcrop of orange-red Wingate Sandstone peeps through the rubbly talus like a glimpse of smooth flesh through a rough robe drawn partially aside. Wingate Formation that stands in sheer cliffs hundreds of feet high in the upper Escalante, at Colorado Monument, and in the Vermillion Cliffs north of Grand Canyon, is here thinned down to mere yards before it (and all the Plateau strata) slips under Grand Mesa.

Curving to the south, the creek has carved for itself a beautiful inner canyon of clean-walled Wingate ornamented with arches, columns, and vaults that are almost caves.

What pushed the creek south is a great plug of geologic debris, Brent Hill. So big it would be called a mountain in a less vertical setting, Brent Hill is the tail end of Sowbelly Ridge, which separates Boyce and Tatum gulches. It is also the tail end of a vast earth slippage in some ice age when Uncompahgre glaciers were melting and soaking into interbedding clays, causing masses of mountain to move down off ridges into canyons that were ready to receive them, having been formed eons before when the world was warmer.

Since Brent Hill is made of different stuff from Sowbelly Ridge, it evidently sloughed from cliffs higher and older than anything still around. It didn't fall gradually, grain by grain and rock by rock in natural erosion; rather it seems to have slid and tumbled down in one vast doughy mass. It is about as homogeneous as a fruitcake, being composed of red boulders, black boulders, white boulders, pockets of dark red dried mud, pockets of bright orange dried mud, blue muds, greenish-purplish muds, creamy pipeclays, and empty holes. It was so much more difficult for the bottled-up stream to deal with this glommy and unstable mass than with hard but cuttable sandstone that the Escalante chewed its way out around the glob, creating this lovely inner canyon.

In early days the road avoided Brent Hill, too, when it could, winding along the canyon bottom, crossing the creek as often as necessary to stay on flat ground between the loops and to avoid places where the creek kissed perpendicular wall or undercut shallow caves. On one of his horse-and-buggy housecalls Dr. Hick counted the crossings—seventeen.

Such a route could hardly be followed now even on horseback; the inner canyon has gone wild, choked with a deep tangle of willow, sage, and greasewood that from above looks solid as a shag rug. You could penetrate it, walking bent double in one of the deer tunnel trails, and if you did you would find evidence in polished stems and branches that deer—and cows—pass through here not only to get somewhere else but also to get their backs scratched.

Even in the old days when the canyon-bottom flats were cleared and planted to little field patches, the wagon road up the creek was often impassable. When the creek ran high in spring or after storms, the only way into or out of the Upper Canyon was over the top of Brent Hill—a steep jumble of precariously balanced boulders, all the binding clay having washed from the surface long ago.

"Nobody now would believe how terrible that road was," Eda Musser says. "The team would jump over rocks two feet high, then pull and jerk the buggy or wagon wheels up over the rock they'd jumped, tipping and teetering. They'd be lathered with sweat, and you'd have to let them stand to rest and get their breath before they tackled the next rocks.

"The year Alice was born Uncle Bob Kelso was just bound to take me and the baby out to the Canyon early, without waiting for the spring flood to go down. He had a new phaeton and a team of light horses, and I guess he wanted to show them off." The phaeton R. S. Kelso boasted was an elegant carriage of delicately curved body and spider wheels.

"First thing, right at the foot of Brent Hill, a front wheel banged down off a rock and broke, almost throwing the buggy over. With the baby in my arms I couldn't hang onto anything. I don't know what kept us from falling out.

"Uncle Bob left us in the shade of a cottonwood while he went back to Huffingtons' for help. He returned with a lumber wagon. Its spring seat, perched way up on top of the sideboards, wasn't much bigger than a plank, and had springs that bounced and swayed. Nothing to hang onto even if I hadn't needed both hands to keep Alice from getting hurt. The wagon inched up that hill like a tall ship pitching and yawing up and down over the boulders. When my side was up, the jagged rocks looked a mile down; when my side went down they seemed to be clawing at me. Uncle Bob managed the team with one hand, feet braced against the dash, grabbing me with the other to keep me from being thrown out."

In the winter of 1918 Canyon cattlemen – the Mussers, Huffingtons, and Calhouns – hired Herb Wells to cut a road out around, rather than over the top. He put it about where the road is now, looping almost level above the inner canyon on the scraped-off top of the Wingate Formation, and exposing in its cutbanks the weird stuff Brent Hill is made of under its surface of iron-black desert varnish boulders.

With Herb Wells ramrodding, several Canyon men worked on the project. Cap Smith was timekeeper, recording in his diary (among sketches of gravestones to be carved) the wages due each at a dollar and half per day per man, two and a half for man and scraper team.

The shelf of road looked down onto the two Walker boys' bachelor homestead cabins. It still does but down into not onto – into topless laid-stone boxes that once had earth-mounded roofs, smoke curling from stovepipes, dishrag and blue shirt hung on a doorside willow to dry.

Escalante Canyon opens wide after the pinch of Brent Hill, the inner canyon pulls back and splits to form a side canyon, leaving pieces of its walls in crimson pillars – a small, lovely pocket of a place, unnamed, unexplored except by cowpunchers hunting strays, and by children hunting adventure. Somewhere in there, in a cave that was playhouse for pioneer kids, is a camelback trunk, with scrolled iron hinges and locks, that came west by covered wagon.

The road comes down off Brent hill in a slant above what was Huffingtons' Upper Orchard until the freeze of 1963. All is pasture and haymeadow now where once were thousands of peach trees, and a village-size layout of houses, bunkhouses, barns, corrals, toolsheds, blacksmith, and packing sheds. Upstairs in the packing sheds were stacks of picking ladders, piles of "shook" (shipping boxes not yet nailed together), columns of nested bushel baskets, and circular forms that "ring packers"–the most skillful women–filled with precise concentrics of the biggest peaches to top off baskets of otherwise run-of-the-orchard fruit.

Left to show for it all are two cabins and a cellar hole–its cool-dark secrets (shelves for jams and jellies, bins for potatoes and apples) open to the hot sun, caving, trying to cover itself with earth again like a pale grub dug up in spring. One cabin has enough white paint left to make it look like a schoolmarm's house, but it is merely the last of several cabins for peachworkers. The other cabin, age-blackened and buried under brambly trees, was the homestead shelter built by Tom Brent, for whom the hill is named.

Brent was one of the waif bachelors so typical of his time, appearing from nowhere, existing without commitment, and disappearing as he had come. He lived for a few years in this cabin, for a while at McHugh down on the river, did trapping and trail cutting for the government, then drifted. Jack Shreeves remembers, "He was kind of peculiar. Didn't take to children or young people much, but would stop and chew the fat with us kids when we were up at cow camp."

In a time when inhospitality was the cardinal sin–because it could be a matter of life or death–Tom Brent somehow got the reputation for it. But Jeff Dillard wrote that on his first trip through the Canyon he stayed here overnight, and welcome. Considering that Brent's guests on this occasion included three trainloads of Texas longhorn cattle and the crew necessary to push them, this was no mean extension of the latchstring.

Tom Brent seemed a man of better-than-average breeding and education, but the only thing about his past he ever divulged was his reason for being a teetotaler. He said, "I got drunk in San Francisco one time and woke up in South America. Never took another drink."

At the bottom of Brent Hill the road swings alongside a sheer sandstone wall with a deep overhang above a sandy floor. The south-facing cliff, cupping the warmth of winter sunlight, is a favorite picnic place for townfolk who are tired of winter indoors. Considering how frequently this "natural patio" is a nooning stop for Canyon residents and visitors, it is surprisingly free of trash. The spot has its own garbage disposal system–its sandy floor is a drywash, and the patio sluices clean every time it rains.

Following a storm, a sheet of water pours off the rim of that overhang, and on occasion serves as a carwash. Bernice Musser says,

"Plowing up around Brent Hill in sloppy weather, mud covers your car till you can't see out the windshield. Luckily the storm also makes a waterfall here. You can pull under and get your car washed slick as a whistle."

In spring prince's plume spurts yellow fountains of bloom from sand pockets in the rocky "arms" of the Winter Patio. On a rise upstream are several unnatural circles of rock half buried in earth and sage. Old enough to be Indian, but not old enough to be prehistoric, the circles were made by Utes to hold tepee poles in place.

The Patio "window" is a beautiful rock-framed view. On the left cliffs juts a shelf of sandstone out across the sky, the opposite thrust of canyon wall is Table Rock. They frame a wide curve of meadow bounded by billowing cottonwoods along the creek. In late summer this view's foreground is a cloud of sweet summer clematis frothing over fences. As if one called the other forth, clematis at its showiest is usually accompanied by a matching froth of real clouds overhead.

Beyond the tepee circles is a later relic, a mongrel fence that starts as a dry-laid rock wall slanting down from the cliff and peters out halfway, ending in a straggle of posts and barbed wire. Scarcely noticeable in a stretch of scrubby sage, it has no apparent raison d'être, separating only stretches of unwatered wasteland. But since in our trip through the Canyon, whether by car seat or recliner, we are using the clues of what we see as passkeys to the world that was, we pause to puzzle the meaning of this bastard fence whose history nobody now alive remembers.

Dismiss the notion that barbed wire was invented between the rockwall start of this fence and its wire finish. Barbed wire was invented a decade before the Utes left; by the time settlers came here wire fences were prevalent and had doomed such great cattle drives as those on the Chisholm Trail.

But cattlemen weren't building them. They opposed fencing in general and barbed wire in particular. When they needed to confine critters for holding, branding, or sorting, or to have a few saddle horses pastured handy, they built stockade corrals of cedar posts, or worm fences of aspens, which come fence rail–shaped by nature, and grow so thick a sufficient supply is obtained incidentally in clearing a fence width through the groves. And no cattleman, except perhaps Oscar

View of the Lowe framed in cliffs, clouds, and sweet summer clematis. ▶

Huffington, would build a rock wall. Cattlemen weren't lazy, they worked prodigiously hard, but preferably aboard a horse, thank you. So this is a homesteader fence. Perhaps the last one in the Canyon, or anywhere.

Like all artifacts in silent places, it whispers questions. Why was it built at such cost of toil in such a worthless spot? Why, starting as a stone wall with a view to eternity, was it finished an ephemeral skeleton of wire?

What did the man run out of? Certainly not rocks!

Out of time? Out of money to hang on? Out of life? Did the rock wall kill him, as wilderness conquering killed by hernia many who took on heavier jobs than man is muscled for; a dead man's fence finished by another with easier ways? Out of doggedness? One fine morning did he wake from his nose-to-grindstone make-do nightmare, buy wire and finish the job in half a day and less than the price of a yearling?

Up ahead where the road again passes between watered places lies a magic meadow—flat and green as lake water, it laps sheer cliff. No transition of talus, no connecting dotted line of fallen boulders; just smooth-cropped grass kissing vertical wall; one of nature's trysting places where opposites meet, touching us with mystery and wonder. The meeting of ocean and land at even the simplest of seashores has it; the meeting of old lava flow and plain country dirt; the place where glacier leaves off and marsh marigolds begin.

Mrs. Burton, who lived at the Lowe place just around the bend, had no truck with mysteries; she used this place. She set up her drying racks against the summer-hot face of the cliff and put solar energy to work preserving fruit for winter and to sell.

Walking briskly along a shortcut path, in her grass-dragging calico skirts, faceless in the shadowy depths of her shoulder-dragging sunbonnet, she carried dishpans full of halved peaches or apricots to spread in this oven place on wood-slat trays. She covered the trays with mosquito-bar gauze to keep off birds, flies, wasps, and bees while the sun sucked the juices from the hemispheres of fruit, turning them into curled leather like mummified ears.

This she did every summer while she lived at the Lowe, both before and after the day her husband went to town and never came back.

Horses doze where Mrs. Burton's fruit-drying racks once caught the sun. ▶

At the bend, where the road squeezes blind between red sand-stone outcrops, you are directly under Table Rock.

In Canyon lore, Table Rock "belongs" to Ben Lowe, who showed off his superb horsemanship by jumping his horse across the gap onto the small square of rock up there, who showed off his crack marks-manship by "writing" his cattle brand in bullet holes high on the west face of Table Rock cliff, and whose name was carved on its base in tombstone-perfect lettering by his friend Cap Smith while Ben still lived and neither of them had any idea his death would be the oftenest-told tale of all the Canyon's history.

In fact, the whole place "belongs" to Ben Lowe, named for all time "the Lowe Place," though he was not the first, last, or longest resident here, and his tragic end is but one of a series of sad events in the lives of people who lived here. If places on the earth's face can draw events, it would seem that the Lowe place from the beginning was getting ready for the Lowe-Sampson duel.

The Lowe doesn't look like a setting for tragedy. Beyond the nar-rowing thrust of Brent Hill, the creek swings to the south, taking cliff and stream-side cottonwoods along with it, opening the canyon wide to a spread of sunny meadows. The cozy cottage-house sits snug under black walnut trees in the warmth-catching niche of Spring Gulch, noted for its flow of cold sweet water.

The view from here is pure peace, spiced with odd bits of geology —just up the road is the Keyhole with its textbook demonstration of orange-red Wingate Sandstone riding on deep ruby-red Chinle Formation, and nearby a jut of cliff built of thin layers like a torte cake, composed entirely of Chinle. These cliffs are the home of doves that fill the Canyon with their soft cooing, a sound that for the whole history of mankind has symbolized serenity and peace.

Yet recurring tendrils of tragedy extend from this place.

The original settler was J. S. Tatum. He came and went before the land was surveyed, never legally had title to the land, but left his name for all time on the map: Tatum Gulch and Tatum Ridge to the north, Tatum Draw to the south, and the Tatum-Burton Ditch that waters the land.

He put his cabin down by the creek and set out orchard trees nearby. Cabin and trees are long gone, but Brownie Blumberg re-members the man: "Tatum would hunt deer and pack them to town to get a bit of cash—cash being something a homesteader seldom saw. But hunting was pretty prevalent. Once he came in with a dozen deer, and at three-quarters of a cent a pound couldn't sell a one. Everybody had their own."

Tatum sold his squatter's right to Kentuckian Jim Burton. For a time the Burtons lived in silver-gold booming Ouray, where Jim engaged in freighting and trading, and where he sharpened his flatlander teamster's skills on the steep, jackknife trails up to the mines, skills needed nowhere more than on the Big Hill when he moved to Escalante Canyon.

By then there was sawmill on 25 Mesa, and Jim Burton hauled saw-squared logs to build a house with straight, tight-fitted walls. It had a big fireplace, and an ample bed-loft above. "I've been in that cabin," Brownie recalls "It was fine, solid-built and roomy for those times."

Later residents moved it up from creek side to the spring. It burned or was dismantled for the timbers, but its site has rewarded artifact hunters with pieces of a way of life—a stove lid, a clevis, a bit of fluted teacup. . . .

On his creek-bottom land Burton planted fields of potatoes, cabbage, turnips, and other cellar "keepers" and enlarged the orchard. Taking advantage of the sun-pocket lay of land—cliffs high enough to shut out cold, but low enough to let in winter sun and extend the growing season at both ends—he experimented with crops usually considered semitropical. He grew tobacco, curing it with Kentucky know-how. He planted peanuts for miners' kids, grew sorghum cane, and bought a horse-powered sorghum mill.

Produce not eaten by the family he hauled to Ouray and Telluride stores and mine boardinghouses. In summer the wagons carried fresh vegetables and fruit, brine-cured beef, smoked pork, eggs, and butter chilled in the spring and rolled in wet leaves to keep it solid. In winter he hauled cellar vegetables, apples, dried fruit, molasses, fresh venison, beef, and pork. Whatever might be hurt by freezing was wrapped in quilts and stowed deep inside the loads.

It was coming back from such a freighting trip that he went over the ledge on the Big Hill, as earlier recounted.

The Burtons had a big family of hard workers, which was a good thing because freighting took him away from home a great deal—from the Canyon to Ouray was several days' travel behind the creeping pace of three or four span of horses or mules pulling two trailer-hitched wagons. At certain steep places he would have to unload and reload, taking several trips to make a climb. Blumberg says four horses were needed to haul one barrel of Burton molasses up the Big Hill.

Much of the planting, all of the irrigating, and the brunt of the harvesting was done by Mrs. Burton and the couple's two sons and five daughters—one of whom was Mary Emma, who would grow up to marry Oscar Huffington.

The kids ran the sorghum mill, one of them stripping fodder from the machete-cut stalks, another feeding stalks into the rollers, a third driving the mule round and round to power the mill. Boiling the water-thin juice down to syrup was an adult job requiring experienced judgment; the syrup must be cooked down long enough to keep it from fermenting, but not so long that profitable gallons had gone up in steam. Everybody got in on the taste testing—sips from the skimmer full of amber, tangy-sweet froth.

The day Jim Burton disappeared was like any other day with an errand in it. He set out for town on horseback and was never seen again. Brown Blumberg says, "They found his horse down at Dominguez between the railroad track and the Gunnison River, and his hat floating in an eddy nearby. They searched and searched, but never found any trace of him."

When, years later the Walker boys found that skull with two bullet holes in it up Tatum Gulch behind the Burton house, people speculated that it was Burton's and that whoever had shot him had tried to cover by planting his horse and hat down there to make it look as if he had either drowned in the river or hopped a train at the water stop. Others speculated he had planted them there himself.

The finding of the skull was almost a relief to the family. Sad, but at least something definite to anchor the span of mourning to. But that wisp of comfort was taken away when the sheriff concluded the skull was too old to fit the time of Burton's disappearance.

Another tragedy, scarcely less mysterious, struck the Burton family while they were living here. One of the two sons died. Without symptom or sickness, he simply died just as he was coming into full growth and responsibility as man of the family.

Mrs. Burton and the other children carried on the farm work and the freighting; but times turned bad, mines shut down, boardinghouses closed. She sold the place to Josiah Barton and moved to town. A confusion of names on legal papers at this time tells the story of financial disasters, people taking on the place with high hopes, unable to meet the payments, the taxes, the hard times, the hard work.

Russell Browning bought the place from Josiah Barton, let it go back again.

When Russell Browning came West he was 23 years old, unmarried, and he never did marry in his 53 years of life. He was sober, honest, and did nothing but work. His neighbors respected him, but never got to know him because, they said, "he spoke and associated with people only when absolutely unavoidable."

Browning was a cattleman on a moderate scale, branding the EXT and running stock on the open range with all the other cattle, but he never joined in the roundups; he worked alone. Cutting cattle out of the herd all by yourself on the open range is about as frustrating as trying to fish bars of soap out of a bathtubful of warm water using one finger, and with no place to park the retrieved soap but the slick wet slant of the tub rim. While you are hazing one cow out of the bunch, another is dodging back in. But that's how Browning did it, working doggedly and, as far as anybody ever knew, without recourse to undue cussing. It was as if he didn't want anybody to know how many cows he had.

He was the same way about money. Didn't trust banks with any of it—if, indeed, he had any; and folks said he must have some stashed someplace because he ran all those cows and sure didn't spend any on himself or anybody else.

His close-mouthed, close-fisted reputation followed him when he sold the Canyon place and moved to a small farm at the north edge of town. And it got him killed.

In 1933 a couple of citizens, Lloyd Frady and William Cody Kelly, were in a speakeasy on Columbia Street discussing the money Browning was supposed to have on his person or premises. After taking on a fair load of liquid courage, they decided tonight was the night to relieve him of it.

With Kelly's wife at the wheel of a borrowed car, they drove into Browning's farmyard. He met the unaccustomed, unwelcome callers lamp in hand to see who they were. The broken lamp was still at hand when his body was found in the hogpen, tied up with barbed wire, the head beaten in.

Whether Browning had any hidden hoard was never known because Frady and Kelly, using twisted paper torches to light their search, set fire to the house, destroying whatever its joist spaces or doorjambs might have contained—more than one house surviving from those times of failing banks was found to have money stuffed behind the door and window trim when, the hoarder having died, the house was sold and demolished to make way for new construction.

The murderers were apprehended by the clue of their tire tracks in Browning's yard, there being so few automobiles in the area then that the Law had only to wait until the right ones came back to town.

As if the details of the "Hogpen Murder" were not gruesome enough, rumors added worse. It was said the killers tried to torture Browning into telling where he kept his money by twisting barbed wire "around certain parts of his body," a rumor so rampant the body was exhumed to verify or dispel it. Untrue. Also untrue was the rumor that the men had tossed Browning bound and alive into the hogpen so the hogs, maddened by the scent of his blood, would devour and destroy the evidence of his body.

Kelly was the first man to die in Colorado's new gas chamber. Frady's death sentence was commuted to life under one governorship, and pardon under another.

The victim of another tragedy that occurred at the Lowe Place did not live long enough to have a name.

When Escalante Canyon women were pregnant they were a long way in hours and miles from medical help. A few of them had their babies at home, gambling that doctor or neighbor-midwife would arrive before the stork, but most of them, when their "time" drew near, moved to town to stay with relatives or in the family's town house.

One woman delayed the move a little too long. Birth pains started unexpectedly early; she was rushed to town as fast as car could take the ruts and bends. At the wheel was a lad in his teens, as tough, unflappable, and prankish a cowboy as ever slapped hot iron on a calf or burrs under a buddy's saddle—Kelly Calhoun.

By the time they reached the Lowe Place, the birthing was imminent; they couldn't go on. Kelly stopped the car and ran to the house for help. No one was home.

He went back to the car, did what he could, and helped the baby into the world. The infant was alive, but just barely. Opening jacket and shirt, he put the baby inside against his skin, trying to keep it alive with the warmth of his body, but could not. The sight of Kelly, tears running down his face, holding the dead child, stayed with the mother all her life.

With the Lowe Place, as with life, it is the tragic not the serene that leaves the lasting impression; but of the transient families—renters and employees of ranchers—who lived here so happily they made no dent on history, the Barkers touched fame because they knew Jack Dempsey. "One of the Barker boys was a school pal of Jack's," Eda Musser says.

But it is another schoolmate, Carl Smith who remembers Dempsey best. He too used to come out to the Canyon to visit the Barkers at the Lowe, exploring the cliff crannies, flirting with the Jump over onto Table Rock.

"That was during the first time the Dempseys lived in Delta, not the other times when Jack was entering his teens, or later when he worked at the Delta Brickyard.

"What I remember best is when Harry Demspey—he wasn't called Jack in those days—was in second grade and I was in first. He was a nice kid, it was his brother that was always throwing the ink wells and having to clean up the floor. Well, I came to school one day with one of those balloons that when you blow it up and turn it loose it goes whistling off into the air.

"Harry said, 'Let me see that!' And he took it and blew it up tight and tied a knot in it so it wouldn't leak, and began boxing it around. He was already into boxing. Well, he boxed it around until it broke, and then he cried.

"I told him never mind, it only cost a nickel.

"He said he would go home and ask his mother for a nickel to buy me another.

"I told him I could get another balloon the next day. Whenever my Dad's racehorses were doing well he gave me a quarter when I left for school. That was a lot of money for a kid in those days, I was the only one on the schoolground that had money. [Carl was probably the only one on the schoolground being raised by a widowed father and indulgent uncles, which accounts for the munificent daily quarter.]

"Well, Harry Dempsey still felt bad, and the next morning he brought a shoebox of hard candy to school. His mother was the Kings' cleaning woman, but she had run an eating house at the construction site when they were building the Gunnison Tunnel and she'd kept a dish of candy on the sideboard for the men to nibble. The candy was left over from that. The Dempseys were very poor, and I guess they'd been keeping it for rare treats for a long time.

"I took one. I'd been taught never to take two.

"'Take a lot! Take a handful,' Harry said, and then he went around among all the others, passing out candy.

"Later, when Harry was older, the Dempseys came back and lived out on California Mesa. There was an outlaw bunch out there, with roughneck boys that wouldn't let other kids ride the school bus — school wagon, that is. The driver was no match for them and knew it; he just kept his eyes over the horses' heads. That bunch tried to kick Harry off the bus, and I guess there were a lot of fights. Harry was into fighting by then. Upshot of it was nobody but Dempseys and Vanbibbers dared ride the bus. All the other families out there took to providing their own buggies and carts for their kids to drive to school.

"Last I heard of Harry, before he became famous as Jack Dempsey, he was training at the Elephant Corral in Montrose."

From the Lowe, two others went to their death by murder.

Frank and Henry Hendrickson, young cowboys employed by the Mussers, batched here. Eda Musser says of them, "They were good boys. Henry was a farmer-type, he did the irrigating for us. Frank cowboyed and hauled stock salt up the mountain. Whenever they came back from town they'd bring candy for our kids, and often gave them rides on their horses."

Details of what happened to Frank and Henry are filled in by several old-timers. It is noteworthy that the accounts of eyewitnesses — not called to testify because apparently no investigation was ever held — do not agree with the officers' account as printed in the papers of the time.

It seems a rancher north of town missed a sack of alfalfa seed, and Henry Hendrickson, who had been working for him, was accused and jailed for stealing it. His brother Frank, having no confidence in the legal justice under the regime then administering the law, took horses to town and sneaked Henry out of jail.

The boys didn't feel guilty of anything very bad, so they didn't ride very far, just across the mountain (and the county line) to the Craig ranch, where they got work with the hay crew. The Craig boy kidded them about wearing guns while haying, so they had left their guns in the bunkhouse when Delta County Law came to the end of their tracks — in Mesa County.

Henry was operating the hay slip, and Frank was working on top of the stack when the sheriff and three deputies came onto the boys, unarmed and in their shirtsleeves, and began shooting. Frank didn't even have time to drop behind the lip of the stack. Henry ran toward the bunkhouse for his gun to try to defend himself, but they shot him between the horses.

That fall when the rancher was cleaning out a shed, he found the sack of alfalfa seed he had mislaid.

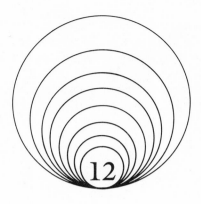

Ben Lowe

Table Rock is Ben Lowe's monument, his towering tombstone, whether or not tombstone carver Cap Smith chisled "Ben Lowe" in beautifully incised letters upon its base before or after Lowe's death by violence.

Few know about that carving, vandals have not discovered it. It isn't really hidden, though tall weeds mask it in summer, but the size of the Rock dwarfs it, and a cliff-pinched, blind kink in the road keeps eyes focused ahead to avoid collision. Canyon people point it out only to those they feel can be trusted to leave it the way they find it.

Because of its eerie, monumental shape, and because of Ben Lowe, Table Rock is the most legendary spot in Escalante Canyon and, by association, in this section of the West.

The legend of the rock itself is endurance in the face of odds. By rights the top-heavy table slab should have shattered the slender neck ages ago, but for a hundred years of white-man history it has stood unmoved above the fleeting dust plumes made by hoof or wheel as men scurried to get their errands done in the brief span between birth and death.

Yet it is the Rock that is diminishing, grain by grain, while the legend of Ben Lowe grows.

Ben Lowe, they say, was a Kentucky gentleman, son of a minis-

Table Rock, Lowe's brand in rifle shots in the center. ▶

ter, tall, blond, graceful and courtly on the dance floor, lordly and centaurean in the saddle. Ben Lowe, they say, was a kind of pioneer Robin Hood who stole (mostly beef) from the rich (often his cattlemen friends) to feed the poor. Ben Lowe, they say, was a rip-snortin', hard-ridin', hard-drinkin', horse-stealin', gun-slingin' bronc buster who was responsible for a great turnover in town marshals.

Table Rock, they say, "belonged" to Ben Lowe by virtue of two deeds, one a deed of homestead, he having taken up the land when the Indians went out, and the other a deed of valor, he being the only man living or dead with the guts to jump a horse out onto the rock.

Well, Ben Lowe never owned Table Rock nor any of the real estate that surrounds it. The Lowe Place belonged to Ruby Lowe, not Ben. Only her name appears in the suit to quiet title going all the way back to Burton's disappearance and including subsequent attempts at ownership.

This ranch in Escalante as well as town lots where they built residence and livery stable—and, according to tax records, apparently all Lowe property that didn't eat grass—was in Ruby's name, either because she was the business manager of the family, or because Ben took that means of insuring his wife and children against the consequences of certain free-handed aspects he recognized in his own nature.

"Ben couldn't hold onto money or things," Nelson Huffington recalls. "He'd give anything he had to a friend or anybody he thought needed it." Ben Lowe's daughter-in-law Frankie uses a phrase that is time-worn precisely because it says it all, "He'd give you the shirt off his back."

Or perhaps these pieces of real estate were in Ruby's name because acquired with her family's financial help.

Ruby was the daughter of Spud and Lady Hutchinson, who staked a homestead on river bottomland just below town about one minute after the Utes trailed out of Colorado ahead of General MacKenzie's troops in 1881. Spud Hutch's real name was R. C. but this was forgotten as his produce began to heat up local prosperity. The D&RG had scarcely replaced its temporary bridges with structures less erodable when Spud was shipping potatoes to Texas, New Mexico, and Nebraska.

Lady wasn't Mrs. Hutchinson's real name, either. She earned her nickname by spending Spud's money—in a manner that put Spud Hutch out of the grubby farmer class, whatever folks called him. When Lady went to town in the shiny black buggy, swaying and jolting up the rutty riverbank road, easing spirited horses down onto the scary ferry ramp, she was wearing jewels, plumes, and silks designed in Paris.

Like her mother, Ruby was tiny and pretty and prone to be nicknamed. Her family called her "Ribbons," Ben's name for her was "Chiquita," a Spanish word meaning something like "my adorably pretty little girl thing," which he usually shortened to Chiquit (pronounced Chi-KEET).

With her family position and looks Ruby could have married anyone—the son of any of dozens of town and country VIP's, bankers, merchants, developers, stockmen. And marrying "well" was so de rigueur that wedding write-ups listed the financial qualifications of the bridegroom: "One of Surface Creek Mesa's wealthiest young ranchers"; "only son of one of the town's foremost bankers."

Growing up in a community so small everybody knew every good and bad thing about everybody else, Ruby Hutchinson knew all about Ben Lowe.

Benjamin A. Lowe was born June 11, 1868, one of eight sons of the Rev. William and Mary (Demmitt) Lowe, who by the time of his birth had come from their native Kentucky to pioneer in Missouri. They saw to it that Benjamin stayed in school to the then-advanced age of sixteen and that he received a proper Kentucky-gentleman type of rearing.

By the time he was twenty-four he had acquired notable skill in training racehorses and in skating excitingly close to the limit of the law, perhaps in traditional PK (preacher's kid) reaction to too much of the straight and narrow. The legends are right about one thing: he was a smooth, courtly man on the dance floor and in the saddle.

He came to western Colorado in 1892 and, with his brother Bert and sidekick Charley Sewell, worked for Roberts Bros. horsebreeders. All three of them broke horses to ride, but Ben also had the training of colts and fillies sired by famous racing studs Briggs and Potter.

Roberts Bros. racetracks were at Buford on Roubideau Creek, across the river from the Spud Hutchinson place. A girl fifteen or so, nearing marrying age, could hardly help noticing such a figure riding the far-side river road to and from town, but he made himself noticeable in other ways. Ben, Bert, Charley, and friends engaged in extracurricular activities that got them labeled "jingle boys"—short for everything implied in "rootin', tootin', gun-slingin' cowboy."

Such cowboy whingdings were so common they didn't rate headlines, but appeared as brief paragraphs in the Local Items. "Ben Lowe flashed his gun on Frank Bishop in Jack's Restaurant Monday evening. Ben has a reputation for that kind of business, in fact it has been a favorite pastime of his for some time. After making the gunplay he left town. Tuesday a warrant was issued and Sheriff Hunt went in search of Lowe but returned without the game."

And another time, "Ben Lowe left town in his usual noisy fashion, both guns."

While still working for Roberts Bros. he began putting together an outfit of his own, a horse and cattle ranch developed on land he homesteaded south of town. The outfit eventually included a spread of buildings, fencing, irrigated hayfields, bunkhouse for a sizable crew of cowhands, and with concomitant cow camps and summer range on the mountain.

This was his fair-weather headquarters. For bad times—when the law was after him for something he'd done or been accused of—he had a hideout cabin in a cranny of the Roubideau where side canyons crack into trackless mazes.

Down in the cranny he put up what old-timers call "a stoop-door cabin"—just enough shelter to keep rain off his bedroll and cooking fire. Roofed and banked with earth, it was scarcely distinguishable from the talus it huddled in.

The cabin site, the trail to it, and the mesa lands above, where he pastured his get-away transportation, still bear his name on the map—Ben Lowe Cabin, Ben Lowe Trail, Ben Lowe Flat—but anytime he felt it expedient to hole up there the law could never seem to find them.

Carl Smith claims the law didn't try very hard. "Those jingle boys had that country triangulated, nobody could come near without being seen—through gunsights. Posse men knew it, they would search around a while, and come back to town explaining they'd lost the trail."

In 1885 Ben Lowe was defendant in a case before the district court —the first of at least three (all acquittals) in his lifetime. *The People* v *Ben Lowe,* grand larceny. The paper did not name the precise crime, but grand larceny in those days usually meant stealing horses.

The case was continued until the following February, and hung over Ben's head the whole year he courted Ruby. Whether Spud and Lady wouldn't let her marry him until it was cleared up, or until she was seventeen, or whether he wouldn't pop the final question "When?" until sure he could offer her something more suitable as a honeymoon cottage than that hideout hut, the fact is they did not marry until May, 1896, two months after the jury pronounced him not guilty.

Since the law had never before been able to get a handle on Ben, it is conceivable that he himself finagled that court case to get the past cleared up before taking on wife and family, gambling that he would be cleared (but not gambling on getting jailed because he always had the hole-up). If so, neither that nor marriage tamed him much. (Ruby didn't try to. For her, as long as she lived, Ben was perfect.) Only a few issues later the paper was reporting, "Ben Lowe was tipped by officers to leave town, and he went without tarrying to say goodbye to the boys."

They set up housekeeping on Ben's ranch and for a while his name appeared in the papers only when he was shipping carloads of horses here and there in the United States, or winning races at state and county meets and fairs.

But just because he wasn't in the papers didn't mean he wasn't into mischief. Along with others of his kind and time he periodically exercised what all cowboys considered a God-given right—a little innocent fun in town, a Saturday night spree concluded by "shooting up Main" one jump ahead of the marshal, guns popping, throats yelling, hooves making hollow thunder on stretches of boardwalk.

And not just Saturday: "A gang of cowpunchers made things noisy in town Tuesday night. What was the night watch doing?" Ben's route after one of these escapades, as Oscar noted was usually up a draw past Sylvester Huffington's brick house at the end of Fifth Street. But Sylvester's protest shot was not the only bullet that went through Ben Lowe's hat before the one that went a little lower.

Ben was in trouble with the law again, and once again the paper neglected to state the nature of the alleged crime. (Court records are incomplete. Some county seats in the days of wooden courthouses and shaky stovepipe elbows lost their records by fire; this county lost records to the town dump by overzealous housecleaning.)

Borrowing team and buckboard, the marshal and deputy drove the seven miles out of town (and incidentally out of their jurisdiction) to Ben's ranch to arrest him for whatever he'd done this time. A couple of days later the team returned minus the officers, the buckboard, and the harness.

As always where Ben was concerned, people jumped to the worst conclusions: He'd killed the officers! Stolen team and rig! The horses got away from him!

Search parties, excited to a lather, were in the act of going off in all directions when the officers telephoned that they were safe but mighty footsore. When at last they straggled into town, this is the story they told, as reported in the paper:

"The two deputies say that when they arrived at Lowe's ranch, they met him in a lane riding a horse bareback, and he immediately wheeled his horse and fled, but owing to the fact that a boy was riding in the road behind him they were unable to shoot with any degree of accuracy."

The proximity of the boy didn't stop the officers from shooting on the fly, or changing their story. "The deputies had fired several shots at the fleeing man and he had returned fire. After following him some distance and gaining on him they came to a canal which Lowe's horse cleared, but the officers had to unhitch and ride their horses bareback. As their horses were both wiry animals that had never been ridden, there was some firstclass bronco busting done which gave Lowe a big start.

"Lowe went to Halley's ranch and secured a Winchester and several rounds of cartridges, saying he had seen a mountain lion nearby. He then started to return, but the officers say they did not see him again, although firing was reported in that direction. Marshal Welch says they would have landed their man if ammunition had not run out, as they had him headed off."

In spite of the apparent whopper that they with team and wagon were gaining on a rider, the officers' talk was not pure face-saving brag; they had indeed almost got their man.

"A Close Shave for Lowe," another news item quipped. "Ben Lowe had a very narrow escape while he and officers were firing at one another about a quarter of a mile apart. Lowe was shot through the hat. The bullet plowed through his hair entering directly above the eyes, just high enough however to do no damage except to the nerves."

Ruby ripped off a public statement, hotly defending Ben. What Ruby wrote is lost, alas, with the issue in which it appeared, but the paper's biased rebuttal remains:

"Mrs. Lowe in a signed statement last week, which was published, made charges against the officers who recently tried to arrest her husband, Ben Lowe.

"She claims the officers shot 17 times at Ben Lowe before he reached Markley's ranch, but witnesses do not bear her out. Only one shot was fired from the rifle, and Officer Welch did not do more than empty the six-shooter [this despite the officers' having gone on record as shooting until they ran out of ammunition].

"Mrs. Lowe claims that both officers were so drunk that parties had to light their pipes for them. Anyone knows that either Welch or Collins are not going out to arrest a man like Lowe while intoxicated."

On the face of it, considering how they tried to ride a couple of unbroken harness horses in pursuit of perhaps the best rider in the country, they do seem to have been a bit fuddled. Perhaps intoxicated *was* the only way they would go out to arrest a man like Lowe.

There were other Ben Lowe escapades on record such as the face-off between him and Beaty over how the last race had been conducted. Half a dozen people were in the two parties that met there on the town's promenade street, tree-arched Eaton Avenue, cutting a wide diagonal down to the ornate new depot. Words led to fists and to pulled guns. Beaty's was the only gun fired, but it was Ben who got arrested. Ruby used to say in fury and despair, "Most of the things they lay to Ben were done by somebody else. If there's a ruckus on the fairground, people say, 'Oh, that's Ben Lowe acting up again.' When he wasn't even there!"

Many of the stories are folklore.

It is popularly believed that it was Ben Lowe's horse that cut those hoof prints you can still see in the wooden floor of the John Davis Clothing store.

John puts the record straight. "No, it was Shorty Gibson, a puncher working for Mussers. I was out sweeping the sidewalk (board-walk in those days). Shorty rode up and said he guessed he would come in for something. I supposed he meant to get off and hitch his horse to the rack, but he just rode right in through the double doors—had a little to drink, of course—whirled his horse to miss the glass counter and rode right on back out."

Then John admits with a grin, "Ben Lowe and Don Musser were in on the same shenanigan, but they rode their horses in the poolhall and the Boardwalk Saloon. Both those buildings have been gone for a long time."

The harvest of trouble his reputation gathered was more serious than mere ruckus and prank. His reckless exploits made him a legend that caused other men's lawless deeds to be attributed to him—both before and after his death—and perhaps helped to cause his death. It enabled criminals (usually horse thieves) to lay their crimes to him.

As time went on, and his reputation got out of hand, he apparently tried to undo it, at least as regards horse stealing. If horses were reported lost or stolen Ben would be first on the trail and last to hang with it until he found and returned them to the owner.

"After several days on the track of the fellow who stole the span of five-year-old geldings from the corrals of William Lance, Ben Lowe came upon the horses in Roubideau canyon country Saturday afternoon."

How do you track a horse thief? Very circumspectly.

"Lowe and I followed the trail from the corral on foot, walking and leading our horses for many miles," Lance said.

When they came onto the stolen horses the thief was nowhere in sight, but they glimpsed him later, struggling to make a getaway through the snow-choked canyons, backtracking, seeking new routes.

Though Lowe and Lance were not deputized and were acting beyond the law, they were criticized for coming back with the horses but not the thief. Lance explained why they made no fight against a man who was armed and in ambush.

"He had a rifle and other weapons, and a thousand places to hide and wait for us. It's one thing to fight and capture highwaymen in a billiard hall or storeroom, but another matter out in the canyons of Colorado. We were perfectly content to let the fellow go his way, and we went ours."

On another occasion Ben Lowe, working alone, found a Palisade ditch rider's saddlehorses a hundred miles from where they had "strayed."

Whether or not these activities did anything to clear Ben Lowe's name, they didn't ease his mind. Though he had more and truer friends than most, he had enemies and knew it.

Nellie Walker Shreeves says, "When Ben's sons were just little boys they carried guns, and practiced shooting. Ben told them 'If anybody tries to kill me, shoot him.'"

Robert and William were still so small they hadn't leg length to reach the stirrups when they were packing food to Ben during those times when something he'd done or was accused of doing drove him to his hideout.

"Ruby would cook up a bunch of stuff, bread and cookies, and start the boys out," Carl Smith says. "Those tykes would wander around like they were hunting rabbits, and shake whoever was trying to get at Ben by trailing them."

Until she had boys big enough for the job, Ruby did it herself, and felt free to tell about it when it was all over and nothing more could happen to her man. "Ruby was best friends to my mother, and I would sit glued when she'd be telling about Ben," Esther Stephens says. "When he was out hiding from some fool thing he'd done, Ruby would take food to him. The law tried to find him by following her, but they should have known better. She gave them the slip every time."

Clarke's *Biographical History of Colorado* describes Ben Lowe as "a cattleman and buyer and shipper of horses . . . who made a specialty of growing alfalfa."

Newspapers noted some of his dealings: "Ben Lowe and Charles Sewell returned from Denver where they sold a couple of cars of horses. It was their intention to take the horses through to Nebraska, but the demand in Denver was such that they disposed the lot there." Denver traffic and draying consumed horseflesh in appalling quantities. Streetcars alone, operating at a killing pace for the convenience of commuters, burned out a thousand horses each year.

"Ben Lowe and one of his men departed Saturday for Fort Lewis, the old Indian Agency, where Ben had purchased three or four cars of horses."

For a few years Ben Lowe was a businessman in town, operating a livery stable on Main Street. It was a clubby place, even more so after he acquired the town Reading Room for his office.

Earlier the good people had noticed that the only heated, lamp-lit, lounging rooms in town were the saloons. So they created the Reading Room to provide a more wholesome option for ranchers, cowpunchers, and wayfarers staying overnight to rest their teams, and for chronic bachelors of all sorts. As is usual with such projects, they stocked it with books they didn't want anymore—"Moore's Complete Poems" and "The Decline and Fall of the Roman Empire." Nobody was using it, so Ben got it cheap. Since people liked to be around Ben Lowe, the Reading Room at last became a success, the most popular hangout in town.

Not long after Ben opened his stable, the town council passed an ordinance against livery barns on Main Street. So Ben and Ruby bought six lots on Dodge—two blocks over from Main and nearer the depot—and built a big new livery barn and two-story house.

One of the young men who worked for Ben Lowe in that livery barn used to tell a story that speaks for a side of Ben's character that has been overshadowed by the more picaresque phases of his life.

Claude Marsh said, "I was fifteen when I came to Delta. Didn't have a cent and didn't know a soul. Me and my horse were hungry, and I guess we showed it. Ben Lowe had a livery stable on Dodge Street. I was riding past, and he came out and said, 'Hi, kid, what's the matter? You look hungry.' Well, Mrs. Lowe fixed me a supper, and Ben fed my horse. He said, 'How'd you like to work for me?' and he handed me a five-dollar bill (that was a week's wage in those days) and told me to go uptown and get some clothes. I didn't have anything but what I had on. I worked for him a long time, slept in a room they fixed up for me in the livery barn."

Not too long after Ben Lowe opened up his new stable, the town council passed an ordinance against livery barns on Dodge Street. This was so patently unjust that Ben ignored it and went right on boarding horses. The city fathers took him to court and fined him a hundred dollars, with promise of more of the same if he did not cease and desist. He appealed the case and lost. The state decreed that a town coucil had the right to pass such an ordinance, and it was not relevant that the council seemed to be following one businessman from street to street to give him a bad time.

This was one of two court cases in which state law would be defined because of Ben Lowe.

After that brush with law and order Ben, Ruby, and the kids moved to the wildest place left in the civilized world this side of Sinbad Basin, Escalante Canyon.

Robert and William were too young for schoolhouse school when the Lowe family moved to this beautiful place. Their older sister, who would grow up to marry a relative of her father's killer, rode down-canyon to the Lower School.

But they had been schooled by Ben almost since birth, though probably neither they nor Ben realized it since both teaching and learning came under the heading of fun. All of them, girls and boys alike, learned to ride—to sit steady and secure yet move easy to the motion of the horse—before they learned to walk. The girls had their pioneer-type domestic management skills to learn from Ruby; but the boys, striving to be exactly like their idolized father, learned not only riding but trick riding, trick roping, trick shooting, trick horse breaking.

Breaking a horse to saddle or harness is a slow, patient task, but Ben had a trick for breaking a horse to the halter in a few minutes. Eda Musser says, "He taught Don Musser how to do that, and they would catch up a bunch of wild range horses, halter-break them and ship them over to Kansas corral auctions. Those plow farmers, sitting on the top rail watching wiry horses being tamely led around and around, would bid each other up pretty high." What happened when the farmers had led their purchases home and discovered the halter was the only thing the broncs would stand still for isn't known on this side of the Continental Divide.

Lowe-trained racehorses were entered at tracks all over the region (and because racing was the main sport of the time, there were a lot of tracks). Many breeders could go to the post with a top horse or two, but Ben's string included so many winners he could enter the five-horse relay, and with such consistent success that not to win was news. Charlie Buzzard remembers, "My brother Ollie and I got a five-horse string together and raced Ben's string in the three-mile. Won once in a while, too!"

A superb horseman, Ben seemed to evoke not mere obedience, but all-out joyous participation from his mount as if the animal exulted in being part of his will and body. At least one horse put his heart on the line for Ben. It happened in a spectacular fashion, before a huge crowd, to match the life-style of the rider. The paper reported:

"Ben Lowe was unlucky enough to lose his horse Flaxie at the Fair last week. Mr. Lowe had just ridden onto the track and was holding his racer near the grandstand when the steed dropped like a bullet, a few spasmodic kicks and all was over. Flaxie had run in the half mile last Thursday and took first money. The week before at Montrose he also made first money for his owner."

First prize in roping events, too, often went to Ben.

Roping and calf tying preparatory to branding is a cowboy specialty, a cowboy exclusive, his daily business and brag. It is thought that Ben Lowe was among the "rimrockers" (the paper carefully named no names) who tore up the town in outrage one County Fair day when a sheepherder delivered the ultimate insult by beating cowboys at their own game.

Sheep, any cowboy would loudly explain (making an obscenity of the word), never require roping or tying. To brand the weevil-shaped things you just slop some paint on the wool as they file docilely out of the pen. Even if you ever had to rope one, there'd be no challenge, no skill or speed involved—sheep just stand there bleating, head up waiting for the rope, or run off bleating, head up to the rope, or huddle in terror, trying to worm under each other, leaving the outer ones head up and bleating. And if you did rope one, it wouldn't give you the satisfaction of fighting back; no need to tie its feet, it'd just lay there playing dead till you got through with it. Nasty. Just a shade less nasty than their keepers. A sheepherder had no *right* knowing how to rope and tie! Much less do it better and faster than the best cowboys in the country!

After shooting up the town in afternoon and early evening, in lieu of shooting up the sheepherder, since they couldn't find him, the rimrockers laid for him in the livery barn where his packhorse was, knowing he'd have to come for it sooner or later. He came, and they had him cornered, dancing a bullet-dodging jig in the straw when the law arrived and took their guns away.

A rimrocker is an extra special tough, rowdy, mean-joke cowboy who gets that way from wrangling steers in and out of tough country — the rims and gashes of canyon breaks. In spite of the paper's carefully anonymous term, everybody just knew the head harasser, the man the law relieved of three guns there in the livery barn, was Ben Lowe.

Ben Lowe was a crack shot with rifle and revolver; and he practiced constantly, perhaps as much to stay abreast of the deadly consequence of his own quick-draw, bull's-eye reputation as for the sport. You can see his cattle brand in bullet holes up there on the face of the cliff above the Lowe house. He stood where you are standing now, sighting with narrow, still eyes, writing with trigger finger.

His best trick shot also combined trick horsemanship. It may have cost him his life or, as people still argue, "might could have saved it." Riding at top speed he would lean down and whip out quick shots at tiny targets from under the neck of his trained horse, which for years was a dappled gray-white gelding he called Cloud.

Whether because he feared the liabilities of his reputation might extend to his sons, or whether he believed every man of whatever age should be able to defend himself, Ben bought handguns for his little boys and taught them marksmanship. Emulating their adored father, they became crack shots. Bill Lowe kept up his skill and was top man in regional trap and rifle shoots as long as he lived.

Two old-timers, who had been their playmates, recall that even while still small, Ben's boys were accustomed to wear .45's, though not as playthings.

"They didn't do much of what you call play, none of us did, but we had good times, though most of it was in connection with work — riding fence, looking for strays. We roamed the mountain, explored, hunted. Bob and Bill were quiet boys, you might say sad, but that's probably only from looking back at what happened to them."

Along with horsemanship and marksmanship, Ben Lowe seems to have instilled in his sons the "Southern Gentleman" ways that made him so popular at Canyon social events. "People talked, but Lowe never gave any trouble to folks in the Canyon. He neighbored well, and his children were mannerly."

When Ben Lowe moved to Escalante he stopped drinking.

This drastic move was probably more an attempt to control the threatening bonfire of his reputation than to get a handle on his own actions, which, even at his drunkest, he'd strictly reined just short of harming anyone. For the last seven years of his life he was virtually a teetotaler. No more Saturday night binges in town, no more juicy little items in the paper about Lowe escapades.

He almost escaped being hostage to his reputation. The newspaper—in the only item about him other than races won or carloads of horses sold—spoke of his life-style in the past tense.

"Ben Lowe came down from his Escalante stock ranch Friday, and went to Grand Junction to take in the Irwin Wild West Show. Ben has seen much of the real wild west, and he wanted to see what Irwin's had in the way of frontier life."

Going on the wagon didn't change Ben Lowe's life-style much; he was still the same flamboyant person, and no less free-handed to anyone in need. On the other side of that barn-size boulder squeezing the road against Table Rock cliff, there are traces of a banked-earth cabin. Ben Lowe built it for an old man who had nowhere else to live.

"His name was Shorty Castle," Nelson Huffington says, "a Batch, too old and sick to live alone, but who'd rather die than go to the County Poor Farm, the only place then for old people with no money and no kin to care for them.

"Ben Lowe built him a snug cabin on the sunny side of that big rock. Private and independent, yet close enough they could look after him. Saw to it he had food and anything else he needed as long as he lived." Ruby kept Shorty's name in the pot, brought him "excess" food—stew, biscuits, baked beans—explaining with tact to match Ben's that she'd done it again, cooked up too much and they needed help to get it eaten before it went bad.

Ben moved the Burton cabin up into the Spring Gulch niche, added a dining room and big kitchen for Ruby, and replaced the mantel with a rock slab carved by neighbor Cap Smith in garlands of oak leaves and acorns like a gravestone.

Ruby stayed in the house as little as possible. Petite lady-girl though she was, Ruby was Ben's kind of woman. A good horsewoman when they married, she became expert. Training on horses he had trained, she won almost as many races as he did, though nothing like his take in cash and prizes – the winner of the top ladies' event, the half-mile dash, was lucky to get a fancy bridle or pair of boots.

"She adored Dad," Bill Lowe said years later. "We kids'd be down at the corral, and one of us would tear to the house yelling, 'Dad's putting on a show at the corral!' and she'd drop what she was doing and run down to watch him."

Ben's best stunt was to jump a horse out onto Table Rock. The Table by eyeball measurement varies according to the eye doing the estimating. Nelson thinks it is about fourteen feet square, Ray says it looks eight to him. Since the tabletop is weather-rounded, the surface a horse can get footing on is smaller than it looks.

"Barely room, if anybody was fool enough to get himself out there, to turn a horse to make the jump back."

The gap is not wide – perhaps three feet – but the distance between hoof-safe footing on either side is wider. The Table stands about eighty feet above the Canyon floor.

One old-timer (not a resident of the Canyon) says Ben Lowe never made that jump, that such a jump is impossible, that this is just another of the myths that form the Ben Lowe legend. Another old-timer swears he did, but doubts anyone else could do it.

"I was working in the Canyon when the Hendrickson boys, Frank and Henry, were living at Lowe – after Ben was killed and before they were. Frank just worshipped Ben, and he set out to do what Ben had done. I watched him try to make his horse Gotch jump over onto that rock. He worked all day, patient and gentle. Face the jump, wheel from it and come back to the edge. For hours. Gotch refused every time.

"A horse knows damn well how risky such a stunt is. Only way he'd do it is if he trusts the rider utterly. Ben Lowe's about the only man could get that kind of trust out of a horse."

Somewhere in this world there is a photograph of Ben Lowe on Cloud's back on top of Table Rock. Cloud is rearing, his front feet pawing air, Ben is standing in the stirrups waving his hat. The photo was taken by Truman Foley while he was with the Forest Service.

The cottage you now see tucked into Spring Gulch niche is not the Burton-Lowe squared-log cabin with the fancy oak-leaf mantel. That was razed to make room for a more modern dwelling after Mussers bought the Lowe Place from Ruby following Ben's death.

With her five children Ruby moved to a ranch she bought west of town, where the land lies flat and open, far from canyon walls. "Mrs. Lowe personally supervises the property," Clarke's *Biographical History of Colorado* noted during her lifetime, "and is making it one of the fine ranches of this section of the State. She has displayed marked business ability and enterprise."

But tragedy was not finished with Ruby Lowe. The new farm had plenty of irrigating water but no spring; domestic water was hauled from town in a wagon tank by Ruby herself. One day as she was driving up Brickyard Hill with a load of water, the team spooked and began lunging, and she was thrown under the wagon. One of the iron tires severed her right arm. One-armed, she continued to run her ranch.

And she continued to keep the memory of Ben Lowe's horsemanship and flare alive. Riding a borrowed sidesaddle or astride, controlling a spirited horse one-handed, Ruby Lowe was the star attraction in fair and rodeo parades for many years.

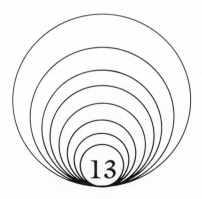

Sandstone Is Not Forever

In a canyon that is superbly photogenic from end to end, but never the same for long, the stretch between the Lowe and Cap Smith's slab-stone cabin has a special kind of beauty. The roadbed of soft red sand loops over talus humps below ever-changing cliff faces; its brilliant color contrasting with the cool bluish green of old-man sage, the hot dark green of juniper, and the stained-glass green or stained-glass gold of sky-shimmering cottonwood leaves overhead.

Thanks to the irrigation ditch that winds alongside the road, pleasant as a natural brook—and to the fact that because this is range for cattle and wildlife, clean-row farming is not practiced—fence rows are a prodigal wealth of wonderful plants called weeds. In summer they are tapestried with flowers, small but vastly intricate to close-up lens. In fall they flaunt assorted seed contrivances, as if trying all possible ways to get the next generation from here to there, equipping seeds to pop, spray, sail, jump, hook a ride, or simply hang until snow pushes them to ground.

Most graceful of these "weeds" is sweet-summer clematis, outlining fences with green tendrils in spring, draping them in white flowers in summer, and burying them in froth of seed plumes in the fall. Along the creek the summer apple-green of willow brush, autumning to lemon yellow, strips to wax-red withes in winter, repeating the reds of cliffs.

Key Hole, orange-red Windgate sandstone over ruby-red Chinle. ►

Up the road from Lowe is the pillar called the Keyhole, most accessible of the Canyon's several "hole in the rock" formations. Soft ruby-crimson Chinle strata eroded to make the hole, scarlet-orange Wingate Sandstone caps and holds it together. As photogenic as the Keyhole itself are the slopes below it, deep red talus backgrounding a yellow spray of prince's plume or the gray sculpture of a dead cedar.

Beyond Keyhole, pilasters of Chinle form another cliff jut that because of its color and horizontal laminations has been dubbed Raspberry Torte. Best view is from beyond the cliff, looking back down the orange road to get the full layer-cake effect. This cliff is shaped precisely to serve as sounding board for Canyon music. Not only does it have music of its own, the cooing of doves or wild pigeons nesting in its innumerable crannies, it also amplifies the murmuring of the creek and the castanet pattering of cottonwood leaves.

Most photographed cottonwood in the Canyon is the one that tops the rise and leans over the road beside Cap Smith's lower field. Classic, when framed by fleecy clouds or framing a piece of sunset.

Just beyond this cottonwood is Cap Smith's walk-in cellar. A hole in the bank, it is faced with a laid-rock wall. Stones bordering the path from road to door, the door itself, were added when the Young Adult Conservation Corps and the Youth Conservation Corps (YCC) did restorative work on Cap's place a few years ago.

About that cellar—Cap, an inventive old codger, wrote in his diary, "Laid pipe underground from lower down toward the creek to create a circlation of air." Yes, circlation. Cap's spelling was as monumental as everything else he did—he could and did spell "stayed" five different ways.

The pole fence around Cap's two cabins was built by the YCC to keep cattle out, the locks on the doors to keep vandals out. Only cows paid any attention, vandals broke the locks almost at once.

"Capt. H. A. Smith" the house says in gravestone letters carved on the outside of the monolith that forms one wall.

Henry A. Smith was a native of Joliet, Illinois, a tombstone cutter by occupation, but was interrupted in his life's work by the outbreak of the Civil War. He fought with Union forces during his late teens and early twenties and was wounded at Antietam, a wound that provoked several decades of feisty correspondence between him and the War Department about the extent of his disability and just how much he had coming to him because of it.

Cap was feisty from the start. Once while posted on guard duty

Cottonwood arch announces Cap Smith's homestead.

he restrained a general, his commanding officer, for not knowing the password, and with weapon at the ready made him walk with him up and down the beat until relief came on duty—or at least that's Cap's version of the incident. He was a corporal, but during a shortage of officers in that very fatal war, he served a month as acting captain before a real one could be found. He turned that month's unofficial duty into a lifetime rank, and thenceforth never signed his name without preceding it by "Capt." even in his personal diary:

"I'm going to retire for the night. Signed, Capt. Henry A. Smith."

He "left home" (his phrase, brash as a teenager's) in 1907 when he was sixty-five and the youngest of his nine sons was fourteen. He came west for his health, and to learn how his fellow stoneworkers, the Indians, made arrowheads.

By then Indians hardly knew what an arrowhead was for, being two generations into gunpowder. Cap never got to watch a native arrowsmith at work, but he had plenty of chances to study the product—Escalante was peppered with arrowheads. "Points" were so prevalent that settlers (having poor opinions of Indians anyhow) didn't bother to pick them up, but the next generation collected them by the shoebox full. They are harder to find now; however, a lot of erosion cover-up has occurred in the thousands of years since prehistoric hunters lost their ammunition here. After spring thaw or gully washer, if you spend enough time, you'll discover a weapon point, bird point, or a chip-worked scraping tool.

Ben Lowe spotted Cap to this place soon after he and Ruby moved to Escalante. Kindred untrammeled spirits, Ben and Cap had neighbored on California Mesa, where, as later here on Table Rock, Cap carved Ben's name ornately on a cliff like marking his place in a book of love or legend.

Though Cap came to the Escalante thirty years late, some pieces of creek bottom were still left for homestead, but none with water rights. His land could only be irrigated with snowmelt runoff or flash floods. Year-round water had long before been decreed and was defended from unrightful tapping by law and, in dry years, by gun.

Cap was undaunted. The creek flowed through his place, didn't it? Well, he had a right to dam up whatever trickle escaped the sooners upstream! And dam he did. At age 69 he lugged rocks, logs, and mud enough to pond-up the flow, then ditched the water (we're talking pick and shovel) down to where his two fields and orchard would be when he'd cleared them of sage, willow, cottonwood, juniper, and boulders. The dam went out, regularly. Exerpted from his diary: Rebuilt dam, cleared lower field, plowed, planted, irrigated, rebuilt dam, harvested grain, hay, garden truck, rebuilt dam.

Nelson Huffington remembers, "That dam went out at least once a year. Cap wasn't much for swearing, his worst cussword was 'By Gee Whivers,' but after a washout he could make 'dam' sound like it had an 'n' and all hell in it."

He set brood hens, bred a couple of sows, milked the cow he sometimes had the use of in exchange for baby-sitting some cattleman's weaner calves. What he raised he canned, dried, cured, and largely gave away. Between farm and household chores he laid up rock buildings for himself (four or five, counting chicken and hog houses) plus several for friends; and hacked off huge slabs of cliff to carve with lettering and wreaths for people less adept at staying alive than he was. If recipients of his incessant complaints to the War Department had happened around, they'd have been astonished.

Obviously, he found health, if not arrowhead craft, in the West. Though some of his grown sons came and helped him now and then, he did most of it himself. Anyhow, they weren't half as work-brickle as Cap. Nearing 75 he wrote, "Otto and I started to dig postholes, but it was awful hot so Otto went for a swim. I got done before time to start supper."

At first Cap had no transportation. When he wanted to go anywhere he walked, and this included walking the thirty miles to Delta for groceries, and the thirty miles back. People still living recall as children seeing the old man trudge by with a gunnysack of grub on his back.

When he did get wheels it was a flashy one-horse buggy with spider wheels, a fold-down top, and side curtains for bad weather—that era's version of today's sports car. Few but Cap admired it. Canyon folks scorned it because it wasn't big enough to bring home more than a sack of flour and the driver. What the horse thought of it, scrambling over high-center rocks and brush in the pathless middle of the road, can only be imagined.

Cap's ready cash came from carving tombstones at a hundred dollars each and the monthly gold coins of his Civil War pension—probably eight to twelve dollars. Even this didn't come without effort; he waged an ongoing battle with the War Department about the size of his pension, about that disability pay, and about the fact that his name was Henry A. Smith not plain Henry Smith, a distinction that seems to have put War Department records into permanent snafu.

Just what the disability pay was supposed to be compensation for is open to question since at three times their age and half their size he could work any two of his sons right down to the ground.

He gave most of his money away—to his sons, to his wife, to his neighbors. "Put a hundred dollars into the bank for my son Otto." "Gave Mrs. Bob Shreeves five dollars for a wedding present." "Gave little Rose Huffington a gold ring and a dress for learning to read so well."

He gave Nelson Huffington a rifle. "I was shooting his 22 repeater one day," Nelson remembers, "and he said when I was fourteen he'd give it to me. Well, I guess he mentally added two more years to his age and doubted he'd be around, so he said, 'By Gee Whivers, you can have it right now!'"

Cap's wife, Dolly, about as independent as Cap, never weaned herself from Joliet and came out to the Canyon only when she felt like it. While there she canned whatever was ready, baked up bread, churned butter, cleaned cupboards, washed and ironed—chores that settled automatically on any female entering the door of any Old Batch's cabin.

Dolly's visits inspired Cap to poetry—an addiction acquired from carving so many rhymed couplets on tombstones (or he carved verses on tombstones because he already had the addiction). He usually ended on a practical note however:

At home with my love
All ready my arms to enfold.
I'll meet you my darling. my dove
    when you get my supper
    take a husle on your self
    for i am hungry

Just how far into his seventies Cap was when he penciled these lines is unknown: the entry appears in his other diary, a workbook of undated pages where he randomly jotted money owed and coming, orders and sketches for tombstones, progress in "whiping the Kizer," and "receets" for such items as boot polish and salve for chapped cow tits.

Rock man that he was, Cap chose his homesite for a huge fin of rock that eons ago had fallen from the cliff, landing on edge and half buried in talus. The slab seduced him. He couldn't resist using it as the fourth wall of his cabin, and as a consequence the house had built-in primitive. Uphill of the slab he dug out a level floor, squared up stones to lay three more walls, bought roofing boards, stovepipe, and window glass—and for as long as he or anybody else lived there, carried domestic water a quarter of a mile from his spring up the next draw (still Cap's Spring on the map). A more practical man would have put the house up by the spring, close enough for piped-in cold water, or even hot water through a coil in the cookstove firebox, but by choosing "wrong," building against that slab, Cap gained immortality—the whole of Escalante Canyon, with all its rich history, fabulous people and scenery is increasingly known as "the place where Cap Smith's cabin is."

If he built against the slab to save rock work, things didn't turn out that way; he immediately began chipping on the slab. On the outside he carved his name and rank big as a signboard and inset an iron hitching ring for visitors to moor their saddlecraft to. On the inside he carved out niches—a tall one for his rifle and shotgun, a smaller niche for his pistol, and a very small niche to hold matches.

Autographed slab forms one wall of Cap's cabin. ▶

Bed niche carved in slab wall, smaller niches for guns and matches.

These latter were conveniently within reach of his bed, a large alcove he carved out of the solid rock. Some say he slept on the bare rock ledge of the alcove, using a chunk of stovewood for pillow, but this was probably just to show off; others remember seeing springs and mattress in the niche.

It was Cap's will that the cabin be his monument (the tombstone carving on the outside wall needed only dates), that his body be crypted here, sealed up in the bed niche. But his longevity foiled him. While visiting a son in California, he sickened for the first recorded time in his 92 years, died there, and was buried under grass like ordinary people.

The sandy clay cabin floor is as it was when Cap lived here, folks say, except that he kept it hard-packed by throwing water on it and tamping it down. Others remember board flooring, but that may have been later.

YCC restorers, misinterpreting the small opening in the northeast corner, built a fireplace there. Cap didn't have a fireplace. He had a potbelly heater and a cook range. The corner crevice was the hidey-hole where he cached venison close to the frypan in the bulk of the year when possession of big game meat was illegal. Similar hidey-holes were common in cabins all up and down the Canyon.

Cap was too sociable to live for long in a one-bed cabin. To the east he laid up another rock house, a bunkhouse, furnished with one big bed below and two in the loft. Just so there would be no doubt about its purpose, he carved "Friendship" on the outside. The rock bearing this beautiful lettering has been chipped out and carried away.

On the back wall of the bunkhouse he built a set of shelves that, hinged to swing out, gave access to a small hidden cellar dug under the talus. This secret "bookcase" panel has also been carried off, but was replaced by the YCC, who, perhaps to make it harder for vandals, built the shelves to swing inward, a mistake that probably has Cap tittering in his grave, because when the deep cabinet is swung in, almost no space for storage is left.

In this hidden cubbyhole Cap kept what he called his "fresh air," a cryptic term that recurs frequently in his diary, as: "Otto went out for some fresh air, but didn't find any." The term is decoded by an accidental reference to Otto's bringing back a hindquarter of fresh air. The secret cellar may also have been used to store Cap's pre-, post-, and duration Prohibition booze, since his diary includes a couple of recipes for cordial, one of which is:

One lb seedless raisins
chop fine. 2 lbs brown sugar
One quart yellow corn meal
mix thoroughly and ad to this
one gallon boiling watter
Alow it to cool to room
temperture and add 1 cake east [yeast]
and three slices of lemon
Do not squeeze the slices of the
lemons. It will ferment in a
bout 4 or 5 days. Then filter it
through a cloth and put in bottles.
Capt. H. A. Smith

Cap loved company and he had a lot of it. Most were stoppers. Apparently, his place was exactly nooning or sleeping distance between the far end of the Canyon and Delta. Fast travelers (on horseback) stopped for the noon meal; slow travelers (in wagons or trailing cows) stayed overnight, parking their stock in his corral, their feet under his table, and their tired bones in one of his beds. Some guests departed without taking all their pets with them. On a spring evening he wrote, "Took all the bedsteads apart and doused them good with gasoline. Not a bedbug left!"

Caps' diary is a roster of Canyon names—cattlemen, punchers, schoolteachers, government officials, lawmen, kids, drifters, remits (remittance men), and visitors from town. Days without company were so rare he entered the fact in his diary. "Nobody here today. Signed Capt. H. A. Smith."

Some stopped expressly "to chew the rag" and try to beat Cap at cards. Pink Blumberg, Oscar Huffington, Tuffy Wells, Bill Shreeves, other temporary or permanent bachelors traveling alone for the night or for life, peered at worn cards by coal oil lamp and contributed to the supply of matches in the niche carved below Cap's bed. The time Oscar won he thought it worth noting in the margin of Cap's diary, which usually lay open on the lid of the trunk where Cap kept his clothes. "Beat Cap Smith this night, Oscar Huffington."

In addition to stoppers, Cap's bunkhouse was occupied by stayers, cronies who came for indefinite stretches. Roy Bowen was one. A Delta blacksmith who, when not tied up in one of their all-day, all-night card set-to's, tinkered at the forge and anvil in front of the cabin where Cap sharpened his stone-cutting chisels. "R. Bowen" elegantly carved on the cliff face above Cap's house commemorated this friendship while Roy was still alive. The star and horseshoe above the name had been the traditional sign language for a blacksmith shop since the days when, English common folk being unable to read, all business signs were pictures.

Amateur carvers, who like Cap cut their initials on the cliff, are kind enough not to encroach on Cap's professional work. Vandals with rifles have not been so considerate.

When Cap wasn't having company, he was being company. He went to Delta so often and stayed so long it's hard to see how he got all that work done. Every few days his diary records, "Went to Delta. Staid with the Freybergs." Nearing 80 Cap was still going to all the Canyon dances and charming the ladies something fierce.

On July 4, 1918, Capt. Henry A. Smith decided to forgo the Fourth of July celebration in Delta—out of patriotism.

To understand what a sacrifice this was, you have to consider the

Cap Smith's swimming hole. ►

times. This was the era when fireworks of all kinds and size of bang were unrestricted. A boy (or boy-hearted man) could fire as big a cracker as he had money to buy. Boys saved pennies all year, agonized over whether to blow it all on a few superbooms or make it last all day in strings of cheap match-crackers. The Fourth was the biggest celebration of the year, especially for boys – and Cap managed to stay a little boy all his life.

Furthermore, Cap was a veteran. In Fourth of July parades of those days war veterans were the heroes, the honorees, and superlatively so in 1918, when the United States was in an ecstasy of patriotism over how it was winning World War I. Cap could have expected to be the Big Man during that particular Fourth – he had five sons serving in Army and Navy – and he would have lapped it up. All during the war Cap was fiercely patriotic, more patriotic than anybody. He bought War Bonds; he went up and down the Canyon selling War Savings Stamps. His diary sputters every other page with "i want the Kizer whiped!"

On July 3 he got ready for the Big Day, washed and polished the buggy, slipped the wheels and filled the hubs with axle grease so they wouldn't squeak and chuck while passing slow and stately down Main Street in the Fourth of July Parade. Then he decided not to go.

"This day i will stay on the ranch," he wrote. "For what money i would spend i am going to help the soldiers that is fighting on land and sea in France, England and Italy. I will help the soldiers till the Kiser is whiped good and hard."

Always a colorful, even flamboyant, little man, Cap Smith hardly needed anything more to make his life spectacular, but he got it. His son Fred presented him with twin albino grandchildren. When their snowhite hair and pink eyes came to national attention, Cecil and Helen toured for a while with a circus.

Along the top edge of a huge boulder just a few steps from the cabin a double row of split drill holes demonstrates how Cap used feather wedging to crack off slabs of rock to work into tombstones. First he drilled the holes with hammer and steel drill rod, turning the drill with each blow to gouge out crumbs of stone. Then he drove wooden wedges in the row of holes, not one at a time but all together, giving each wedge a tap or two, then back over the row, evenly, delicately, like playing a marimba. Suddenly, without warning, the slab would break off in a straight line exactly where he planned.

Cemeteries all over the west slope of the Rockies had specimens of his work—one of them was for his friend and neighbor Ben Lowe, commissioned by Ruby after the shooting. His work diary notes:

"Aug. 1, 1917. Mrs. Ben Lowe $100, two vace shells like the one on the Shreeve lot and one tablet for baby. To be put up befour Decoration day 1918."

When this child of Ben and Ruby was born and died is not remembered. Almost every family those days lost one or more infants, a fact that did not make the anguish less, nor the need to perpetuate the memory of brief life in eternal stone.

Stone is not eternal, especially sandstone. Nothing remains of Ben Lowe's and the baby's markers, nor of any other of Cap's delicate carvings of tree trunks twined with ivy, roses, or oak-and-acorn sprays except the penciled drawings in the pages of his workbook diary. Sandstone weathers badly even in the rare rainfall of desert lands; after the advent of cemetery sprinkling systems, Cap's tombstones melted to shapeless flaking lumps. Most are now merely sandy patches in graveyard grass.

In the same cemetery is the wreck of a gravestone carved in the shape of a saddle, every floret and scroll of the leather tooling had been reproduced in chisled rock, but the name and all but a few protected florets have eroded away. This saddle-shaped stone is popularly (erroneously) believed to have been erected to the memory of Ben Lowe.

Ben Lowe's true monument is Table Rock, and it is fitting that the best surviving specimen of Cap's work is the "Ben Lowe" carved on its base.

Others since Cap have lived in this rock-slab house. Harvey Head remembers a golden boyhood spent here while his father was trying to make a living on good land but little water. "Dad had to let it go back. Only twelve-hundred dollars from having it paid out, but that was in the Great Depression, couldn't sell anything, couldn't borrow a dime."

Oscar Huffington bought the place from Cap's son LeRoy in California, who was managing Cap's "estate." Oscar made it pay out because he had reservoir water up on the mountain. He housed his hired men here. One of them converted the meat scaffold there in the yard into a swing for his children.

Present owner of Cap Smith's place is the State of Colorado. The Fish and Game Department (now the Colorado Division of Wildlife) acquired it from Nelson Huffington in 1957 to provide habitat for small game and winter browse for deer. Nelson waters it and keeps the fences up in exchange for part of the graze for his cattle.

For the convenience of Cap's present-day visitors, a picnic table, shelter, and fire grill have been set up. The Division's responsibilities do not include preservation of buildings and carvings; it yielded this phase of management to the Montrose Historical Society, which is also unable to keep a twenty-four-hour guard on the place.

Attempting to save the unique historic site from complete destruction, several people including Cap's albino grandson, Cecil Smith, have proposed that it be made a national monument; but unless such an action also finances a live-on guard it would provide no more defense against vandals than the pole fence. Costs of salary for an official guard, and construction of a nearby modern dwelling for himself and family, have been deemed prohibitive.

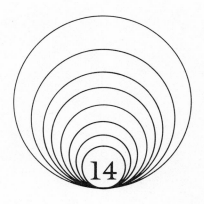

14

Underwater Death Trap

The Upper Escalante Canyon road is as full of ups, downs, and twists as a roller coaster, but the rise just beyond Cap Smith's cabin leaps right off into space, geologically speaking, skipping 300 million years of the earth's history.

At this point the Canyon has cut down to the foundation of the Uncompahgre Uplift—Precambrian granite estimated to be more than 600 million years old. Resting directly on it is Chinle formation said to be "only" 250 million years old. All the missing strata washed or blew away during one of several times this mountain heaved up then wore down to a nubbin. The granite itself had been smoothed by erosion when red-velvet Chinle began to sift gently down upon it.

If you walk to the creek from the rise west of Cap's place, you'll see it at the bottom of a black granite gorge.

Tumbling off granite to sandstone the stream has cut itself a waterfall. A small dam wedged in the slot above the rapids diverts irrigation water by a short tunnel through granite onto meadows below. Cap didn't bore the tunnel, though he could have watered one field higher if he had.

Rock man though he was, he left granite alone. The theory of tombstones is that they are forever, making the names of the dead and the craft of the carver immortal. Then why, with all that eternal granite just up the road, did he settle for sandstone that wouldn't last much longer than he did? Well, he didn't know it wouldn't last. He saw Indian writing, shallowly pecked into sandstone cliffs thousands of years ago, still so fresh the strokes of the stone chisel could

be seen and felt. In the dry climate of this part of the world sandstone is obviously durable past worrying about. How was he to know that the fashion in graveyards, even in the desert West, would turn toward grass—falsely green, unfalsely ephemeral—and that the beating sweep of the sprinkler would wash his work away. All that is left of Cap's handiwork is in this Canyon, doodling he did for fun—his own name and those of his friends Ben Lowe and R. Bowen.

Cap put his diversion dam below the rapids and replaced it every spring (or oftener) when floods, pressured through the narrowing granite gate like water from a nozzle, ripped it out. From the lip of this little black inner canyon you look back at a few dying and dead apple trees, Cap's orchard. Floods and beavers took most of the trees long ago.

"Beavers!" Kel Musser cussed, "People think they're such cute creatures. They are wantonly destructive. They cut trees they've no use for just to keep their teeth sharp."

For miles you have had cliffs towering overhead and have detoured huge blocks of fallen cliff beside the road. Maybe you thought those barn-size boulders fell a thousand years ago, and no more will fall for another thousand. Well, that great spill of boulders up ahead, stretching from cliff wall to creek, crashed down a year ago last Christmas night.

When Frank Ward left for the outside to eat Christmas dinner in town, that tumbled mass was all in one piece, a smooth rampart of the cliff face up there on the skyline. It hadn't fallen at twilight when Fish and Game official was making his way home. But when Frank returned after dark, his headlights suddenly bounced off a wall of jumbled rocks blocking the road, most of them twice as big as his pickup.

"By daylight I might have found a way around the lower end between the slide and the lip of the granite canyon, but in the dark I thought I'd better go back to town and wait for the road crew to blast a way through."

Though Canyon folks still retain the cowboy delight in laying prankish names on people and places, they haven't yet dubbed this rock fall "Frank's Near Miss." But farther ahead are Frank's Draw and Bert's Draw, where Ward and Shreeves, respectively, survived turn-

◄ Creek straddles 350 million years in jumping from granite to sandstone.

ing their vehicles wheelside-up. Negligence, speed, and inebriation are neither implied nor ruled out in this chuckling kind of landscape memoranda.

After passing Frank's Near Miss you will be less trusting of these Canyon cliffs, eyeing them for the top-to-bottom crevice that, pried wider by expanding ice or merely a change in temperature from day to night, might topple a canyon-span of boulders where you are. Don't worry, chances are somewhat less than winning the Irish Sweepstakes.

Beyond the recent boulders of Frank's Near Miss is a rock that was here eons before wheels came through. Indian Sign Rock bears the pecked outline of what seems to be a campfire with curling smoke. A prehistoric signboard directing wayfarers to traditional camp-grounds? Indeed, two campsites (besides the hidden one at Cap's place) have been discovered on up the Canyon; two slopes show evidence of being dwelling sites for thousands of years. You have to look for Indian Sign Rock because it is not large, resembles other rocks nearby, and is usually splashed with dried road mud. Perhaps because of this disguise it has not been vandalized.

At many places in the next several miles, you can drive your car off the red Chinle roadbed and onto the bench of granite above the inner canyon.

Granite, which often is monotonous gray-black, is full of surprises in Escalante Canyon. Some is blue-gray and fine-grained as petrified modeling clay. Some is porphyry, a fruitcake of big varicolored crystals. Some is rotten gneiss, sparkling with mica, black as banks of coal slack—good place to look for fairy crosses' twin crystals studded with tiny garnets. Some is veined with quartz, splintered to glittering white chips that drive arrowhead hunters crazy.

From the granite rim in low-water season you look down upon works of art—free-form sculptures created by eons of soft water grinding hard rock. Potholes, swirls, braids, arches, tunnels, globes attached by slender pedicles. Blue-gray stone polished to the curves and sheen-less velvet of flesh. A rock trapped in the bottom of a hole, revealing how one shape is being hollowed, hints at how the others happened—waterpower, driving it round and round like a tool.

Though at low stage the water is so clear you can see the bottom sculpture four and five feet below the surface, some pools are deeper than sight can pierce. Fishermen clamber down the granite walls to fish in these pools, swimmers to swim and dive in them.

Favorite swimming place is the Potholes, where a water-chute, a sheet of water rushing down a steep slope of clean granite, slides into a crystal pool. Open to the sun, harmless as a smile. It kills people. "The pool is thirty-one feet deep," Nelson explains, "and has an underwater shelf. If you don't come down just right, the chute-current drives you under that ledge and pins you there."

During a certain week in spring, the Potholes is the rendezvous of hippies from almost every state and several nations. One day the sheriff (of one or another of the counties Escalante Canyon bisects) was passing by and thought he ought to look into the whys and wherefores of that many out-of-state license plates in such an out-of-the-way spot. Frank Ward said, "Nobody was around the cars, so the sheriff walked over to the rim. Saw them lying around down there on the rocks like a lot of naked seals. Got back into his car and drove off. Said they were too many for him!"

The Potholes is all the more dangerous when the decision to swim is made by chemically short-circuited brainpower.

Nelson Huffington came onto one of them out of season and stopped to see if help was needed, the way you'd check the well-being of a downed bird that had missed the migration. "It was February, snow on the ground, ice in the creek. He was stretched out by his car, stoned and nearly naked. Said he was considering a swim. I didn't see much use trying to talk him out of it. If ice wouldn't stop him, an old fellow telling about that ledge sure wouldn't, even if he could hear me talking. Well, next day the car was gone, so I suppose he, or somebody, had enough life left to drive it off."

From time to time, especially after a drowning, there is a furor in the press to have the granite walls blasted down, making the Potholes pools safe by eliminating them. This rouses such a counterfuror among the many who use the place repeatedly (knowing how to live to return) that nothing comes of it. Someone once posted a sign describing the danger; it survived bullets and bonfire about two weeks.

The rims of these granite benches have a gardened look because plants and trees grow mainly in crevices, with clean-swept granite between. Little plants do well, each in its niche living on rain runoff stored in the cracks; but cedars and pinyon pines, striving in cramped quarters to fulfill the size pattern of their genes, grope and grapple like oriental bonsai specimens. If someone were to set a Japanese garden lamp on one of these lichened rocks, it would look at home.

Several varieties and colors of cactus nuzzle among the granite bulges and gravel interstices—opuntia's ears and hedgehog's mounds.

Parasite Indian paintbrush peeps from the sage it feeds upon. Found all over the lower Uncompahgre, but especially nice in this spot is the little white daisy thing botanists call the Townsendia aster, spreading a flat doily of gray-green leaves embroidered with yellow-centered white petals. More than most plants it seems to have a good time growing—fresh and pert as if it had been prettied up for Sunday School. Common folks, with delicious aptness, call it the Easter daisy.

Groundwater under the Uncompahgre Plateau, at least in the Escalante region, flows from north to south. Where the Canyon cuts through the strata, only the north cliffs ooze water, which is why the North Fork of the Escalante is also called Spring Fork, and what might be called the South Fork is known as Dry Fork. Snowmelt and other forms of sky water percolate as far down as the watertight granite and feel along until finding some place to come out. The gash of the Canyon provides such places—water faucets in the aquifer.

The water doesn't flow through the aquifer in a sheet, apparently, because springs are more frequent in some areas than others, but in the area between Cap's Spring and Cottonwood Spring the water-bearing rock stratum does seem to carry a sheet of water. Between those two sweet-water springs are the Alkali Beds formed by a different groundwater bearing such a burden of chalky minerals that in places it has built up rounded mounds on top of the granite. These domes are haired over with a sparse crew cut of salt grass, scalps showing through all dandruffy with alkali.

Somewhere on the Alkali Beds the first car ever to make tracks in the Canyon got stuck so thoroughly the passengers had to spend a day and a night within its side curtains. The vehicle was being piloted by a dealer who hoped during this trial run to sell it to one of the passengers—Dr. Hick or nurse June Musser—or to some other Musser at the Forks, where they were headed to make an emergency housecall on Eda.

It was the kind of place (creeping underground water) and the time of year (spring thaw) that in cowboy parlance would "bog a saddle blanket." Despairing of rescue—no rider with lariat and horsepower had the bad judgment to be out and around—they eventually rescued themselves, with fenceposts and brute push. In the process June Musser pushed her shoes so deep she could only retrieve her feet. Undaunted, the Mussers did buy one of the contraptions, thus becoming, Eda says, the first in the Canyon to own a car, and thereby putting themselves on call every time an emergency required a fast (anyhow, faster than horseback) trip to town.

Several decades earlier those three trainloads of Texas longhorn cattle got "stuck" here in the Alkali Beds, but in a different way. The longhorns were merely passing through on their way over the mountain to the San Miguel River. The etiquette in pushing thousands of cows across somebody else's range is to do it as fast as possible, otherwise such a herd can harvest an entire season of grass at one pass. From the moment the herd hit the Escalante, the drivers had trouble conforming to this courtesy.

Dillard wasn't the only flatlander on the drive; the cows were flatlanders, too. Presumably while negotiating Big Hill, follow-the-leader, head-to-tail, they'd had eyes only for safe spots to set hoof. But once they got their fill of creek water and looked up to see what kind of fix they were in this time—the bottom of a slot in solid rock—they didn't know what to do except get up out of it as quick and in as many ways as they could individually discover. Dillard and crew worked hours hazing them down off the taluses, through brush, and in and out of Brent Hill boulders.

Nightriders held the restless herd, bedded in grassland that would eventually be Oscar Huffington's Upper Orchard, while the rest of the crew shared campfire grub, yarns, and everything but liquor with their host, teetotaler Tom Brent. At dawn the cattle were up and bawling back at their echoes from the Canyon walls. Coffee and woodsmoke sweetened the Canyon airflow, rank with cow. The battle to keep boss cows from dashing into side gulches, or detouring up talus ramps—taking half the herd with them—resumed as the vast herd was pushed past the gash in the wall that would someday be the Lowe, past the fin of rock that would someday be the fourth wall of Cap's cabin, and up onto the granite benches.

But when the longhorns got to the Alkali Beds they settled down on the scruffy white domes and wouldn't budge. Jeff Dillard explained, "Those cows had been drinking soft water and going without salt ever since we left the Arkansas River, so they went after that alkali like licking salt blocks." If there is anything harder than trying to bunch cattle that are tearing off in all directions, it is trying to move them when they are dead set to stay. "We worked all day getting them pried off the Alkali Beds."

The ground flow at Alkali is bounded on both sides by sweetwater springs. Cap's Spring on the east has been boxed to put the water where stockmen want it to go, in the trough. But the spring ignores the box, finding its own way down through the talus slope underground. As you walk up into the cavelike cove, you hear it underfoot, under the firm dry earth that supports your weight, gurgling along in some hidden channel, chuckling at having eluded the trap. Show-off, nonconformist, like everything else that had anything to do with Cap.

Because there is more water and it lasts longer in the season, the stretch between Cap's Spring and Cottonwood, the second sweetwater spring, is notable for wild flowers—asters, sego lilies, prince's plume, and columbine. But even here the season is short. Flowers, knowing exactly how little time they have between last frost and first sizzle of summer, get the leafing, flowering, seeding job done in a hurry.

Like most other cliff springs, Cottonwood issues from a grotto. The deep red water-bearing Chinle is so much softer than the orange cliff-forming Wingate Sandstone above it that the moving water erodes from under, creating moist shallow caves and hanging gardens where grow mosses, ferny plants, and rare flowers. Lifting from damp crevices are the brownish-pink flowers of the chatterbox orchid and the red flowers of *Mimulus eastwoodiae*. The latter is a monkey flower found in this grotto and a similar cove around the next point, in two other places in Colorado, and in only three states in the Union, according to James Ratzloff, BLM botanist. It blooms through August and is pollinated by hummingbirds.

Both these flowers are clowns. Chatterbox is so called because its lower petal looks like a stuck-out tongue, and the word *Mimulus* actually means mimic. The fragile *Mimulus eastwoodiae* is barely clinging to existence. In fact, just the trampling involved in reaching them can harm the grotto environment, Ratzloff warns. "Enjoy through binoculars and photograph with tele lenses at compassionate distances."

Up the road from Cottonwood Spring is Canfield Flat, a goneback-to-nature clearing in the juniper-pinyon woods that have been thickening as you climb. It is named for "an old couple who built a lean-to and plowed a few ditches. There wasn't enough water to

Standing Slab. ▶

tie a future to, even the little future the old Canfields had left, so they drifted off."

You can tell you are in Canfield Flat by a skyscraper triangle of rock rearing on end beyond it—the Standing Slab. If you can pull your eyes away from the Slab, as you walk toward it up the slant of the Flat, you will see a small depression in the red earth with a few posts sticking out of it. This is all that is left of the half-dugout log homestead cabin of the Canfields' successors, Mr. and Mrs. Bill Faircloth. Bill seems not to have made much impact on old-timers' memories, but his wife did. "Largest woman I ever saw," Eda Musser remembers. "When you'd drive by in the evening she would be sitting in front of the dugout door to enjoy the cool, and it didn't seem possible she could squeeze herself back into that little cellar house."

Large, generous, and jolly, Mrs. Faircloth was beloved by many friends and all her nieces and nephews, ten of whom were the children of Bert and Emma Shreeves. Jack Shreeves says, "She weighed over three hundred pounds, and we kids loved every ounce of her. She ran a rooming house in Delta and always had something baked up for kids. Usually face cookies with raisin eyes, nose, and mouth." Nelson Huffington adds, "The Faircloth rooming house was over Freyberg's Steam Laundry, and right under the tin roof. Hot as you know where! Dad and I stayed there when we went to town to attend the funerals of Ben Lowe and Cash Sampson."

Which brings up a problem of the time: When travel by saddle or wagon meant a daylong dusty ride to get from somewhere in the Canyon to attend something somewhat formal in town, you were in no shape to attend unless you had a room at your disposal where you could clean up and change into your "best clothes." Lacking friends or kin in town, or preferring not to bother them, you went to a hotel or rooming house; consequently, rooming houses and hotels were more numerous than the population of a town would seem to warrant.

Barbershops had public baths in back where men cleaned up in preparation for legitimate or other activities. As to the latter, there was no red light district in town and only one mention of commercial sex in five decades of the newspaper. When a photographer aptly named Pratt was jailed for peddling dirty pictures, it was hinted that

Hole in the cliff where Standing Slab was. ▶

he was also being supported by the pretty ladies in his rooming house over Mathers Kandy Kitchen. The postcards cost him a $300 fine, but the matter of the women could not be investigated without involving some city fathers, so it was dropped.

Standing Slab is impressive from the road, but seen up close and edge-on from the west it is breathtaking, towering into the sky as slender and straight-edged as the Washington Monument. How tall is it? Nelson Huffington says, "I tried to find out once. Stood on top of my saddlehorse, and threw a 35-foot rope and couldn't touch anywhere near the top."

When did it fall? No one knows. It was there when the first settlers came, but bears no Indian writing. It seems unlikely the Indians would have overlooked such a noticeable "tablet" for recording their messages if it was here during the time they were leaving messages on the scenery. So that gives us a couple hundred years of conjecture room.

Look up at the cliff and you'll see the immense hole where the Slab and its entourage of boulders came from. The scar, as fresh as if everything fell out only last night, gives some idea how long it takes cliffs to acquire desert varnish and that weathered look.

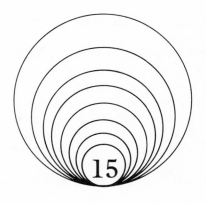

Antique Dynamite

Beyond Cottonwood Spring the road for the first time gets out of sight of the creek or the Inner Canyon rim, swinging back behind erosion-isolated knobs. These red remnants of talus, steep and pointed, affording views up and down the Canyon, were apparently lookout posts where tribal guards also did a little on-duty arrowhead manufacturing. Flakes of chert and agate, brought from elsewhere, are found by eyes-on-the-ground tribes of arrowhead buffs, but as is usual in work sites, few finished points.

After the Knobs, the red cliff wall crowds the road back down toward the Inner Canyon. Scrub timber is thicker now; it obscures picnic places along the granite rim and masks pull-out access, mere tire tracks in the sand, leading to fishing spots. The Wingate Sandstone cliff overhead thrusts forward in fins, pilasters, and spires that often bear fantastic resemblance to persons or things—an Indian profile, an urn, a hat-over-face figure slumped against the wall asleep. Each is recognizable from a certain angle, from a certain direction coming or going. None are named. Try your hand at naming one. If you describe often enough, to enough people, the sun-warmed winter picnic you enjoyed at the base of the "Ballpoint Pen," for instance, that spire may eventually be so named on the map forever; a name surely as valid as Sowbelly Ridge.

All along the south side of this stretch of the Canyon are great talus fans, whitish in this red land, like white drapery pinned by a corner to the skyline and sweeping all the way down from rim to canyon floor. Between them the sheer red cliffs stand clean in alternating points and coves.

Evidently at one time there was a solid mass of this whitish stuff burying the Wingate walls, perhaps filling the already geologically old canyon. Whatever lofty white cliffs it was sloughed from (or was gouged from by glaciers in some ice age) are long gone from the plateau. An interesting theory is that these white taluses are all the Uncompahgre retained of the Green River deposits that once covered this part of the West when that side-slipping river started skinning off the plateau.

The beauty of the white talus fans is best seen in the slanting light of morning or afternoon when junipers and pinyons that clothe them like dotted veiling over rounded flesh cast long shadows accentuating curves and hollows. The walls of the Canyon here are hung with Peter Hurd paintings!

During snowmelt or after a summer storm a waterfall drops sheer over every cliff cove between the talus fans, but that's the only time you'll see water there. That is the dry side of the Canyon, no perpetual seeps and springs over there to create grotto gardens of water-loving plants. Instead, we have the Little People Pinnacles.

All the Little People are wearing hats. Where a slab of fallen rock rests on the talus slope it protects the soft stuff under it. Hard rain or trickling snowmelt, unable to budge the rock, erodes the soil around it, and eventually a pinnacle is carved out, capped by the rock that saved it. The rock on its slender neck maintains the same angle it had when lying on the talus slope, often a ridiculously rakish angle in its new imposing circumstances.

In some of the coves the Little People Pinnacles seem to be spectators in an arena, watching an incredibly slow-motion game going on in the gully between them; in others they line up, chins over a ridge, to watch you pass down the road. In some they mimic sky-scrapers or Indian cliff dwellings; in others they stand on opposite slopes facing each other across a dry gulch, hats pulled down over eyebrows, each side waiting eternally for the other to draw first.

From Cottonwood Springs to Escalante Forks, least-tamed stretch of the Canyon accessible by car, the road tunnels through tangles of sage and juniper. A number of efforts have been made to subdue it but there's little to show.

When bricklayer Harry Walker went out of the horse business his mares wintered here, resisting for years all efforts of cattleman to

eradicate them. Unemployed mine burros, laid off during some depression or other, hid out here through prosperous times, stupidly
blowing their cover every dawn by bouncing squeaky braying off the
Canyon walls.

Deer find winter browse here and manage population control
with mysterious efficiency. Warren Reams says, "There's one band of
exactly seven. Year after year. Never six, never eight, no matter how
many fawning seasons go by."

Parts of the motion picture *Tribute to a Bad Man,* starring James
Cagney, were filmed here in the 1950's without denting the wildness
any.

By rights, the last instance of cattle rustling (rather, the latest
known instance, since cattle rustling is an ongoing industry) should
have happened in this wild section, but it took place down in the
"civilized" end of the Canyon, near what used to be Huffington's
Upper Orchard.

"The game warden had stopped between our two ranches," Eda
Musser says, "when a car came around a bend. The car stopped, then
did a quick reverse." Unsuspicious until then, the warden investigated this guilty-looking maneuver and saw two men running up
through the brush. Abandoned in the trunk of the car were their
guns, knives, and a young beef—gutted but stilll wearing hide and
head. "The warden called us, thinking it was Musser beef, but it
was Nelson's, the second steer he'd had rustled that year."

Most cattle rustling in this area is done on a commercial basis
by the semi-truckload, but this case was small and amateurish enough
to seem easy to solve—the sheriff had the car as bait to lure the owner
back, and the culprits were afoot on the roadless side of the river
with only two ways out, across bridges easy to guard. But the men
never did claim their car, and nobody expected them to after it was
discovered they had first done a bit of car rustling.

When anything illegal occurs in a certain section of Escalante
Canyon, it is difficult to determine which sheriff to call—Montrose
or Mesa. There is ulterior motive for this vagueness. Little Cottonwood Creek slashes down from the north cliff about where the county
line crosses the road. In flood it is a bearcat, tearing up the scenery,
wide, deep, and boulder-riddled. Each county would just as soon
the other was saddled with fixing the road after one of Little Cottonwood's big tantrums, and the usual way of passing the maintenance
buck is to move the county line sign one way or the other. With
untypical triteness, Canyon folks call this vague area No Man's Land.

The spot where Ben Lowe and Cash Sampson finished their lives to end their quarrel is known—but in which county it occurred was one of the complicating uncertainties of the unwitnessed tragedy.

Near No Man's Land is the beginning of an expensive wire fence around a quarter section that is known as the Old Herb Wells Place, presently owned by a Grand Junction man. The fence is as mysterious as anything else in the Canyon—multistranded, taut and ready; barbed four-square outward since there is little to enclose within but a ruined cabin, sage, juniper, and unfencible history. Deer leap over the wires to sip springwater at its grotto source rather than down at the roadside where it offers openly. People crawl under the wires to wander and muse and project upon the Canyon scene imaginary happenings evoked by the bits of things they find—the brush-blind site of the Lowe-Sampson shoot-out, ancient Indian campgrounds and hunting posts, the Wells cabin itself.

Herb Wells came to the Canyon in 1898. He had married Sylvester Huffington's daughter, Sylvie, by more or less eloping with her— that is, he rode up to the door, she climbed on the saddle behind him, and they rode off.

Their first home was the cabin Oscar Huffington built on the claim he was still too young to homestead. Kids though they were, Herb and Oscar went into a man-size partnership, grubbing brush and leveling farmlands along the creek, building rip-gut fences and camps on the Plateau, going into debt for ninety-two cows and three bulls at $30 each. Herb and Sylvie held down the Huffington place while Oscar lived and labored almost everywhere else on the mountain.

After eight years it was evident the outfit would never support two families (Herb and Sylvie were busy making what promised to be a big one), so Oscar offered to buy or sell half-interest for a thousand dollars. Herb couldn't buy so he sold. Oscar really couldn't buy either, but there was something about the single-purpose, bulldog way he bit into hard work and held on that made banks trust him all his life.

Just when Herb Wells moved here on the 120 acres now enclosed by wire is not known because he never proved up. Nor is it known when he built this cabin, or where he got such huge logs, or how

Wells' cabin. Hand-adzed log walls housed abandoned dynamite. ▶

he hoisted them into place. That he was an artist with an adz, you can see for yourself.

Like Oscar he was an ingenious man. Morgan Hendrickson tells about the time Herb and Oscar, up on the mountain and tired of cooking between two rocks on the ground, were bound to get a cookstove up to cow camp though there was no way except muleback, and no mule big enough to carry that stove. "They took a wagon up that horse trail. Whenever they came to a sideslant so steep the wagon couldn't stand up, they'd put a twenty-foot pole on the up side, and Oscar would hang his weight out on the end of it to keep the wagon from turning over while Herb drove it across."

Source of domestic water for the Wells cabin is a good spring behind it. Irrigation water was brought around from the Little Cottonwood, but there was never enough water for the land, nor land enough to support anybody.

Selling their preemption right to Bill Shreeves, Herb and Sylvie—with however many children they had by then—moved up onto the Calhoun cattle spread where both were employed for several years, Herb in the saddle or with irrigating shovel, and Sylvie at ranchhouse cookstove, washboard, and churn.

The snug, thick-walled Wells cabin was seldom without occupants, though over and over the land itself proved so profitless it was sold for back taxes. Hunger and plague visited it at least once.

The plague was the deadly influenza epidemic that, in the final years of World War I, filled the front pages of local papers with obituaries. This virulent strain of flu singled out young adults, boys in army camps and those not yet drafted, girls in their teens to late twenties. So many died so suddenly that the nation's population was terrified. Superstitious folk wore charms around their necks to ward it off—little bags of foul-smelling asafetida. Not a family in the Canyon but felt the touch of this killer; few that did not lose at least one member of it.

The young mother who was then living in Wells cabin was in the fatal age bracket. She and her daughters, six and seven, were already weak and undernourished because the father had not only given up farming here, but had given up trying to feed his family by any means whatever. In desperation the mother filed nonsupport charges, and the law put him in jail, which did nothing to help her situation.

Mother and daughters came down with flu. Caring for her children, the mother was unable to care for her own illness—there was the water bucket to fill at the spring, wood to chop for keeping the cabin warm, ashes and chamber pots to carry out. The wind of early spring was cutting cold; she developed pneumonia. Two cowboys discovered her plight and urged her to let herself be taken out of the Canyon to the hospital. One of them promised to stay and care for the children until a nurse or doctor could come.

Doctors and nurses were working day and night, there was little chance of getting a doctor to come to the Canyon when the twelve-hour trip would deprive dozens of desperately ill patients of his attention. The children were too small to understand what might seem to be desertion by their remaining parent and, in their condition they might, literally, be frightened to death. The mother refused to leave. In three days she was dead.

Some of the cowhands using this as a batch cabin from time to time were Herb and Sylvie's sons—Harry, Merle, and Marion, who was universally known as Tuffy Wells, a nickname hard to understand now, so tender were the things he did.

It was Tuffy Wells who was beauing the schoolteacher, Miss Millie Simineo, the year of the diphtheria epidemic. It was Tuffy Wells who got the loan of a spring wagon and the gift of a mattress from the Mussers and took Miss Millie's body to Delta after she died, choosing to make the long sad journey alone. It was Tuffy Wells, they say, who when no marker was placed on her grave, himself ordered and paid for a marble tombstone for her.

The 1919 Big Snow that dumped thirty inches of water-heavy snow in one night, collapsing roofs and driving cattlemen out on skis to find snowed-in stock, caught another Wells boy and another schoolteacher out in the open.

Cleo Compton, teacher at the Lower School, wanted to be with her folks in town on Thanksgiving and was set to leave right after school on Wednesday. At the Rogerses, where she boarded, Joe reluctantly saddled a horse for her; it was snowing and he felt she shouldn't make the long ride alone.

Rogers was only slightly reassured when Merle Wells happened by and offered to accompany her. Merle was still just a big kid and he hadn't fully recovered from an accident a few weeks earlier when he had chopped off two toes while cutting poles fifty miles and two days' grueling ride from help.

It was after four o'clock, the ride would take five hours at best. The young people weren't worried; there wasn't a breath of wind at the bottom of the Canyon, the snow came straight down, soft and pretty as a Christmas card. But when they topped the Big Hill the wind struck with blizzard force. It was at their backs so they kept on. Fourteen miles and Cleo would be home.

The snow thickened, coming so hard and fast the air was dense with it, too thick to see anything, too thick to breathe. The trail was invisible, buried in drifts and scuds of swirling snow. Crouched in the saddle, scarves pulled over nose and mouth, Cleo and Merle gave the horses their heads, relying on the animals' ability to find their way to town over a trail they had traveled many times.

But the horses drifted with the storm.

When dark came they were lost. The horses had stopped on a brink of rimrock (it turned out to be Cottonwood Canyon, far out of the way). The boy and girl groped down the cliff and into the lee of an overhanging rock where they huddled, near freezing, through the endless hours of winter night.

How they came to make the remainder of the trip on foot is not known. Oscar Huffington's diary says that when morning came, the storm had cleared, but their horses were gone. The paper says they remounted and rode through belly-deep snow until the horses played out.

"They came to Negro Gulch about ten o'clock, decided to hitch the horses to a cedar where they would be protected, and try to reach some ranch on foot."

The snow was twenty-six inches deep on the level, waist-deep in drifts that must be floundered through or laboriously detoured. It was heavy and yielding, at each step the foot sank all the way and must be heaved out to make the next.

Merle's wound, which had been partially numbed with cold while he was in the saddle and crouching under cliff, was roused to fierce pain by the heavy, slogging gait, then numbed again as his feet began to freeze.

It was nightfall when they reached McMullin ranch at the forks of Roubideau and Buttermilk creeks. Merle's feet were frozen and so swollen his boots had to be cut away.

When John Schorn, known in the Canyon as the Dutchman, acquired the Old Wells Place he had figured out a way to get water up onto his land from Escalante Creek down in its narrow inner canyon. What he had in mind was to blast off enough of those granite walls to dam the creek and then ditch the raised water by gravity flow to his land on the bench. Simple. Nothing to move, nothing to haul, nothing to build. Just dynamite, stuffed in strategic crevices of rock.

"It was Fourth of July in Escalante every Sunday"—Schorn had a Monday through Saturday job somewhere, leaving only weekends for dam building. "You'd hear those blasts going off, echoing back and forth from the canyon walls till you couldn't tell where they came from. He was with the Bureau of Reclamation, or knew somebody who was, and could get free dynamite. We thought that Dutchman just liked to listen to the bang. He sure did put a lot of rock into the creek. But high water eventually took it out. That creek can move boulders big as a truck when it gets its dander up."

Schorn quit before he used all his dynamite, as I found out. All along I was just an observer in the Canyon, looking and listening, but I almost became an Escalante statistic.

I hadn't yet heard about Old Dutch Schorn when the Morgan Hendricksons, the Lloyd Brutons, and I picknicked at the then-unfenced Old Wells Place. Since the place lacked doors as well as fences, I did a little "research" exploring inside the cabin. At that time it had remnants of a roof, rags of cedar bark with holes full of sky; the windows were gaps rimmed with shards of glass. Where the floor had been, my boots made dents in sand.

Across from the door was a lidless box trunk made of rough boards with loops of rope for handles. At the bottom of it, half buried in dust, were what looked like rolls of old newspaper. History hound that I am, I was eager for any clue they might provide about the cabin's occupants and had one of the rolls in hand, poised to strike it across the edge of the trunk to knock the dust off before unrolling it, when I realized by the greasy feel that it was dynamite, old and crystallized, just waiting for a wink to go off spontaneously.

How do you lay a stick of crystallized dynamite back down? V-e-r-y gently. Morgan, standing nearby, let his breath out.

You won't find it there now. Morgan notified the Civil Defense, which has crews trained to explode such overdue explosives harmlessly.

To the east of Wells cabin is a long black slope that might be taken for one of the crumbling gneiss granite outcrops except that this stuff is too powdery and too high in the Chinle Formation. It is deep ash, an ancient Indian campground, blackened by thousands of years of cooking fires, speckled with the flint chips of generations of arrowsmiths. The site has yielded countless arrowheads and stone tools, but the deposit of archeological debris is so deep, and the slope is so steep, that almost every storm unearths new pre-historic treasures.

Could this be the camping ground the Indian Smoke Sign Rock down by Cap's was pointing toward?

An ancient trail—first Indian, then cattle, and always deer—to the top of the cliff enters near the west gate in the wire fence. It goes up by the cabin, past the spring, and up a little draw to the top of the Escalante Rim.

Warren Reams says, "Huffington tells me there are Indian hunting blinds and lookout posts up on those rims, but there are a couple of hazards to finding them—crumbly rock along the edge, and wild Brahma cows." Wells homestead has its own private grotto, the watering place (to judge by sign) of bobcats, coyote, and mountain lion.

A tangled line of downed trees and brush, sagging toward the ground with age, is the remains of a rip-gut fence that marks where the road used to be, closer to cliff and cabin, when Lowe and Sampson faced each other for the last time.

West of the Old Wells Place the Canyon walls begin to pull back on either side, making room for what is known as the Park, and pre-saging the great open space where all the Escalante streams come together. Stands of cedar and pinyon give way to sage and grass.

The plume of dust from your wheels has already announced your coming to anyone living at Escalante Forks.

Eda Musser says, "From the house we could always see travel in the Park—anybody a horseback, cows being trailed up, a car or a truck—in time to have the coffee ready."

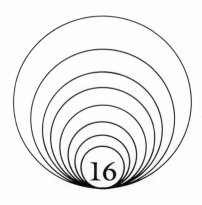

16

Vein Gold

Encircling the great, grassy park known as the Escalante Forks, sheer walls of Wingate Sandstone rise, slotted through with canyons where the creeks have cut dark passage and emerge to join their rippling waters here like surprised laughter mingling in a sudden openness of sunny hayfields.

Roads bore into the red walls along each of the creeks, but only the Escalante Main Fork is open to the public. The other two—branching up Kelso Creek and the North Fork—cross private property that nowadays is often closed off by locked gates. In former times, when Canyon travel was rarer, gates like door latches opened to a tug; you had only to lift a wire loop or slide a wooden bar. Travelers then were usually people with Canyon business to attend to, friends or relatives to visit, or they were hunters and pleasure riders who understood the etiquette of the range—that you leave things the way you find them, gates closed, cabin woodbox refilled, dishes washed and back on the shelf.

But as population thickened, jeeps proliferated and people changed, stockmen had to protect themselves from the few who make problems for all—people so irked at having to get out and open a gate that they leave it open, apparently out of spite; people who can't tell the difference between a deer and a steer in the rifle sights; people who rustle cattle or remove furnishings (even doors and windows) from seasonally used cow camps that, finding them momentarily unoccupied, they rationalize must be "abandoned."

Annie Huffington gives an instance.

"A friend came tearing down to our home place, yelling that somebody was robbing our house at the Upper Ranch.

"When we got there they were loading the last of the furniture, our cookstove, onto their truck. California license plates; a man and woman and their children. They weren't scared or embarrassed at getting caught. Just mad. Like they had some right, and we didn't. Real peeved that we expected them to put it all back. In fact they didn't, just piled it out in our lane and roared off. We had to carry it all back in. Dressers, beds, table, stove. Everything.

"Lamps are hardest to keep. Up in the cow camps there's no electricity. You have to have coal oil lamps, and even though they're not antique—just lamps you can buy right now in a hardware store for three or four dollars—people will steal them."

Traditionally cow camp cabins in high country were never locked and were kept stocked with a minimum of things vital to life for anyone caught out by sudden deep snow or by injury. Stove wood and kindling, chopped and in the dry. Matches and staple groceries in tight-lidded lard buckets to keep the wood mice out. Lamp and lantern, coal oil, ax, shovel and a bit of rope. Kettles, skillet, tin plates and cups, cutlery in apple-box cupboards nailed to the logs. Bedding.

Eda Musser says quilts were hardest to keep. "There has to be bedding in those camps. If one of the cowboys gets caught up there on the mountain two miles above sea level, snowed in or sick, there has to be warm bedding at hand.

"When Kel and I were first married and operating with almost no cash income, I thought I'd save us some money by making quilts out of discarded clothing instead of buying expensive blankets for the cowboys in the camps. So I cut up the men's worn-out coats and pants and made pieced quilts. They weren't pretty, just drab old colors, but they were warm. Well, those quilts disappeared right away. People who wouldn't dream of stealing a nice blanket will walk off with a dingy old pieced quilt, thinking it's antique."

The ranch spread that crowns the sweep of meadow under the sundown shadow of Long Point—houses, barns, corrals curving down—is the original Musser homestead. Since it is the knot that ties the strung-out Musser holdings together, the way the Forks knots the branching streams into Escalante Creek, we will come back to it later, after we have explored the other creek branches and the lives of people who left visible mark and invisible mood upon them.

Except for the two homesteads still owned by descendants of the original pioneering families—Huffington and Musser—all the land along the creeks diverging from the Forks has changed hands, three outfits just once and only after three generations; other places as often as twice in a summer. Not all the brief owners left lasting mark on Canyon or memory.

Kenneth Campbell did. He homesteaded north of the willowy marsh inelegantly called Ward Mudhole and is remembered as "an oldish bachelor of imposing appearance with a snow-white, meticulously trimmed Van Dyke beard"; not your stereotypical homesteader! Neither was his cabin. He built it eight-sided, a shape that encloses a larger space with shorter logs than a rectangular cabin that could only be as large as the longest top-plate logs tying the walls together over door and window openings.

Campbell may have modeled his unconventional cabin on the Navajo hogan, which may have been modeled on the Indian tepee, which (since the Indian came to this continent by way of the Bering Strait) may have been patterned on the Eskimo igloo, which may have been patterned on the Mongolian felt-tent yurt—all invented without benefit of engineers to tell them that the roomiest space-to-materials ratio is obtained by building as nearly round as possible.

Whether he brought his octagonal roof to a peak by cribbing shorter and shorter logs as the Navajo does—weaving a kind of inverted log basket—or whether he rested radiating rafters on a central post, no one remembers. Theoretically, a structure is stronger the nearer it approaches the circular, so Kenneth Campbell's cabin, of all the cabins in the Canyon, should be the best preserved. Since not a stick remains of it, nor even the clue of ashes, one must assume it was coveted for its timbers.

The scraps of a pioneer's life that happened to be recorded in newspaper "Locals" are sometimes all that is left of him, especially if he never took the risk of linking his life to a woman and consequent children to carry memories a generation further. Six lines of newspaper stringer can say a lot about a man. The paper notes that one day Kenneth Campbell got word the Grand Junction sheriff was holding rustled stock bearing his brand. They neglected to mention it was just one steer, so he made the two-day, sixty-odd-mile saddle trip down there to round them up and drive them back.

When he saw just one steer, he scratched his head. A range bovine is a social animal. A herd will file down a trail docile as pulled string, kept in forward motion by the leader-dictator cow as much as by the rider in the rear. But a lone cow will try to break around and get back to the spot where she last saw cows, convinced to the end of the journey that if she doesn't she will never see a cow again.

Kenneth figured that steer would dodge enough extra miles to double the distance home and run off more fat than he could put back in a winter's feeding. If it had been a bull or a cow creature, now, with some calving future to her. . . . So he did a good thing for an expedient reason—just as in shaping his cabin—he told the sheriff to have the steer dressed out for the folks at the Poor Farm.

Homesteading upstream from Kenneth was his brother Cum, whose two sons, Pete and Kenny, eked out their grade-school education, during terms when the Upper School had no teacher, by camping in a tent pitched in Cap Smith's yard within riding distance of the Lower School. Apparently it was enough—Pete went on to become state representative. But before that he and his wife, Mabel, "hired out" at nearby ranches, he as cowboy, she as cook-housekeeper.

Cash Sampson was on his way to pay Mabel Campbell for some baking she had done for him, he told Kel Musser on that fatal day. Had he not veered from his errand, he might have lived to die an old man.

Kenneth Campbell didn't build that remnant of board-and-batten cabin on the slope above Ward Mudhole. That's what's left of the house Banker Helmke built after buying Campbell's preemption right.

William Helmke was not called Banker Helmke, and he had no marble-silled teller's grill, but he lived by lending money just the same. He may even have had some kind of license; in those unregulated days it was about as easy to become a banker as to become an ex-banker—that is, banks started up and folded up with frequency and insouciance (the latter also in its literal sense, without a sou), as cashiers and presidents fooled around with depositors' money, and upon discovery escaped, made token restitution, committed suicide, or brazened it out, according to their natures.

Helmke's cash turnover was mostly among up-coming young Escalante men such as Oscar Huffington, who for several years operated on "Helmke money," borrowing to buy cows, prove up on claims, and to buy out his partner, Herb Wells. "Banker" Helmke lent on character, quite safely as it turned out, having character enough of his own to know it when he saw it.

This is not to say Helmke was rich; his house was not large, he dug irrigating ditches and scrambled in dung-dirt branding calves like anybody else; but he had a little patch of money growing on the side which returned a bit of harvest if he sowed and weeded carefully. With William Helmke money wasn't everything. One room of his and Gusty's house was the Escalante School for a time, provided free until settlers had their own families housed weather-tight and could turn mind and muscle to building a schoolhouse.

Helmke put up a swing for the children, a shed to shelter their saddle horses, and heavy netting over the windows on two sides of his house so they could play "Anty Anty Over" across the roof without the trauma of crashing the ball through one of his windows. First teacher was a tiny woman, Zora Convers of Galesburg, Illinois, who married across the road, becoming Zora Ward. Arthur Ward took the Helmke schoolteacher at the end of her first year; he took somewhat longer to acquire the Helmke land.

The corrals silhouetted against the sky on the rise to the left, and the tops of yard trees hiding house and barns, mark the Ward Place.

Isaac Arthur Ward, a Canadian who entered the United States the moment he was of age, came to Escalante in 1893. Not a first-comer; but his partner was—Uncle Bob Smith, the Uncle being the customary title for nice old bachelors with harmless eccentricities. Uncle Bob's eccentricity was neatening up his part of the Canyon by squaring off the bottoms of native cedars with pruning shears. The native cedar (juniper) is a ground-dragging tree with a long life and a long memory—some of Uncle Bob's cedars still resemble ladies with their skirts hiked up to go wading.

Arthur and Uncle Bob resolved their different notions about how a cattle outfit should be run by dissolving the partnership, Uncle Bob taking up the Missler homestead just above on Kelso Creek Fork.

Having secured title to his homestead in 1901 and to a wife in 1904, Arthur slowly added other holdings—slowly because his nature was to avoid the risk of debt. He got the Helmke place, then some public land sold at auction, then a section on the mountain for summer pasture. The six Ward children came faster, all but one born in the Canyon, Don or Kel Musser riding out to fetch the doctor for Zora.

Arthur Ward had a reputation for staying a mile away from anything that wasn't his business. Writing about the Delta County Sheep War, Carl Gilbert noted that the only Escalante Canyon ranch not represented among the night raiders was Arthur Ward's. When word of the Sampson-Lowe shoot-out reached the Forks, Kel Musser got Arthur to ride with him to see about it; as they were approaching the last few hundred yards—cautiously because one of the gunmen might still be alive—Arthur offered nervously, "I'll just ride to town for the sheriff."

Yet Arthur could go the whole way in cowboy-type fun and games. Nelson Huffington retells a story Arthur told him:

"Bert Enore was in Delta one night and saw Guy Blair sitting on the boardwalk in front of the hardware store, his legs hanging over the edge. Enore invited Blair to get up and do a little dancing, and put a few shots in the vicinity of his britches to underscore the invitation.

"Guy was doing a pretty fair job of dancing when Arthur Ward came along. Guy appealed to him for help. Instead, Ward pulled his own gun and told Guy to dance faster. 'Between the two of us,' Arthur told me, 'we really had him doing some fancy steps. To this day Guy won't speak to me.'"

For thirty years the Escalante "post office" was literally that—a post holding a large wooden box here beside the road on Ward property. Every passerby was mailman, looking in the box not only for his own mail, but for any letter or package addressed to anybody in the direction he was headed—upcanyon, downcanyon, or all the way to town. Anyone actually going to town was expected to bring back whatever Canyon mail had accumulated, depositing Lower Escalante mail in a similar box at the foot of the Big Hill and bringing the remainder here.

When the Canyon got a real United States Post Office in 1917—fourth-class with weekly service—it was in Zora Ward's kitchen. As first postmistress she had the privilege of naming it, "Escalante Forks P.O.," and, incidentally, the privilege of feeding most of her customers once a week. For free. Since the mail route stopped here, all the people living above it on the three branch creeks came here to get their mail. Traveling horseback, they usually arrived at noon and, of course, must be pressed to join the family at dinner; but even if they came later it was unthinkable, according to rigid Canyon etiquette, to let them start the return journey unfed. So they had pie, coffee, hot bread and new butter at the oilcloth-covered table near the pigeonholes that constituted the post office.

The mail-carrying Walker kid remembers: "I'd bring in the mail sack—my Dad had the mail contract, but when he was on a bricklaying job I took his place. Well, she'd have the table cleared off ready, and the first thing she'd do, she'd hoist the mail sack over her head—

she was a little woman with a husband to match—dump the mail out on the table, and read the postcards. Laughed and laughed over the things people'd said to each other on the postcards." The mail stage (a wagon or buckboard) left on Friday with freight and passengers as well as mail, put up at hotel and livery stable overnight, and returned on Saturday.

After the post office was moved into a little store that Kel built at the Musser ranch, Arthur Ward was mailman. Never was mail delivery so punctual. Folks could set their clocks by when Arthur's stage team pulled up at the mailbox.

One Friday morning Arthur Ward was late. Eda Musser remembers, "We had the mail made up and ready to go, as usual, and Kel had saddled to start his day's work with the stock, but he came back in. 'Something's wrong at Wards. I can see them running around over there, but nobody's hitching up.' So he rode over to see what was the matter.

"Arthur was missing. Not just off doing something with the cattle. Missing. Eventually Kel rigged up some grapple hooks and started dragging the deep holes along the creek. The water was high, but not in flood. Clear, cold snowmelt. They found Arthur in one of those potholes."

Nevertheless, the mail must go.

"While they were still searching, Buddy Cowger drove by in a wagon, and Kel commandeered him to carry the mail to Delta. Buddy was too young to be a legal carrier, just nine or ten, so Kel told me to ride with him." Changing to her riding skirt, Eda reluctantly prepared to set out on the two-day ride. She says it was one of perhaps three or four times she rode horseback in her half century as mistress of a cattle outfit. Her ordeal lasted no further than the Lowe, where Brownie Blumberg offered to ride shotgun on the mail in her place.

"Arthur's body was left in the snowmelt water, fastened in an eddy in the shade of trees. It was summer, very hot, and they didn't think it best to take the body all that slow long way to town in a wagon. So the undertaker came out, bringing his equipment, and did the embalming where he was."

As with other pothole drownings, there was an investigation. During it tiny Eda Musser put the law in its place. "The sheriff and his men slept and took meals at our house. Armed, of course, like they always were. Strutting around so important, and I said, 'Sheriff, you just put your guns away, outside some place. We've got children here, and there might be an accident.' And he did."

There is no Escalante post office now. Twice a week the mail lady drives out from the post office in town, braking her station wagon to a dust-cloud stop at fewer than half a dozen rural mailboxes. It was dwindling population, not petty graft, that did for the Escalante Post Office—unlike some other fourth-class post offices that were discontinued for abuse of "cancellation-and-a-half" pay.

A fourth-class post office was usually just a couple dozen wooden cubbyholes on the wall of a farm kitchen or in one corner of a country store. The postmistress was paid for her trouble, reports, and time (she had to be there all day of any mail day), not with a salary but with the amount of stamps she canceled plus one-half. That is, if you bought a two-cent stamp for your letter, the government paid her three cents. At that kind of margin, a few postmistresses could not resist the temptation to expand, paying postage out of their own pockets to mail stuff to anybody they could get an address for. One lady in Utah, they say, mailed enough bricks (one at a time and neatly wrapped) to build an entire church. A lady in Arizona had such financial success getting rid of surplus squash by mailing them to people she thought didn't have any that she began boxing up and mailing the basic raw material—garden soil.

After forty or fifty years the government tumbled to what was going on and put an end to this kind of creative enterprise by paying ladies a flat monthly sum. Almost all fourth-class post offices were run by women, as a kind of cottage industry that didn't pay enough to make it worth a man's while to stay home.

The Ward house is almost empty. Once not half big enough for Arthur and Zora's children, now it is too big for their son Frank, who lives there sole and alone. The bride of his young years, Alice Calhoun, died early; his children have grown and moved away; and his wife of his later years is terminally ill in town. Though the land now belongs to the Mussers, the house is his as long as he lives.

Frank Ward must be an old man, but he doesn't look it. He has the erect grace, the flat belly, and the piercing eyes of a cowman who has spent a lifetime in the saddle looking for sign that the creatures in his care may be in need or trouble. He runs no cattle now, but he has another charge. Early every evening, like clockwork, he comes out of his gate in his pickup, driving the forty miles to the nursing home where his wife has existed since a stroke closed a door on her mind a decade or so ago. He sits with her and puts supper into her mouth in delicate spoonfuls. At seven-thirty, never late or missing, because any night may be the one when she will come to herself and know who he is.

Beyond the Ward place the road is relatively new, a purple-red scar gouged out of the looping Chinle taluses along the base of the left-hand cliff. The original road lay on the sunny side of the creek, crossing private land (and through gates) most of the way. When the Fish and Game Department acquired Picket Corral, this new road was built to provide public access to public land. Red cliffs close in, narrowing the sky overhead; the creek is near, but out of sight, almost straight down. The Main Fork has continued to burrow deeper into its inner granite canyon, and it is in this black stuff that the Crabills found gold.

The gold is in a narrow vein of whitish, pinkish quartz that spans the granite canyon from rim to rim, looking like a sag of paint down over the edge and back up again on the other side. Over there the vein looks thin as a twist of string, but in the clarity of mountain air distance deceives; it is two to five feet wide just as it is here where eroded crystals spangle the granite underfoot.

According to the books and old prospectors, you would look to find precious metal richest along the edges of the vein where the hot young intrusion (young relative to the ancient granite) met older colder stuff, and fuming gases crystallized into maybe money. But to get at it, to get body room in the working hole, you'd have to take out the whole vein. It is hard. Flint hard. Pocket knife doesn't faze it.

There have been veins of quartz in the granite, netting across creek and road ever since the Potholes. Why is gold found only up here? Has anyone really tested all the other places? Did the Crabills go all out to find the lode?

A Crabill of this generation thinks not. "We always believed mining gold was just an excuse the men used to get away from home and responsibilities in summer. Sometimes the women didn't go, glad to get the men out from underfoot, but usually they went, they and all the kids. They'd camp up there for six or eight weeks. Took a cow, and put the milk and cream in the creek to keep sweet and cold. Made butter, fished, hunted, and just generally had a good vacation time. This went on for, oh, about twenty-five summers."

The Crabills, A. B., Aden, Joe, and Fred, were not the burro-and-sourdough-type of gold prospectors. They came from Virginia, where Mrs. Joe was friends with future first Lady Mrs. Woodrow

Wilson. There was a banker in the family somewhere, and Aden Crabill had the Delta Flour Mill, which kept right on grinding out
money. Besides, they raised hogs by the carload—a profitable but low-
life enterprise that acquired status when some (well, at least one) were
rustled just like cows. Funds abounded to equip the offspring for
any field they faniced—when Tish showed unusual musical ability
they sent her to Oberlin. Even when they were pranked it was on
the lavish side: on Aden's wedding night his bachelor cronies shiva-
reed him with his favorite ginger cookies—a barrelful delivered on a
dray wagon shortly after the light went out in the nuptial window.

The Crabills couldn't have been too desperately seeking gold. On
the other hand, look at that black hole in the vein over there across
the Canyon. It goes back into granite about four hundred feet, and
is only one of several mines they dug. That represents a pretty serious
amount of sweat.

"Fred was a small child when they started working the vein," says
his widow, "they were still at it when he was a grown man. When
they'd be about to give up, they'd strike a bit of rich ore and get all
fired up again. Just pockets, never anything worth starting a mining
operation on."

One day Mrs. Joe found a piece of rock on the dump heavy
enough to be high-grade; it was, assaying almost pure gold. But they
had no idea which tunnel, shaft or pockhole it came from. That
rock stirred up a lot of excitement; for a while the Canyon was, as
one disgusted stockman put it, "weevilly with men crawling around
pecking at the quartz veins."

Another time, after the blasting dust settled, the Crabills went
into their tunnel and found a hunk of what looked like pure silver,
but assayed worthless. "That's when they quit," Mrs. Fred says.

Frank Ward took up where they left off, digging shafts along vein
after vein on this side of the granite canyon. An expert among the
"weevilly prospectors" had told him to look for "a certain vein, thin
as a broomstick and with a certain slant to the east. There'll be gold
there. A lot of gold." Only one of Frank's many prospect shafts is
visible because he filled each shaft in turn with waste rock from the
new one.

Down along the creek, not far from the mines, is a tall stand of
ratty-looking pines that were turkey roosts when there were big flocks
of the wild gobblers on the Plateau.

"I was hunting with a game warden along here," Nelson Huffington remembers, "and he worked a turkey call. Seven turkeys lifted

Picket Corral, built in 1882.

off the rim of Dry Mesa way up there, must be a mile and a half, set their wings and came sailing down to us. It was beautiful."

Where Escalante Creek splits into East and Middle forks, another open park is created, Picket Corral. The red walls have pulled back and East Fork cuts through them like a window letting a low sun in; here a man might build his cabin and cellar cave on the summer-cool north slope without living in a snowbank all winter.

The raw road gentles, curving down and away past clumps of trees like a road in a painted scene, crosses the small bridge over the creek, and curves up again through yellow grass to the ancient, silver-gray stockade corral. Framing the palm of hollow, like the upright fingers of sheltering hands, are the ramparts of the Canyon walls, paled by the sun to the rosy orange of living flesh. Where Oscar Huffington's hand-adzed cabin-house stood you look out across one of those places on this earth that say, "Home! Home at last!" though you never before set eyes on it. That Oscar Huffington loved this place with passion and tenderness, the way man loves woman, his diary discloses though it does not state.

The actual corral from which the place gets its name was built in 1882, according to Oscar's diary. It was built by John Musser, according to Musser tradition. Both can't be right, because John Musser did not come until 1886. Perhaps it was built in 1882 by John's brother-in-law, R. S. Kelso, and the fact that it is still standing more than a century later refutes for all time the newspapers' frequent teasing remarks about his disinclination to work.

"It was built sound," Oscar Huffington wrote when it was fifty years old, "with cedar posts set on end close together, two feet deep into the ground."

Neither Kelso nor Musser filed on the land; they grazed it and used the corral, as did everyone else going up or down the mountain. It was a place to make sure the saddle horses would be there in the morning when the drive resumed, a place to separate weaners, to hold steers overnight on the trek to the railroad stockyards.

Oscar first used Picket Corral as a base of operations in 1901 when he put up a tent here and built a rip-gut fence just below the old corral from cliff to cliff, thereby taking sole possession of a canyonful of pasture that he did not really own. A rip-gut fence was made by felling whole trees and leaning them against each other, butt down, in a piggy-back rick. Branches and stobs were left attached, sticking out like javelins in all directions. The fence got its name from the fact that any horse or cow that attempted to jump over it, and didn't clear, was slit open.

Twelve years later Oscar filed on the 160 acres that includes the corral. By this time the National Forest was in firm control of the land, and homesteading within its boundaries forbidden, but something—perhaps the corral itself witnessing decades of private use—made an exception of this piece.

"Uncle Bob Smith knew where there was a cornerstone to start surveying from," Oscar wrote, "and he and Forest Ranger Billy Stell helped me lay out the boundaries."

The next year he started the house. "I am snaking out my house logs from East Fork, using my Kernel horse and my Dock workhorse. I put Kernel on a log and Dock on one, then I start Kernel out ahead of me and lead Dock. Once I happened to get Kernel on a light log and he didn't stop to rest at the house site like he'd been doing. Dock's log was heavier, and when I topped the rise, Kernel had gone on over to the corral and was dragging his log round and round it."

Oscar himself adzed the logs square, but when it came to the finish work on this his best-loved house–doors and windows, floors and cupboards–he hired neighbor-carpenter Paul Harvey of Kelso Creek. Winter kept interrupting the work (and the homesteading–Oscar applied twice for winter "abeyance" to cover absences from the live-in homestead requirements), but on June 28, 1915, he wrote with a glow of satisfaction that still comes through the penciled pages, "We got through shingling the house. Now it can rain!"

Until three years ago that house stood, looking down on the creek, the famous corral, looking up at red cliffs, hawks and eagles soaring. The Division of Wildlife sold it to guide and outfitter "Straw" Berry who took it apart, hauled it to Delta and put it together again, log by numbered log.

Still here, and as sound as when Oscar built it more than fifty years ago, is his walk-in cellar–dug back into the bank, lined with peeled cedar posts, thatched with the bark stripped from them, and covered with earth. Recent hunters have built double bunks of aspen poles and installed a stove. Packrats have liked the mattresses they left.

Oscar's bridge over the creek is built on the same principle–peeled cedar timbers separated from the devouring earth by thick padding of cedar bark. Except for one worm creature that chews harmless patterns in the cambium tissue between bark and wood of new-cut logs, cedars seem antiseptically immune to termites, worms, insects, molds, and bacteria. Indeed, Indians used the antiseptic bark, softly shredded, as bandages.

Living or dead, cedarwood seems to last forever. Just up the Canyon is a slope of cedar trees firmly rooted in the ground though they died over a century ago. "Those charred trees have been standing as long as anybody can remember," Nelson says. "Since the Indians set fire to the Plateau forest in 1879 just before they were banished to Utah."

Back the other way is something infinitely older: Dry Mesa Dinosaur Dig high on the east skyline, where each summer for years students from Brigham Young University excavated a still-larger "largest bone in the world," under the supervision of Dinosaur Jim Jensen.

Picket Corral is well into bear country–some 310 bears roam the Plateau, an approximate figure that depends on who had twins last year–but there used to be many more. It was common to step out of the cabin here and see sign that a bear had been snuffling around the door during the night.

Crouching behind this stacked-rock shooting blind, Utes waited for deer.

One November morning a skiff of snow outside the door recorded bear tracks that had sinister meaning for Oscar and his hired man, J. B. Thompson. They recognized the prints, a stock killer.

"We tracked him to a rock slide, tied our horses, took our rifles and started to climb. I topped the edge and there he sat in the mouth of his den, about five feet from my face. Couldn't see the top of his head, so I shot him in the mouth.

"J. B. put his rope on the bear's front feet but his horse couldn't pull the bear out of the den. I knew my horse Blazer would be afraid of the bear, so after I put my rope around the bear's neck, I just wrapped it around the saddlehorn, ready to turn it loose when the bear came out. And it was a good thing. When Blazer saw that bear coming out, he left there tearing down through the trees with me.

"J. B. and I dressed him out—big black bear with thick glossy fur. I rendered out nine gallons of bear lard while J. B. sat around nursing his sprained wrist that he got in the bear chase. A harness maker once told me that bear grease is the oiliest stuff there is."

Above Picket Corral the creek bed has gone back to the wild, choked with trees and brush, threaded with deer runnels.

Traces of Indian occupation remain. Overgrown, and thus hidden from vandals, are lodgepoles still angled together in tepee shape. And still in place on the ledges are dry-laid rock wall hunting blinds where prehistoric hunters armed with bows and arrows crouched waiting for deer to trail down off the mesa to drink at the stream.

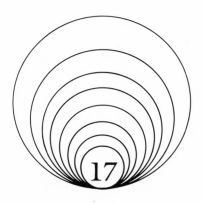

Wrong-End Ditch

For a cattle outfit to remain in the family generation after generation, the family must have sons, and the sons must prefer punching cows to other livelihoods. Calhoun, the largest cattle outfit headquartered in Escalante Canyon, didn't last through the second generation because, folks said, Alex Calhoun married a schoolteacher. Other cattlemen married teachers without such a dead end to dreams of family dynasty; but Alex Calhoun and Rhea Leeka produced sons that neighbor Eda Musser described as "mathematical geniuses."

Alex tried. Starting when they weren't much more than out of diapers, Alex made cowboys of his five sons, gave them early responsibility, a taste for hard work, and a mountainside of cows and horses to practice on.

Rhea never adjusted to ranch life. Not that she'd ever had to experience the real grind of pioneering—Alex provided her with a fine new house in the Canyon, a really splendid house in town, and a hired girl in both.

And she didn't like what it was doing to her sons. She was the epitome of what Wes Massey meant when he said, "them old gals got a car and the vote, they left the wilderness and all that hard work. They put their kids in school so they wouldn't have that life. Made doctors and lawyers of 'em. Completely unfitted 'em for cattle ranching."

With her sons, Alex said, Rhea put the wrong end of the ditch in the dam. The expression stemmed from a long and permanently dry irrigation ditch on the Missler homestead that was to become Calhoun headquarters.

An earlycomer, having his pick of land and water rights, Missler chose one of four south-facing cliff coves along Kelso Creek where wide meadows lay open to the sun but with a stream that dried up in summer. For water he chose the North Fork, which flowed year-round but was squeezed in sun-blocking cliffs. His idea was to dam the North Fork and ditch the water down around Long Point and back up to his land on Kelso. It was a matter of miles and years, and he didn't discover until he had it done that the water would have to run uphill, the outlet being higher than the intake. He'd put, as the Canyon saying was, the wrong end of his ditch in the dam.

When Uncle Bob Smith acquired Missler's preemption, he let the wrong-end ditch alone—there are only traces of it now out around the points where erosion is slighter. He made do with what water came down Kelso Creek, and with Missler's cabin as it was. It looks very much today as it did in 1885—a one-room, dirt-roof log hut that housed several of Calhoun's hired cowboy-cook couples before being converted to the ranch blacksmith shop. For this purpose the board floor was removed, exposing deep soft earth to quench dropped hunks of red-hot iron—the blacksmith's fire insurance.

A metal stovepipe pokes up through the red dirt of the roof just as when cats sought there a bare, dry circle in a snowy world. "Uncle Bob liked cats and he had a lot of them," Nelson Huffington remembers. "In winter they'd lay up on the dirt roof near the stovepipe to keep warm. When they'd hear his chair scrape back from the table, they piled off and jammed around the door meowing to be fed."

Uncle Bob Smith has been described as a small man with red hair, a little white-streaked red beard, a squeaky voice that he used incessantly, and a driving need to keep busy whether what he did was profitable or even sensible—as those trimmed cedars still testify.

He slept with a gun under his pillow. There was some doubt that Robert Smith was his real name.

Oscar Huffington noted in his diary that when Mr. and Mrs. Burton were coming west by covered wagon they traveled briefly with a man who looked like Bob Smith. He seemed wary and suspicious. "Grandma Burton got the idea he was hiding from somebody."

What he was hiding from is revealed by another Smith, Carl. No relation. "Uncle Bob Smith was from Tennessee. He brought two

Uncle Bob Smith's cabin.

carloads of heavy draft horses to sell in Denver—Denver wasn't big then, but it was known as a good market for horses because it used them up so fast on the streetcars and the dray wagons.

"Well, Uncle Bob sold the horses, got drunk and spent or lost the money. It wasn't really his, some men in Tennessee had an interest in the horses. He couldn't go back home without the money, so he went farther West.

"He hit Delta in the fall, made friends with my Dad, and stayed with him and me until spring, then he went out to the Escalante and homesteaded. He raised Percheron draft horses, saved his money, and after some years he got enough together to pay back those men in Tennessee, but they'd all gone away, and he never could find them.

"After what happened to him in Denver, Uncle Bob lived so he got the reputation for never taking a drink, but I noticed he didn't put up any fight when my Dad took him out a bottle of whiskey now and then. He loved children, and never had any. Made a fuss over me when I was little. Once he gave me three hides, two coyote and a skunk pelt that he'd tanned silky soft on the fur side, silky suede underneath.

224

"But he had a special place for the Burton family. When he'd go down to 'the Indian,' as he called Mrs. Burton, he always took something for the Burton kids—strawberries he grew, candy when he'd been to town to sell some of the horses he raised—stockings to go with their new school shoes, pencils and tablets, tin dinner buckets with painted pictures on the side."

If anyone else in the Canyon called Mrs. Burton "the Indian" it wasn't with Uncle Bob Smith's deference. In that, he was a man ahead of his times. Most pioneers were still too close to the usurper's guilty bias against the people they had ousted to be tolerant of them.

A cryptic item in the newspaper in 1888 speaks for the attitude of that time: "A dusky daughter of the noble Cherokee struck this hamlet last week, and already some of the hardened sinners are beginning to slobber. Why, Bert, you ought . . . Wow!"

Uncle Bob slowed down toward afternoon of his life, content on summer evenings to sit in the doorway here watching wild turkeys down in the meadow by the creek—dozens of them, strutting and preening in the park he had made by clipping the cedars.

Then he took to leaving the Canyon come fall. Carl says, "My Dad and Aden Crabill had the Delta Flour Mill, and Uncle Bob Smith had a little house below the millstream where he wintered as he got older."

His red beard gone white, his muscle no match for a Percheron geld resisting harness, Uncle Bob Smith sold his homestead to Alex Calhoun. After that he summered up on Middle Point, pitching a tent, eating dutch oven biscuit, and getting on with his retirement busywork—fishing.

Every few days Oscar Huffington stopped by to see how the old fellow was doing and take him down to Picket Corral for a spell of stove cooking. "I gave him my Blaze horse," Oscar wrote, "and he'd fish his way down from his tent to Picket Corral, stay all night, and fish his way back."

Uncle Bob's independence grew fiercer as he grew frailer. Oscar would help with the heavy chore of setting up or knocking down the Middle Point camp in spring and fall—when he could do it without hurting the old man's pride. But there came the autumn day when Uncle Bob ordered Oscar off the place. Alone, mumbling and grumbling, furious at his dwindling strength, he dismantled camp, packed up grub and cooking gear, rolled tent and bedding, heaved it all onto packhorses, and roped it down. Overheated from the labor, he became fatally ill. Chilling though wrapped in blankets beside Oscar's cookstove at Picket Corral, he still refused help of either medicine or doctor. Finally Oscar picked him up, carried him to a mattress in the wagon, took him down as far as the Mussers, who rushed him the rest of the way to town in their car. Too late, he died next day.

He had no known family. Oscar noted in his diary, "I had Uncle Bob put away in an aluminum casket. Best in Delta. And later I had a nice granite headstone put up."

Kelso Creek and Kelso Point are named for Robert Shaw Kelso, delightful but feckless brother-in-law of John Musser.

"The place right at the foot of the mountain where you go up to Kelso Point was originally R. S. Kelso's," J. D. Dillard notes. "R. S. had a pretty good little cabin there, corrals, fences, alfalfa patch for his horses; ditched water out of the creek and developed the spring. But he never proved up on it. Paul Harvey found that out, jumped his claim, and took it himself. That was done a lot. My Dad said anyplace earlycomers camped or built a corral or boxed a spring, someone else came along and jumped it."

It was perfectly legal. The law wouldn't have allowed a stockman to file on as many places as he required for holding and watering. Some stockmen hired homesteaders to file on coveted property, and some homesteaders thus hired didn't turn over the property when the time came, knowing such a prior agreement was illegal and couldn't be put into writing.

But only an R. S. Kelso would lose his home place, fully improved, residence requirement met, simply because he put off going to town to make final proof.

It didn't faze R. S. He just moved one cove farther down the creek to the middle homestead of what is now known as the Calhoun Spread. This he managed to stay with long enough to own it, or at least sell it.

When William and Mattie Cowger acquired R. S. Kelso's ranch they had two little boys with skin so white and cheeks so rosy that Mattie was unable to refrain from calling one of them "Peaches." This, of course, is the one that grew up to be a horse wrangler and bear killer. The other one, Don, joined the Navy and disappeared into outer space, as far as the Canyon was concerned, by entering the electronics field.

When he was in his early teens Peaches, by then known as Buddy, took on the job of ridding the mountain of the horses that had gone wild after being turned loose by Old Onion Eye, and others unintentionally lost by stockmen. There were a lot of them. Wild horse bands increase at an amazing rate considering that it takes a mare eleven months to make a foal, and she usually makes them one at a time.

Buddy Cowger got a little money for the horses he roped and brought to the sales, and he got a bit of bounty for removing their appetites from range that was more profitable when consumed by cows. Mainly he did it for the hell of it.

Nelson Huffington recalls, "Buddy and Noan White's boy would run those bands of mares and studs day and night—Buddy riding nights—sometimes for two weeks straight. Frazzled 'em to a standstill. They got some by hanging rope snares in the trails."

When it came to single horses—when it came down to the very last horse—Buddy went it alone, a kind of Captain Ahab—Moby Dick battle of skills and wills. "Buddy got that last one by himself out in Negro Gulch. I came onto him one night near Christmas.

"'I'll catch him in the morning,' he said. 'Been following him two days and nights.' I asked him how he kept going, and he said, 'I build a fire, heat a flat rock, and lean against a tree with the saddle blanket.'

"Roping wild horses on open range is man's, not kid's work, but not many men care to take it on. When you finally get a rope on the bronc he hauls back so hard he chokes off, and you've got a second or two to put halter on him before he comes to and rares up fighting. Once you get the halter on, you can tie him to a packsaddle and hope he will want to stay with the other horse enough to follow along.

"When Buddy and Claude Marsh were running wild horses on Dry Mesa they traced a bear to her den. They made a pitch-pine torch and crawled right in there after her. Her all the time growling something fierce back there in the dark.

"Buddy, in the lead, got off a shot at a glint he hoped was eyes. After the shot blast died down, silence. 'Thank God,' Claude whispered, 'she shut up.'"

Later Buddy Cowger worked for the government, trapping, shooting, and poisoning predators—bear, coyotes, wildcats, and mountain lions. It cost him both his legs. Gradually.

Annie Huffington, a relative, explains the cause of the repeated amputations. "He'd had to handle the cyanide cartridges they shot predators with. I guess the government agreed that's what caused his feet and then his legs to go, at least the government has taken care of him all along."

Not content to sit back and live on compensation, Buddy Cowger went over the mountain to Cisco and opened a grocery store–gas station beside what someday would be I-70. While he still had feet to stump along on, he prospected for uranium and drilled for it with two rigs he bought and operated himself, though by then badly crippled. His rigs didn't tap any uranium rich enough to be worth talking about, but he staked a man who did.

During the years Charlie Steen was living on beans or less, while scouring the Colorado Plateau for uranium, Buddy Cowger was one of several who staked him to enough grub and gas to keep on with the search. And it was Buddy Cowger's Geiger counter that told Steen when he had struck it rich.

Steen didn't own a counter. A geologist, he relied on his knowledge of formations to tell him where to drill, not attempting to lay electronic stethoscope on every inch of Utah to discover where the ticker was. His geology hadn't done him much good—a long series of high hopes and wipeout disappointments culminated in a final shoestring drill site in a formation that just had to have carnotite in it. It didn't. Instead of the bright yellow earth he expected, only worthless gray stuff came up in the cores. At last, broke for the final time, he gave up and pulled out, resigned to direct his life toward something less chancy. He almost didn't bother to throw in a few pieces of the gray core.

They sent Buddy's Geiger counter crazy.

As with others who had helped him during his lean years, Charlie Steen staked claims for Buddy Cowger at the fabulous find. Though Buddy didn't become a multimillionaire like Steen, he sold his claims for more than enough to equip his home with contrivances that compensate his disabilities, enabling him to live alone and self-sufficient.

Buddy Cowger's tragic-heroic story brings up a protest by many readers of pioneer accounts. "Why so much about hard times and trouble; why not dwell on the good times instead?"

In writing memories, one writes what people remember. And it is an unhappy fact that bad experiences cut deepest in the mind. Happy recollections come back in generalities—"Oh, we had such good times in the Canyon!" fervent, but vague as to specifics.

An old man remembers in sharp detail the morning two days after his twelfth birthday when his sorrel mare, Keech, spooked by a rattlesnake buzz on the northeast rim of Dry Mesa, bucked him off and bolted, leaving him afoot, his left leg broken just below the knee, five miles of sage flats and two deep arroyos between him and help.

He does not remember in equally sharp detail one particular hour out of a thousand happy hours in the saddle when a buckskin carried him up through the fragrance of cedars and wild roses, good leather creaking under him, sage wrens fluttering and chirping ahead of him, the sun lying warm on the back of his shirt, a downflow of mountain air moving like cool water past his mouth and eyelids.

These joys, like eating country bread every day and being in on corral joshing, suffuse pleasure into and over everything, each instance as unmemorable as a single drop of water in the ocean. It is the bad times that stick up like dark, jagged, unforgettable rocks out of the sea of experience.

Alex Calhoun bought the three Kelso Creek ranches after he sold the Club outfit in 1915, bought E. J. Mathews' cattle, and found himself with more cows than land to base them on.

A Canadian, born on the St. Lawrence in 1854, Alexander Calhoun came west by degrees, gaining cattle capital as he came. Working across the Dakotas on ranches and trail drives, he arrived in Colorado in 1878 during the mine boom in the San Juan Range. The Utes had just treatied away those mountains of gold and silver to the whites and, backs to the wall, were fighting white encroachment in the remaining valleys where they wintered and their ponies grazed.

The energy crunch of that time and place was fuel for the manpower that operated pick and shovel—the fuel of choice being beef heaped on platters in mine boardinghouses. To cash in on this demand, young Alex (he was 24) built up a sizable cattle outfit in the Dove Creek–Blue Mountain range, now known as Four Corners Country.

He did all right, but couldn't help noticing the wide disparity between what he was getting for beef on the hoof and what the miners were paying for beef on the plate. Besides, from where he sat (in the saddle more hours of the day than not) the retail end of the business not only looked more profitable but also freer of hassles such as cattle rustlers, horse thieves, dry years, deep snows, and hired hands with designs on his cattle, designs they executed with their own branding irons when he wasn't looking.

So Alex sold the Blue Mountain outfit and set up a slaughterhouse–meat market in Telluride. Of those years when he was buying cows all over the Uncompahgre Plateau and converting them into steaks and stews, only one incident is remembered: "The slaughterhouse waste, entrails and stuff, was thrown out on grass or snow for the wild creatures to clean up. Alex had a big old bulldog that set himself to guard the offal for some reason, and the coyotes got a kick out of teasing him. They'd sneak in, snap, slash, and run. He'd just take it until he got a chance to sink teeth in one. When he did, he never let go."

Somewhere in there Alex ran a packmule freight line that he acquired without really meaning to. Happening by when a hundred mules with pack saddles were being sold at auction, he put in a for-the-hell-of-it bid of ten dollars each for mule with saddle. He made the bid and left, knowing how ridiculous it was—horses and mules, the chief power source of the time, were worth about as much in gold-based dollars then as they are in paper now. He was called back and informed he had just bought the outfit.

Dividing the mules into four trains, and hiring nine skinners, he began packing supplies up the mines. In one year of especially deep snow, his outfit was the only one to get through to Silverton. The merchandise never reached the store shelves; people crowded into the snow-piled street to buy directly off the pack animals while the store clerk stood by writing down the purchases.

One of the reasons mine populations in such desperate, cut-off situations had to pay as much as ten (gold) dollars for a pound of flour was that the mules had to carry along enough feed to get them there and get back, reducing the payload and upping the overhead.

The year Alex was 52 saw two big changes in his life—he got married and he went back into the cattle-raising business. He was so enmeshed in the latter that, on one occasion at least, he completely forgot the former.

Soon after the wedding, business took him to Denver, and his bride went along—young, pretty Rhea Leeka, Telluride schoolteacher. Since it was a trip he made frequently, he was used to the connections—change to narrow-gauge at Montrose, back to standard, breakfast stop at Palmer Lake. At Palmer Lake he was talking business with some cattlemen, got off with them, ate a hearty meal, caught the train as it was pulling out, and did not remember his breakfastless bride until he saw her sitting there.

That same year, having had time to discover that the retail end of the cattle industry was not without hassles (chiefly involving drunk

butchers), Alex bought the Club outfit, largest and most famous cattle outfit in the region.

The Club got its name from the cloverleaf shape of the brand,
the Ace of Clubs, which was first the deuce of clubs, the brand being
burned twice on the critter. Whether that was too much trouble or
whether the operators had qualms about applying that much heat
to the rump roasts while still ambulatory, the brand became the
Ace, symbol of the outfit's size and status. Club cattle ranged "from
hell to breakfast," says Dillard. "From headquarters at Uravan, up
over the mountain and down to the outskirts of Delta, from the
Tabeguache almost to Unaweep. Just about the entire 100-mile-long
mountain.

The Club was started by the San Miguel Cattle Co., originally
the San Miguel Placermining Co., organized by Doctors Johnson
and Seward of Johnson & Johnson surgical supply house (yes, the
Band-Aid people). Gold there was (and is) in those fabulous gravels,
but they couldn't extract enough to pay for the miles of flume and
sluice ditching. So, to appease their stockholders, they switched from
gold to cows. They didn't have much luck there either, mainly because of absentee ownership and ambitious ranch managers who built
up outfits for themselves by running their own brands on some of
the boss's calf crop.

In 1906 the Club was up for sale. Dillard described Alex's purchase of the outfit: "Alex was about ready to quit the butcher business and get back into cattle. A Telluride gambler named Selby wanted
to go in with him, so when Alex heard the Club was for sale he went
and looked it over.

"You never could range-tally that outfit, so he told Wetzel, who
was operating the Club, 'Give me your calf tally and I'll figure what
you've got.' Alex went back over the past two years' tally and figured the Club probably owned a little more than Wetzel said they
had, so they made a deal.

"Then Wetzel said, 'Oh, I forgot. We got about forty head of
wild cattle to add on the count.'

"Alex said, 'I wouldn't give a dime for a wild cow. If you want
me to buy the wild cattle you'll have to find another buyer.' Wetzel
said, 'I'm not going to let thirty or forty head of wild cattle spoil
the deal.'

"Back when Alex ran cattle on Blue Mountain he'd had his eye
on a big old kid named Fred Sharp that was catching wild cattle with

the McClure boys. Sharp was with another outfit, so Alex had to wait a year to get him. He told Sharp if he knew anyone anywhere near his caliber to get him and pay him what he was worth. Sharp knew a fellow in Arizona, Joe Landers, and those two started in on the wild cows."

Because of the kind of work (among other things) they were doing, Sharp and Landers and their crew were dubbed the "Wild West Boys." Their modus operandi was to rope the critters, hobble them head-to-foot, and put them with gentle cattle until they got the hang of proper range deportment.

"In the meantime, Alex was buying horses, all the good horses there was over in the country from Disapointment to Telluride. I'll tell you he had a string of horses that was! That first year, in place of forty head of wild cattle he went to market with four hundred, and before they got through they had sold over a thousand head of wild cattle."

Of course there were those who, in view of the Wild West Boys' reputation, mumbled that not all the wild cattle were really wild, and that any bovine late in getting its owner's trademark was head-hobbled and hauled off with the wild ones.

"Alex cleaned the outfit down to good cattle—sold all that Texas longhorn stock my Dad came in with. When he got through he had five thousand head of really good cattle.

"His partner, the gambler who'd put up a share of the money, would come out to the mountain and ride once in a while. He and Alex got along fine, but Selby's wife was a bit of a nuisance, always wanting to manage things, so one day Alex told him, 'One of us should buy it.' Selby said, 'Let's go looking for money and see who finds it.' And Alex said 'Go ahead,' knowing the bank people weren't about to lend the gambler money to buy him out, no more knowledge than Selby had about cattle and the range. Selby came back saying, 'I can't rustle the money.' So Alex borrowed from the Telluride bank and bought the outfit.

"Many years later Alex told me, 'That outfit never done nothing but awful good for me!' If it hadn't been for miners crowding his Uravan headquarters, Alex never would have sold the Club, but it looked like mining was taking over."

When Alex Calhoun came to the Escalante his life had already crested. He was sixty-one, the age when a man begins to look to his sons to take over and ease him of the load.

His oldest son was six. Perhaps because Alex was getting such a late start at producing sons he started training them early—at six George Calhoun had several years' experience in the saddle. Oscar Huffington wrote August 1, 1915, concerning the last Calhoun round-up at the Club: "Nelson and I came over to Mr. Calhoun's to help him ride his range and brand up his calves. Just Mr. Calhoun, his two little boys, George and Frank, and Bert Carver. Nelson and I are doing the riding." Nelson Huffington, at ten, was the "old man" of the second generation. Frank couldn't have been more than four.

Kelly Calhoun says of this entry about his older brothers, "Oscar was probably right. I don't know how early George started riding with the crew, but Frank was on a horse punching cows before he could walk."

Even if these babes merely rode flank, held bunch, or cut weaners, the work was hard, responsible, and long hours. They loved it. In his old age George said, "Every fall when we came back to town, I left cow camp with tears in my eyes."

To get them (and herself) away from it, to give them other options, Rhea wintered her brood in town, starting with the September the oldest, Margaret Alice, was six—no Calhoun attended the Escalante school. Alex bought her the "Killian mansion," the town's showplace, a turreted house topping the bluff, pillared verandas, music and drawing rooms, and a divided stairway perfect for pausing to show off the sweeping gowns of the day.

If Rhea had any inclination to play the lady showing off Edwardian gowns, she had little chance. Whether in the "mansion" or in the comfortable two-story house Alex built just up the hill from Uncle Bob's cabin in Escalante Canyon, those five boys drove her out of her mind.

One of them swallowed calf black-leg pills and nearly died; one of them rode bareback through a barbed-wire fence and nearly died; one of them ate all the icing off two party cakes and nearly died; one of them conducted an experiment to see how big his belly would bloat if he stuffed it to capacity with dried apricots and drank a quart of water—and nearly died. To jump into the bathtub fully clothed and booted was not unusual, to jump into the burning fireplace to see if it was possible to jump out again fast enough to avoid being singed was tried not more than once each.

Rhea couldn't cope, she couldn't cope with them or with the succession of hired women that were supposed to help her cope with them. She couldn't cope with the Case car Alex bought so she could get from Canyon to town quickly in summer. No one knew how to drive it, least of all Alex, who never did learn to drive; so Rhea drove, and on the first trip burnt up the motor going all the way to town in low gear.

She herself suffered a broken arm and a ruptured appendix—each a day's drive from a doctor.

When Rhea's last baby was born, Margaret Alice, who'd seen this as her final chance to get a sister, stormed into her best friend's house, "Guess what, I got another one of those damn brothers!" Margaret Alice got married, to Frank Ward down the road; Rhea, whenever things got too much, escaped to the hot springs in Pueblo for her rheumatism.

All the boys could cook and keep house. Whether because of hired girls' unreliability or Rhea's helplessness, they cooked, washed dishes, washed clothes, ironed, and mended as needed. All without becoming even faintly feminine—Calhoun boys swept prizes at rodeos and races. Naturally, with the infant headstart they had! One of them, Kelly, was perhaps the initiator of the rodeo clown, riding a bucking bronc at a Norwood rodeo wearing sunbonnet and Mother Hubbard dress.

The Calhoun outfit dwindled after it came to the Escalante; perhaps the slot of the Canyon narrowed Alex's scope to its size. The range he bought with Mathews cattle included Twenty-five Mile Mesa, but he sold it almost at once. He still had mountain range and the strip of ranches on Kelso Creek but . . . Perhaps he had spent too much on houses. A townsman said, "He sold the Club and came here with $85,000 and a checkbook" . . . or the cattle-killing winter of 1919 . . . a war . . . a depression. . . .

He was an old man. Always slow and deliberate in making decisions, he got slower, standing long moments jingling coins in his pocket, reliving old days of glory on the Club.

Rhea was beside herself. "This outfit will never make enough to educate those boys!" she told Eda Musser. It didn't. The ones who wanted college and could get away made it on their own. Uphill all the way, like the wrong-end ditch. John became a certified public accountant, halving his life span with work and deprivation in doing it. George started toward his CPA, but about that time the ranch almost went under. He and Frank saved it for the family, then other obligations kept him from his dream. Frank, who was punching cows before he could walk, is punching still, but for another man, without the stresses of ownership.

Kelly, as he put it, "wore out three colleges getting a law degree," then before he could go into practice he was yanked into World War II, where he served on a PT boat—riding outside bronc-style, his shipmates reported—nonchalantly bringing home like rodeo trophies the Purple Heart, Silver Star, and a lieutenant commander's insignia. Eventually Kelly became district judge, somewhat on the order of Judge Bean of the Pecos. When Kelly's court was in session the paper never lacked for spicy news, though not everything that transpired appeared in print.

On one occasion—the first of the current generation's marijuana trials here—I was covering the case and after the trial asked for a look at the evidence. Kelly handed me the sack of pot, "Hell, you can have it!"

Naturally, I handed it right back. Nothing would have tickled Kelly more than to have me arrested for "possession" two blinks after he gave it to me.

Kelly's funeral last year was as unconventional as his life. Instead of a church service, his friends crowded into the stockyard sales barn and gave him a "roast." So many had a "Kelly story" to tell that the "Service" lasted for hours, and Kelly left town the way he would have wanted, in roars of laughter.

Ray, the youngest of the Calhoun sons, stayed with the ranch and ran it until his health gave out. It was sold. What was the Calhoun ranch is now "outside owned." A tenant occupies the Big House below the scar of the wrong-end ditch.

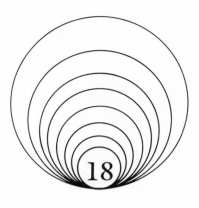

The Water Wall

Of all the canyons that branch from Escalante Forks, only the North Fork has perennial water. Known also as Spring Fork, the canyon slices through the mountain's south-flowing aquifer strata, tapping underground "water pipes" as reliable as faucets. But not as matter-of-fact as faucets. The mystery of a spring, of eternal water flowing from the depths of earth has evoked awe and worship from millennia of men, and still has magic. In the case of Escalante springs, we get a few tantalizing clues to what may be happening.

We can guess the direction of the water flow because it emerges only along the north wall of this canyon, and there are no springs in canyons that cut the same strata south of this one. And we can guess the contour of the hidden water-carrying strata by clues where canyon cuts expose the impervious granite that blocks water from percolating farther down. Contour maps at such canyon cuts show granite a thousand feet higher a few miles north at Unaweep Canyon than here where springs emerge. (Paradoxically, the crest of the Plateau slants the opposite way.) So what we envision is the profile of an underground mountain range, ancient worn-down granite, its slope still acting as a watershed, grooved with gullies that were formed when the mountain was open to sky and storms; gullies that though since filled and covered with millennial depths of more porous stone still funnel streams of water and emerge as springs where the canyon cuts across.

Water that dependable in a dry land was snatched first when homesteads were up for grabs. Before the Indians left, the Blumberg brothers and sisters staked all the land in the largest wide place in this branch canyon and built mud-and-stick dams prior to everyone, entitling them to First and Second Decrees on the entire Escalante water system.

A little later the Barclays arrived.

On our way to the Barclay Place we thread magnificent scenery. The cliffs to the right, sheer orange-red sandstone, are rimmed with a thin layer of pure white stone like icing on red-velvet cake. The road runs along the base, past the place where Kenneth Campbell's eight-sided cabin was; past meadows where Cum Campbell's boys finagled cows into obedience, somehow thereby getting the hang of politics; past ash where Upper Escalante Schoolhouse was burned to destroy diphtheria germs.

Eda Musser describes that schoolhouse: "Primitive! Tiny, dim, and so hard to heat that on cold days the children had to study in coats, caps, and mittens."

It was used for more than thirty years, mostly by children whose parents could not afford a second house in town, or who suspected that excessive book-learning unfitted a boy to punch cows, a girl to cook for punchers. Teacher also was in coat, cap, and mittens, suffering the added frustration of having to stoke the inadequate stove. Oblivious members of the Upper Escalante school board complained, "We had trouble keeping teachers. Unreliable, wouldn't renew their contracts at the end of the first year."

A narrow peninsula of cliff—a quarter of a mile long, several hundred feet high, and only a few strides wide—thrusts out from the blunt end of Sowbelly Ridge, pushing the road aside. It is called the Pinnacle—or the Castle, a Canyon-joke contrast with the name of the ridge.

Beyond is the homestead of the man the ridge is named for: Jess (Sowbelly) Barclay.

Jess Barclay was a Welshman who came to America to get out of the coal mines, and got into them again in Nova Scotia. Starving himself, with a frugality so fierce it became ingrained for life, he saved enough to buy freight wagon and ox team. His own boss at last, he was freighting out of Old Fort Sage, Kansas, when he met and married a schoolteacher, Miss Roxie, soon after the Civil War. With Roxie beside him he worked his way west.

By the time he rimmed out above the Big Hill he had acquired a family. Freighter that he was, Barclay couldn't bear to be without a wagon, but this was '81 or '82, years before the pack trail down the cliff would be dug wide enough for wheels. Nevertheless, he put a wagon down there, packed the pieces down on the backs of mules, and reassembled it when he reached his homestead at the far end of the Canyon.

Beyond the Pinnacle the cliff draws back in a great semicircle scalloped with V-shaped bays that sweep down in meadows like narrowing segments of a fan joined at the creek. Barclay filed on it all, putting his log cabin in the flowery cove he named Elk Horn Springs. Though neither he nor any of his family seem to have realized it, so fiercely did the toil of homesteading clamp their vision to the task, this lush dell is the most beautiful homesite in the Canyon, relinquished grievingly by all its owners but the first.

Barclay's cabin still stands, notable for its huge logs. It then had the usual dirt floor and roof; pole bunks, split-log table, sawed-stump chairs—but no cookstove. The man who packed a wagon down the Big Hill trail didn't think it necessary to lug a stove down it—after all, you can make money with a wagon, but a cookstove is a mere convenience.

"Grandmother Roxie cooked in the fireplace," Emily Blumberg Grooms says. "Not for the whole sixteen years she lived there, but for a long time." What she cooked in the fireplace, what Barclay provided, was mainly beans and saltside pork—sowbelly—even after he had herds of beef grazing the ridge named for him.

Sowbelly is not bacon which is streaked with lean and grows on the ribs of the pig; it is what it says, the layer of skin and lard that holds the hog together underneath. Crystalline with salt, it is simmered with beans, or sliced, desalted in boiling water, and fried. It is what folks mean when they speak of hard times as living low on the hog.

"The Blumbergs named him Sowbelly," Frank Ward said, "and they named Sowbelly Ridge and Sowbelly Creek for where he ranged his stock. Blumbergs were good at tagging Canyon people with names."

Perhaps scarred by those early years of self-imposed deprivation, Jess Barclay was unable to ameliorate Canyon isolation and hardships for his womenfolk. To the third generation Barclay women hate the Canyon. His granddughter Emily Grooms says, "My mother Elizabeth was three when they went out there. An old Delta doctor who would come horseback to deliver the babies once asked her, watching her eyes, 'Little girl, can you see any farther through these rocks than when you came?' As for me," Emily adds, "I hate even what that Canyon's made of—rocks."

When Roxie had lived at Elk Horn Springs sixteen years she'd had enough. She took the children and moved to a place she traded from Sam Maupin west of town. "Granddad Barclay went back to Nova Scotia," Emily says.

Elk Horn Springs is also known as the XVX, the only ranch in the Canyon named for a cattle brand. Among its many owners— before the Shreeves family acquired it as the jewel in their spread— was Cash Sampson, who, some folks still say, only bought it so he would have an "in" with the cattlemen and find out who had taken part in the Sheep War.

Squeezing the Canyon shut again, after Elk Horn Springs, is a steep slant of rocks and tangled growth that gives Brushy Ridge Trail access to the canyon rim and eventually to the top of the mountain. If the Big Hill was the front door to the Canyon, and the mouth of Escalante Creek is the basement entrance, Brushy Ridge is the ladder to the loft. "That trail was terrible, nothing but rocks and clay held together by scrub-oak roots," Eda Musser remembers, "but Ruby Lowe drove a buckboard up and down it to Ben's cow camp. The only woman ever did it."

Because of its slick clays, heave of boulders and slips, the trail was as arduous and dangerous to descend as to climb. It was down this trail, in breakneck desperation, that Bill and Nellie Shreeves wore out the team in bringing little Wilma to medical help.

Today, Brushy Ridge Jeep Trail varies from challenging to hair-raising, depending on what weathers have hit it lately.

Beyond the foot of the Brushy Ridge "staircase," the Canyon opens out again, making room for the Blumberg ranch.

There were a lot of Blumbergs—five brothers and four sisters. They came to the Escalante from Germany by way of Oshkosh, Wisconsin, and the Telluride gold mines. Fred Blumberg's son Brown described their soonering. "My father was nineteen. He and R. S. Kelso slipped in early. Spring of 1881. Three other Blumberg brothers came that fall after the Indians had been removed and it was legal.

"Those first years the Indians used to come through to hunt. They wintered in the pinyons in wickiups supported by lodge-pole pines they dragged from up around Gunnison. They built better shelter for their dogs—low and warm, lined with cedar bark inside and banked with earth. This was economics, not kindness, because that was their emergency food supply. When times got hard they ate their dogs."

Fred and brothers Dick and Bill staked squatter claims and drifted their cows onto the mountain. Brother Charlie left for a place called Tranquility Basin nearer town. Fifth brother Emil came late, old, and nowhere near the Canyon.

Times were hard for the Blumbergs, and their women suffered from the disinclination of menfolks to lug anything bulky (and unprofitable) down the Big Hill. A visitor left this memory: "They didn't have a washtub. The men had dug a hole in the ground and lined it with a tarp. One of the women was down washing clothes in that holeful of water."

But the Blumberg sense of humor got them through, erupting in creative names. In addition to Sowbelly Barclay, other Blumberg labels that became common usage were Old Onion Eye, Old Black Bill, Silk Hat Harry, Uncle Windy, Wind River, and Mr. Ain't-so-good, who let his wife do all the work. They gave their own sons names like Ellsworth, Paul, Earl, and Harvey, then never called them anything but Pink, Boss, Brown, and Monk. Pink and his twin, Whitey, were tagged for the color of their hair. A girl, Cleo, answered to Barney; Doris had the only conventional nickname among them, Dory.

Marrying neighbors, the Blumbergs briefly meshed the Canyon together—Fred married Elizabeth Barclay, Gusty Blumberg married William (Banker) Helmke, Mary Blumberg married Joe Harvey up on Kelso Creek—then they all left the Canyon for ranches near town.

Fred, on his Roubideau ranch, settled down to making money and did so well that he became one of the bank's biggest shareholders just in time for the crash of 1929. Charley in Tranquility, mixing hobby with potato growing, got newspaper notice for capturing wild infants to display in the billiard hall—bear cubs and lynx kittens.

William spent most of his life in the Canyon but was never quite contained by it. In 1894, watching hordes of Coxey's Army ride freights through Delta on their way to Washington, he went to Denver headquarters to see if he should "enlist" in this effort to get the government straightened out. He came back disillusioned, reporting, "The majority were Italians, Irish, Swedes, Huns, and only a few real people—Germans and Americans." Then he was off placer mining, a venture that apparently made ranching look good by contrast, for next spring he was signing notes to buy more cattle.

While other Blumbergs worked the Canyon ranches off and on, Dick was the one who stayed through it all, hanging onto the family holdings with bulldog grip through bad times, adding to them in good. But he was tempted. The year he went to town to prove up on his homestead he announced that if anybody wanted to reach him they'd have to write to Klondike because he was off to the gold-fields. If Dick really turned loose and went, he wasn't gone long because he shortly had his back teeth in a lawsuit against Ben Lowe.

The Canyon consumed the life spans of second-generation Blumbergs Brownie and Pink. For Brownie, cowboy life in the Canyon seems to have been a pleasant somnambulance from which he woke only when past retirement age. He said, his voice tinged with surprise, "Used up my life chasing other people's cows up and down that slot hole. Nothing to show.

"You could say times were easier then, those years when our fathers were getting started in the Canyon. Grass was higher, thicker, and richer. Dad would put a calf out on winter range and by March he'd be beef worth $18. Doesn't seem like much now, but it was clear, and bought about as much in the way of necessities as the price of a steer will bring today. No grazing fees, not much taxes.

"When the tax inspector came by he'd ask how many cows you had. If you had a hundred you'd say twenty-five, and be taxed for that many. He didn't count and didn't care."

The Blumbergs weren't prejudiced about what a cattle ranch was supposed to produce; any year cows weren't paying out they grew hogs. Nelson Huffington says, "They raised so many hogs they drove them to market. They'd get as far as Wards' the first day, then as far as our place, and the third day make it up the Big Hill and down to Roubideau where they loaded them into boxcars." Picture that kind of Wild West trail drive looping down this beautiful movie-set canyon! The same dust and noise, but squealing and oinking instead of bawling; and double the volume of cowboy cussing, the hog being the world's most independent-minded quadruped.

From a cabin without even a washtub, the Blumbergs prospered until eventually they were living in what was described as "the finest house in the Canyon"—two-story, with ample porches, wide lawns, truck garden, and orchards.

Apple trees they planted are still bearing. "One is a Wolf River apple," Brown's wife, Louise, says, "a big apple that puffs up like a balloon when baked. You can still pick them there, if the bears haven't beat you to it."

Dick, of all the Blumberg brothers and sisters who pioneered this place, struggled most doggedly to keep it in the family. "Nobody but a Blumberg will ever own *this* place!" he growled like knocking wood, as he saw homesteads sold, one after another, to outsiders; as his body began to betray him by getting old; as times worsened and nothing solid remained except the land. "Nobody but a Blumberg!"

But the next generation had other goals. "We received letters from his sons asking us to buy the place," Eda says.

No one has lived here for a long, long time. The yard is a forest of sucker cottonwood saplings, the clapboards in the gables soften and sag like rotting cloth.

In this ghost place clasped in cliffs, the stillness is tangible. A mourning dove caresses silence with two slow notes, a raven's caw cleaves it sharply. If the day is warm, a column of ravens rises, spiraling on motionless wings, the shape of their flight giving visible form to the shaft of thermal air that lifts and drifts them away like smoke.

Except for a strip of cliff-boxed thickety browse called the Sagebrush that Morgan Hendrickson homesteaded for (he says) sentimental reasons, the last private property on the North Fork of the Escalante is the Sawtell.

Unlike other Canyon ranches it is named for its last, not first owners. And well it may be, because nothing is known about the firstcomers except that they arrived some ten thousand years ago, lived here off and on until about the time the Pilgrims were landing on Plymouth Rock, then left for good. Like the Mesa Verde peoples of which they were a part.

Their village spanned the creek from cliff to cliff. Though drifted with sand in the centuries since they left, stone dwellings and underground kivas were visible when our pioneers came, and still may be seen on the far side of the creek, where it was harder for the pioneers to get at them. Pioneers had no interest in the Indians they displaced; they called them "noble savages" in sarcasm, taking the term from romantic Eastern writers they considered the crackpots of their time. When the first settler saw those archeologically precious remnants, he saw only nice flat rocks that would make a dandy wall for his cellar. The cellar is still intact; the kiva he robbed is a mere depresion in the dirt mound above it. The part of the prehistoric

◄ Blumberg Big House. The kitchen that made it a saltbox is gone.

ruins that lies across the creek, being out of handy reach, was still there to be scientifically excavated by archeologists from the Colorado Museum of Natural History fifty years ago.

Probably it was the second owner, Emil, one of the carpenter Harveys up Kelso Creek, who built the fine house that once stood here. Eda Musser describes it in telling about the first Canyon dance she attended after Kel brought her as a bride to the Canyon. "It was the Fourth of July, 1916. The Gilberts were living on that place then. We hitched the team to the light wagon and left the Forks just before dusk. The road up the creek was so rough and scary I couldn't bear to think of coming back over it in complete dark, so I suggested we stay all night with the Gilberts.

"Kel said, 'Oh, we will dance till daylight!'"

"It was a nice house, five-room log with bedrooms above and polished oak floors. They opened double doors to make a big room for dancing. Next morning when I went outside I thought it was the most beautiful place I had ever seen, the cliffs towering all around like a theater, like some of the big theaters I had attended in the East."

This was three months after the host and several guests had secretly ridden in the Sheep War. Gilbert's daughter said her father, who never wore sidearms, wore a holster gun all that summer. Either he laid it aside to host the dance, or it was unnoticeable because all the men were wearing guns—Eda's recollections did not include this detail.

Sawtell, the kind of homesite everybody longed to own and nobody could make a living on, has had more owners than any other place in the Canyon. They number three separate cattle outfits, a couple of reluctant banks, and half a dozen small operators who had it by the fingernails on a string of debt. R. S. Kelso, by then married and a man of money, owned it twice, once on purpose and once by default. Bad markets, bad judgment, hard times, foreclosures, back taxes, and perpetrated "discouragements" kept it shuffling around.

Marcus Doty owned it long enough to bring a daughter within marrying reach of the Canyon. When Louise Doty married Brown Blumberg down the road, they lived here until they had a child of six and had to move to put her in school.

Louise Blumberg cites a problem school tots faced twice a day.

Horse-drawn rake. Apples in the nearby orchard are now eaten only by bears. ▶

"Even though we moved to a place nearer school Betty still had several miles to ride, and a lot of gates—the Canyon road wasn't unfenced like it is now. Brown set rock mounting blocks at every gate so she could get back on her horse after she'd opened the gate and closed it behind her.

"The teacher they had then was a man. He raised a fuss about our dog following Betty to school, said it caused a distraction. But we wanted the dog to go with her because he would let us know if anything happened to her—she was so *little*. The teacher finally gave in, but it wouldn't have done him any good not to, that dog would have chewed the rope or hung himself to go with her."

The Sawtell brothers, Walter and Marion, were the last owners here before the Mussers. Knowing they'd never pay out with the cattle they had grazing permits for, they diversified in an unlikely combination, strawberries and hogs—acres of each—and moonlighted by feeding Musser cattle.

Since these activities came in bursts (the sows thoughtfully farrowed before strawberry season, and the latter was generally over before the calves had to be trademarked) they required batches of temporary labor—especially to pick all those strawberries. Sawtell's hired help was usually high school boys from town who, though the work was hard, hot, and not too well paid, would probably have done it for free and their meals just to spend the summer in such a wild, beautiful place replete with hunting, fishing, and the chance now and then to play cowboy for real.

Cooking for the hired boys, and for anyone else who happened by, were the Sawtell bachelors, or just one of them after World War II yanked Marion off to Europe. Walter could shake up a good meal —all Canyon men could; who else do you think did the cooking while wives were wintering in town to put the kids in school? That didn't mean he liked to.

He remembers, "Seems like you'd just get into the morning's work and you'd have to quit and go fix dinner.

"Raymond Tyler was working for me, helping me dig ditch. Young, good-looking fellow. When it came time I had to go to the kitchen I threw down my shovel and said, 'Why in the world don't you marry us a cook!'

"And durned if he didn't," Walter Sawtell says now, not knowing that Raymond had been, as the Canyon saying goes, watching pretty Ione Edwards for quite some time.

The beautiful old house is gone; it burned one night when hunt-

Of the Sawtell Big House only the cookstove remains.

ers, taking the house for abandoned because it was seasonally unoccupied, prepared supper on a gasoline grill. Only ash-dark earth, a
cookstove, a cellar wall are left—relic artifacts, like the prehistoric ruins
across the creek.

Within its inverted bell tower of red walls, Sawtell dreams on,
silent except for the tolling echo of cattle speaking the one syllable
of their tongue.

Up the mountainside beyond the Canyon, but tied to it by strings
of cattle going up or down and strands of conflict between men, is
one of those grassy valleys entered through a notch where if a man
builds fences from side to side he can prevent ready access by other
men's cattle and secure a private monopoly of public grazing land.
Oscar Huffington did this at Picket Corral years before he homesteaded
there, and without any ruckus arising so far as is known. But when
Bert and Ben Lowe did it, there was a to-do.

The grazing rights of several cattlemen were involved, but it was the Blumbergs who acted. In an era given to settling disputes by gouge or by gun, the Blumbergs were notable for going to law. They were in court at least seven times in two decades, usually as plaintiffs. This says a lot about the trusting nature of the Blumbergs because even if you could get a judgment it was next to impossible to get a sheriff to come into the Canyon to enforce it.

Details are sketchy. (As noted earlier, some county records were housecleaned out of existence.) Newspaper coverage of entire court proceedings was often mere one-liners, "X vs Y. For the defendant," or "The people vs X. For the people." Blumberg cases dealt mainly with foreclosure, boundary lines, and good name. Though the paper did not specify, apparently the recipient of a Blumberg nickname — Old Onion Eye, Sowbelly, Uncle Windy — had learned what he was being called and surmised who was to blame for it.

Or perhaps Mr. Ainseworth discovered he was a living, walking pun.

Mr. Ainseworth was transmogrified to Mr. Ain't-so-good soon after he and his wife filed on their Canyon claim. People began remarking that when there was anything really laborious around the place, such as building a fence around it in order to prove up (two solid miles of post holes dug in mostly rock), Mrs. Ainseworth usually did it, because at such times Mr. Ainseworth had a tendency toward urgent errands in town or a bad back.

Whether Ain't-so-good or somebody else brought that suit, the Blumbergs won it; but they didn't win the one against the Lowe brothers. That case began when Ben and Bert Lowe fenced off two thousand acres at the head of Escalante Creek.

This was a few years before Ben Lowe moved to Escalante, and during the hey-day of his tag games with the law. Bert Lowe also was feeling his oats. Not too long before, he had come home from Manila all covered with glory, having served with the First Colorado Regiment in the Spanish-American War. But the two rip-snorters were showing signs of settling down. They had got themselves married, had developed homestead ranches in the Uncompahgre Valley, and in fencing off mountain range were building with an eye to the future like other responsible stockmen. But the Lowe brothers were not counted among responsible men; furthermore, the land they fenced off had been accustomed — though not entitled — range for other men's cows.

The fence was "obnoxious to the Mesa County Cattle Growers' Association," which seems to have jockeyed the Blumbergs into brunt position in the matter, or perhaps that's where they wanted to be.

The opening skirmish was to charge Bert Lowe with burning down the Ed Wetzel cow camp cabin—though what that had to do with anything isn't clear. Bert countered by suing the Blumbergs $5,000 for false arrest. He was subsequently cleared of the arson charge, but the jury couldn't make up its mind about the damage suit.

Then six members of the Mesa County Cattlemen's Association met the Lowe brothers in the road and ordered them out of the country.

The Lowes refused to go, at least unless paid for improvements they had made. Their $750 fence had been cut all around and posts pulled up.

Ben Lowe said he "would defend himself if they attempted to force him out of the country," adding, "but if they would let him alone, he would let them alone."

Interpreting this as a threat, the Association hailed the Lowes into court again as "dangerous men who had made threats against Blumberg and others."

The judge dismissed the case, assessed all costs against the complaining witness, Blumberg, and gave the Mesa County Cattlemen's Association a scolding that took up half a column in the Grand Junction *Daily Sentinel.* After citing recent cases in Wyoming where the Cattle Grower's Association had hired thugs to murder people who were obnoxious to the Association, the judge summed: "No individual or aggregate of individuals had the right to order any man out of the country."

This was one of at least two times when law was judicially defined by a confrontation involving Ben Lowe.

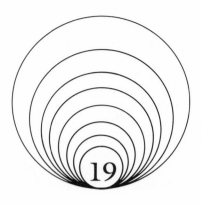

Escalante Forks

"When Kel and I were married and he brought me to the ranch, every cowboy and rancher in the Canyon found excuse to come to the Forks and look me over. At least that's what Kel said they came for. 'They want to get a look at you while they can. They're betting you won't stick it long.'

"Well, I guess they saw plenty to raise their bets on. Kel was teaching me how to cook."

There was good reason to doubt Eda's staying powers. A tiny girl who spoke French (learned at her Parisian grandmother's knee) as fluently as English, and whose English had a cultured inflection learned in elocution classes at a finishing school for young ladies in the East; who could drive harness racing horses, but couldn't sit a western saddle; who could play three musical instruments, but hadn't the rudiments of cooking, cleaning, or managing a household because there had always been day servants to do such chores.

Odds on Kel weren't much better.

Though he was born on the ranch, he seemed unfitted for the harsh, ruthless life of early-day cattle ranching. For one thing, like his father he hadn't wanted to be a cattleman; for another he didn't look physically strong enough. A small man, slender and deceptively frail-looking, he'd got off to a bad start, born premature to a woman who had not lived to finish the job of rearing him.

Anna Kelso and brother R. S., themselves orphans, were reared delicately by a group of well-to-do unmarried relatives known as "the old uncles," though some of them were aunts. R. S. came West for his health and fortune and found both, living to be 92 and, what with one thing and another that came along–marriage, inheritances, free grass, and Naturita mines–becoming rich enough to winter in California rather than in town, all without noticeable effort on his part. But Anna Kelso Musser came because her husband had made her brother a bad loan on cattle.

The home he brought Anna to–after that harrowing trip down the Big Hill–was the usual log cabin: one room, dirt floor, dirt roof. Anna didn't rough it for long, however. By spring John had built her a house in town and eased her summers by flooring the cabin, adding another, and screening the breezeway between the two.

Her last child, Kelso, was born in that cabin in 1894; too soon, before she had moved back to town for the winter.

The first of the deaths that shadowed Kel's childhood occurred just before his birth; his brother Albert died of a kidney complication. From time to time Anna took the children by train over the Rockies to visit "the old uncles" or, upon word of a death among them, to settle an estate. On one of these trips Kel's sister Edith died. A year later Anna herself died. Kel was nine.

Tied to the ranch, John Musser was unable to live in town with his three young children–sixteen-year-old Don was doing a man's work at the ranch. The housekeeper John hired was unsuited or disinclined to mother children, so at fourteen, Hazel took over the raising of her little brother. June, just older than Kel, seems not to have required "raising," being already sturdily aimed at a nursing career.

"Hazel set her heart on Kel and was bound he'd turn out just about right, and he did," Eda says now. "He was diplomatic but stood up for himself."

On her last trip Anna had brought back one of the old uncles to mother, and he was still there. Because the Musser town property didn't have barn room enough for his horses, he had built a larger house for Anna, up on the bluff above town where there was room for corrals and stalls for his horses, Anna's, and the teams and saddle horses that must rest overnight between coming from and returning to the Canyon.

A rosebush Anna had planted was moved to the new house. All his life, it evoked from Kel the only outlet he allowed his sorrow. "Mother's rose. Mother's little white rose," he would say when he passed.

"I don't think Kel ever was a child," Eda says. "In town he had

to look after the old uncle, ease out of bed so as to let him sleep till nine, listen to his complaints about his failing body and times getting worse. And out on the ranch it was even harder. Dad Musser didn't trust Hazel to raise his son, and kept Kel with him as much as possible. 'Chap' he called Kel, short for 'Little Chap,' his nickname as baby of the family. He would have Kel up on the mountain with him six or seven months of the year—from a month or so before school was out until mid-November. They lived in a tent. So cold. No comforts whatever. So lonely for a little boy. To the end of his life Kel hated camping out."

Kel vowed to escape it, go to college, be an architect.

When Kel was twenty, John was sixty-four and decided to retire. Though his oldest son and namesake (Don was only a nickname for John W. Musser, Jr.) was thirty and with years of experience in cattle raising, it was on Kel he unloaded the burden he had never liked. One Sunday afternoon, at the end of a weekend in the luxurious town house, he said, "Chap, are you going out to that place, or do I have to?"

"All Dad Musser did after that was take care of his garden and town team and read the *Rocky Mountain News*. Musser Brothers Cattle Co. was in its second generation."

The brothers complemented each other—Don, "man of the Old West," doing the cowpunching up and down the mountain, psyching out the horse trades and the deals, holding up the outfit's end at cowboy Saturday night sprees in town; Kel, the steady one, farming Musser ranches as they were acquired.

Kel decided not to do it alone. At the Baker home near Chicago, Fleming Baker, one of the town's "summer people," received a letter asking for his daughter's hand in marriage.

Eda Baker first came to Delta she was thirteen. An old uncle of her own was the cause of her coming. "Father's brother Homer had come west, hoping the high dry air would cure his tuberculosis. It was thought that walls hindered the flow of air, so lungers lived in tent houses. It was too late for Uncle Homer, all Father could do was take his body back East." Nevertheless, Eda remembers it as a happy summer. So did her parents; they returned again and again.

◄ "Modern" hand-crank gas pump keeps company with a century-old cabin at the Forks.

"We rented the top floor of the Hammonds' house, and had some of our own furnishings shipped out. We couldn't get the piano upstairs so Father had a tent house set up for it in the backyard."

Furniture as well as road and racing buggies traveled at the other end of an immigrant car carrying Fleming Baker's saddle and sulky racehorses. An immigrant car was rented as a unit, and was so called because it was the means used by many pioneers in moving all their possessions West—household goods, farm implements, livestock. Contents of the car must be unloaded and reloaded as the track changed from broad to narrow gauge in crossing the Rockies. Females of the family rode coach on the same train, but usually the men stayed with the stock, to see that no animal was down and trampled, and to feed them if finances did not permit the expense of having it done by railroad employees.

Either Fleming Baker did not always ride with his horses or on one trip was unable to face down a minor official bent on fulfilling to the letter a law requiring vaccination of horses crossing state lines. "With horses of this quality, such laws were waived, because, of course, owners had already protected their valuable animals that way. But Father's horses were vaccinated anyway, and one of them died of it."

Welcoming the new girl in town, Judge King's wife sent her chauffeur around with what was one of the area's first automobiles to take Eda and next-door friend Jeanette Amsbury for a drive. "Mrs. King sat in back with us, describing the pioneer history of the countryside we were passing."

Just who the chauffeur was, riding in front under open sky and whatever weather was happening, isn't known—perhaps he came with the car. But a "day lady" who did cleaning, laundry, and cooking for the King family, is known. She was Mrs. Hyrum Dempsey, mother of thirteen children, one of whom was William Harrison Dempsey, known as Jack after he entered the prize-fight ring.

The Dempseys had drifted up from Manassa by way of Creede to the Delta area where Hyrum, described as not very "work brickle," intermittently hired out as a farm or brickyard hand. Jack, who adored his mother and resented the kind of work she had to do to support her family, evened the social score by chasing the King boys all the way home from school every night or so. Kel Musser was in the same grade as Jack, and partner in at least one of his pranks—the two of them going for an unsanitized swim in the town water tank.

Eda continues, "All that summer my new friend Jeanette and I went riding together—we thought it was simply fate that our horses, coming from so far apart, were look-alike sorrels. Mrs. Coleman told Kel about me, said she'd found just the girl for him—new in town. But at thirteen we weren't interested in the opposite sex. Jeanette and I did nothing all summer but ride our horses and play paper dolls.

"Young people at any age didn't date. Why, once when I was 16 I had a date and Father wouldn't let me go! Everything was in groups. One of the groups where nice young people could get to know each other was dancing school. That's where I first noticed Kel—the year I was sixteen and Father decided we would stay over the winter.

"Mrs. Coleman's dancing school had ten boys and ten girls, meeting every Saturday afternoon. She taught the steps—schottische, waltz, two-step—and etiquette. Boys learned how to bow and ask a girl for a dance, and how to thank her afterward.

"She said to me, 'I've found just the right boy for you! So nice, just your age.' But I didn't pay much attention to Kel then. He wasn't the best dancer. I did get to know his sister June. Father had a sleigh, a cutter, and he would take us flying up the snowy mountainside as far as Cedaredge.

"After that summer we always rented a house. The first one was on Main Street, and we would sit on the porch every evening until ten o'clock, when they turned off the street lights. People would stop, visit, and pass on to another porch. One who stopped to chat with Father every evening was the night marshal, Cash Sampson. It was said Cash had a girl over on one of the dark streets—all streets except Main were unlighted—but he never brought her by.

"Another summer we rented Ben Lowe's house on Dodge Street. Like other cattlemen's wives, Ruby Lowe lived in town in the winter to put the children in school and moved back to their ranch in the summer. There were always a lot of empty houses in town during the summers.

"Father entered his horses, trotters and pacers, at all the area racing meets—Grand Junction, Denver, Pueblo, Salt Lake City. Of course, when the horses weren't on the train or being raced they had to be exercised—so I would do my turn at driving them up and down the country roads. I'd always earned pocket money by walking his horses to cool them down."

Eda Baker's driving experience began when not much past babyhood she drove her Shetland pony hitched to a tiny cart she calls a two-seater. Also she "showed" Shetlands for a neighbor who raised them, driving a miniature replica of a fashionable buggy that he had

had built to scale for the purpose. The size of her rig grew with her and eventually was a gleaming brown-varnished phaeton. "Father preferred me to drive a runabout, cut under, because you could turn so short."

When pampered Eda Baker was seventeen her destiny in the uncouth Canyon was challenged by an even stranger possibility—marrying into polygamy.

"We'd rented a little house in Salt Lake City where Father was racing, furnished with the camping kind of furniture we always brought when we came West. None of our nice furniture—our home was in the East and we didn't disturb it. I got to be good friends with a Mormon girl who had a 'cousin' that was obviously a half-sister, and a father who lived in another house about half the time. He took a liking to me and kept saying, 'Oh, just wait till my son gets home from his mission! I want him to meet you.'

"That boy was so good-looking in his pictures that I was scared. I told Mother I didn't want to be around when he got home from his mission. I didn't want to risk being attracted to him and getting into that kind of situation."

When Fleming Baker received Kel Musser's proposal he asked Eda, "Is this what you really want to do, marry Kel and live out there on a ranch in that canyon?"

"I had never been in Escalante Canyon nor seen the ranch, and I hadn't seen Kel for nearly two years, but I was sure. I knew we were a lot alike. The ranch was a challenge; both of us always liked a challenge.

"Kel sent my ring in a big package—jewelers always sent jewelry in big weighted boxes, so nobody would know what it was and steal it—and we went to Delta in November.

"I'd known the Musser young folks because they lived in town, but the first time I saw Dad Musser was after Kel and I were engaged, when he took me to the family home for dinner."

Eda still gets a chuckle from the gesture her father-in-law-to-be made to impress her. "It was thought our family had money, and I guess we did, but somehow there wasn't much at the end. Well, he said to June, 'Write a check for a thousand dollars. Chap [Kel] wants to buy some cattle.'

"My sons laugh now at the idea that a thousand dollars is flourish money. But it was quite a flourish, at that; in dollars of that day, the check would have bought fifty head."

Eda describes the home Kel brought her to at Escalante Forks: "There were three cabins, two set close together with a screened breezeway between where we would set the table and eat in the summertime. One cabin was the kitchen, the other had a little table to hold the Victrola, and three beds where the men slept. The third cabin was our bedroom.

"Kel said there'd be only him and the hired man, Shorty Gibson, while I was learning to cook. But Calhouns had just bought Uncle Bob Smith's place; Uncle Bob didn't move out of his cabin, so the Calhoun cowboys, Ray Lockhart and Hooly Hoover, lived with us until a house was built up there. None of the men could seem to eat at the same time, so I got a lot of practice, cooking five or six meals a day. Then of course there were the stoppers. Nobody had told me that Kel was expected to offer the hospitality of his table to anybody who stopped at corral or hayfield to pass the time of day.

"The cabin walls were covered with newspaper, funnies and rotogravure, pasted up when Hazel or June had been summering there. In a storm the dirt roof would leak and run mud like chocolate pudding, but that was exciting, part of the fun, finding a dry place."

Eda could afford to think of it as a lark because unlike Roxie Barclay, she knew she wasn't stuck in it forever. Within the year Kel had built an eight-room house on a proud rise of land above the irrigation stream.

"We didn't plan on a housewarming. We'd stopped going to dances because Kel thought it was unseemly once we'd started a family. But we had one anyway. Several, in fact. Before the four bedrooms were partitioned off, the whole upstairs was open – a wonderful big place to dance – so people just came, bringing refreshments and music along.

Except for going to town to have babies, Eda lived in the Canyon year-round until the oldest was in sixth grade, but her children – Alice, Jack, and Tom – did not attend Escalante School. "Kel was on the school board, and we enrolled our children so they'd count toward the number needed to get a teacher, but I taught them at home with Calvert School courses. Calvert is still used by families who live in far-away places, such as mining engineers.

"I don't suppose I saw another woman more than two or three times a year – Mrs. Ward came over about that often.

"Not that we didn't have company! We had lots of stoppers. By the time riders reached the Forks from town or cow camp it was too late in the day to go on, so we bunked and fed them. And the Forks was just 'meal distance' from other Canyon ranches in all directions. I cooked for cowboys, ranchers, and Forest Service people all hours of the day."

If she missed woman talk—this very feminine person who had attended only schools for girls, except for one winter at co-ed Delta High School, where she felt "simply surrounded by boys"—she was too busy to notice the lack. But it shaped her. The cooking she learned was cowboy cooking, and remained cowboy cooking for life, she says —meat, gravy, beans, potatoes, pie. Her thoughts, as she worked, did not float free into quiet eddies of books, fashion, theater, or even her beloved music; they grappled with the problems of ranching discussed at table—hoof disease, black leg, the risk of borrowing to buy sprung heifers, the risk of not borrowing and coming short of steers to meet next year's payment on the current mortgage.

When Kel and Eda had been married about eighteen months, the outfit took a new direction. During the three decades of John Musser's management its holdings hadn't grown; there'd been only the ranch at the Forks, Short Point cow camp, public grazing on the mountain, and rented winter pasture along the river. Now, with one purchase, the outfit began the expansion that would eventually take in most of the Canyon. It almost doubled the outfit's size—and its liabilities.

Eda wasn't told or asked. "Don Musser just came home one day and said, 'Well, I bought the Lowe Place.' That's when I learned for sure it was Musser *Brothers!*"

Don Musser's purchase of the Lowe Place was notable because he paid widow Mrs. Ben Lowe her full asking price, contrary to the customary practice of the day in buying ranch real estate, which was to wait until the seller was in desperate straits—widowed, ill, or behind with the taxes—and willing to sell for a "reasonable" price. Other instances of Don's generosity earned him the nickname "Writer of the Family" because of notes he signed to help family men struggling to get a start in the Canyon. Whenever one of these defaulted and it was suggested Don do some dunning, his response was, "He knows he owes it to me."

The next Musser Brothers acquisition definitely cut Eda in—the McHugh Place down on the river, taken in trade for Cedaredge land she had inherited.

During the bank crashes of 1929, when a thousand dollars of Musser money "disappeared," it was Eda who caught the discrepancy —the brothers were too busy with the cattle to pay much attention.

Because of this and the fact that by then she was living in town all winter, handy to banks and commission houses, it was decided she should handle the checkbook. Soon she was keeping the outfit's books and knew better than the men when they were in a position to risk the purchase of more land or cattle. Eventually she was planning some of the purchases herself.

"A few summers ago I noticed an ad for a piece of land adjoining one of our pastures up on the mountain. It was about to be bought by a group planning to develop a youth camp. We just couldn't have that—hordes of people coming and going, hazing the cattle, leaving gates open—so I told the boys [by that time the Musser Brothers were her sons Tom and Jack] that we'd better buy it."

In the six decades of its expansion Musser Brothers acquired the Lowe Place and Shingle Roof cow camp and pasture, the Campbell Place, McHugh, the Blumberg holdings in Canyon and Mountain-top, Bridgeport, the four Canyon ranches that with mountain acreage made up the Shreeves spread, the Welland Smith Place, the Ward Place, and the Sawtell—along with the forest grazing permits that came with each.

"It sounds easy when you put it all into one sentence like that," Eda says. "But we worked hard. Oh, so hard! And when other people were going under during depressions, bank failures, killing weather, and bad markets, we almost did. Just held on by the skin of our teeth. I remember we had to borrow on Kel's life insurance to keep Alice in college."

Kel and Eda had lived in the new house just seven years when it burned to the ground.

"A fire in the Canyon is terrible! No equipment, no help! We hadn't had sense enough to build the house below the irrigation ditch.

"Afterward we figured one of the cowboys, getting supplies together for packing to cow camp, had left a candle stub burning in the storeroom, stuck to a board or table by its own grease, then went off and forgot it.

"Kel and I were in the garden planting dahlias when we looked up and saw smoke coming from the roof. My first thought was, 'Mother's asleep in there!'

"We put the three little children over in a field, and told them to stay there. Kel grabbed the buckets and ran down to the ditch for water, but the fire was already too big to put out. He got upstairs somehow and began throwing dresser drawers of clothing out the

Mussers trail cattle down off the mountain.

bedroom windows. Mother rolled a trunk out the door, saving some precious mementoes. Much as I hate feather beds I saved two or three.

"The house was lined with beaverboard. It burned like paper. The stairs went, and Kel jumped from an upper window.

"Then we stood and watched everything we had saved burn on the lawn before our eyes—the back chimney fell over on the stuff. Out of it all, we saved ourselves, a clock that was at the jeweler's to be repaired, and two singed pictures that came floating down out of the heat and smoke—Kel and his dog when he was a boy.

"With the insurance money, $2,550 we bought a mail-order house. We looked through a catalogue of ready-cut houses, found one with three bedrooms and ordered it. It came with everything, like a kit—boards cut to the right lengths and numbered, furnace, paint, window shades, bundles of lath and sacks of plaster. Kel put it together himself."

Ham Hendrickson came to the Forks at a time when the Mussers —their children away at school—needed a roomy house less than they needed a good, reliable man to help farm the ranches they were acquiring. Leaving the Forks to the new foreman and his family, Kel and Eda moved down to the cottage they had built at the Lowe, and had another of their honeymoons. Ham also ran the Escalante Forks Post Office and Store, in which the hottest article was horseshoe nails.

Ham seems to have been one of those people who do the right things so consistently and pleasantly that like a summerful of June days they are always just summed up "Wonderful!" not itemized in grim or spicy detail like the vagaries of a March morning or an old hermit.

Mrs. Ham, on the other hand, escaped a similar beatific anonymity by shooting a bear through the screen porch.

The bear was clawing and devouring the garden that she, with much labor, had just raised to harvesting stage. Outrage getting the better of judgment, she hauled off and pulled the trigger. Faced with a dead bear, she panicked. It wasn't bear season, even if she'd had a license; game wardens and Forest Service personnel were frequent stoppers because the cooking was so good. One might pop in sight at any moment.

She tried to hide the bear by covering him with a tarp; he made a very suspicious-looking hump on the lawn. She would have dug a hole and buried him if he hadn't outweighed her five or six times over.

That's all there is to the story; she wasn't arrested or hanged, but she did gain a more specific kind of fame.

Mr. and Mrs. Ham Hendrickson brought two children to the Canyon, or rather one of their children brought them. Morgan Hendrickson began punching Musser cattle while still in high school and continued with the outfit in various capacities—with time off to serve as Delta mayor once or twice.

As far as Kel and Eda were concerned, the four Hendricksons were always "family." The bond became official when their son Jack married Bernice Hendrickson.

With the Hendricksons at the Fork, and other reliable workers coming to occupy various ranch sites, Kel had time to devote to the welfare of the industry as a whole. He headed several local and state stockmen's associations, served as Colorado representative for the National Cattlemen's Association for several years, and was district adviser for the Bureau of Land Management, Department of the Interior. Jack and Bernice Musser have carried on this tradition, representing the cattle industry and their specialty, Beefmaster breeding stock, at the national level.

Kel Musser's work with national stockmen's organizations sometimes took him to Washington and New York, and on one of these trips they had dinner at Jack Dempsey's restaurant.

"He came to our table," Eda remembers. "He and Kel talked over school days, and he asked about his special friends, the Barker boys he used to play with at the Lowe."

Dempsey didn't ask about the King family. Realizing as he grew older their kindness to his mother, he had kept in touch with them, knew they had moved to Denver, knew who'd been born among them, who had died. It is one of the nice ironies of life that the most prestigious and cherished memento of the eminent King family is a letter of condolences from Jack Dempsey at the time of Mrs. King's death.

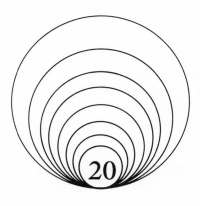

The Sheep War

Fifty-six years after Kel and Eda were married an old man came to the Forks and, without making a point of it, managed to talk to Kel alone. They talked a long time.

When he had gone Eda asked what it was all about. Kel said only that many years before there had been some trouble on the range about sheep, and the old man wanted permission to use Don Musser's name in an article about the incident.

"Until Carl Gilbert's article came out," Eda says, "I didn't know about the Sheep War, as they call it. Or that our Don had been involved in shooing those sheep away from cattle winter pasture down by the river."

Could this be? The raid happened the very year she came to the Canyon, and the armed raiders met here at the Musser ranch before riding out into the night. Didn't she read the newspapers? Didn't people discuss the sheep slaughter then or during all the years afterward?

Well, the raid was in March, 1916; she and Kel were married in April; she came to the Escalante in May (perhaps the Musser cabin had been chosen for the rendezvous precisely because there was no wife in it). Newspaper accounts placed the raids downriver at Dominguez, and though it was known that Dominguez was Escalante cattle wintering country, neither that fact nor anything else implicating Escalante stockmen was mentioned. Never having been in the Canyon, Eda may have been unaware that she was moving to an area where Wild West ways still prevailed. Out of fear or loyalty, the raids were not discussed, most especially not with someone whose family might be thought to have taken part.

For more than half a century the men who rode that night were so close-mouthed that not even their wives were told the identities of the riders. At Ben Lowe's suggestion they had sworn death to any man who talked, a melodramatic vow they probably wouldn't have carried out—but in fact nobody did talk until all but one of them was dead.

Sheepmen from farther west—from as far as Oregon, but mostly from Utah—had been accustomed to sweep their immense herds through Colorado grazing lands annually. Taxed in their home states, these man paid no Colorado state or county taxes, though their sheep —tens of thousands of nibbling mouths—vacuumed up Colorado grass, leaving the range more depleted with each spring and fall sweep.

Wherever animals graze, the plants they like best are eaten off first and closest. This gives less tasty, less nourishing plants an edge in the competition for space and moisture. They take over. Eventually, if overgrazing by a species is not halted, its range grows nothing but forage it can't or won't eat. This is true even in wild herds such as deer—deer can starve in otherwise lush-looking areas where over-populating bands have eaten to extinction the kinds of browse they like or have the digestive apparatus to handle.

Before the Forest Service established grazing rules limiting bellies to range capacity, cows had so defoliated the range it took years to bring grasslands back.

Sheep do the job quicker. Sheep eat right down to the ground, and they eat almost any green thing that puts up leaf. Western range where they have grazed for generations grows little except a certain sage that nothing eats. In the intermountain Colorado Plateau are hundreds of miles of this gnarly brush that, according to old-timers, was not here when they arrived, or could not be seen for the tall, thick grass.

About eight years before the Escalante Sheep War, Utah sheep-men stopped bringing their herds into Western Colorado, "discour-aged" by various shooting, knifing, and clubbing episodes in which masked riders killed hundreds of sheep and a few men. None of this affected Escalante Canyon except to raise the apprehension level. There was a tacit agreement—you couldn't call it a gentleman's agree-ment because it was implemented by fear—that sheep would stay the hell the other side of the Gunnison River. Escalante country, and the whole back slope of the Uncompahgre Plateau, was off limits.

Local sheep battles were fought over range still in question beyond the river—two hundred head shot at State Bridge, fifteen run over a cliff at Dry Creek, thirty-five ewe throats slashed at Whitewater. Pete Swanson was killed in his sheep camp across the river at Kannah Creek. Pete was not a Utah sheepman, he was a local man from Montrose.

And so was Howard Lathrop. When word came that Howard Lathrop's men were building a sheep bridge across the Gunnison, four Escalante men rode down to stop it: Ben Lowe, Don Musser, Tom Brent, and Zoe Gilbert. The cable-swung bridge was over a hundred feet long and one sheep wide. Planks laid endwise in a double row ribboned a narrow floor along the bottom of a wire netting trough about shoulder high to a man. Swaying and fragile-looking as a spider web, it was stronger than it looked; bridges like it lasted through decades of use in sheep country. Obviously Lathrop meant to use it more than just that one winter. (Stories vary about how the sheep crossed the river—by ice, raft, or a railroad track on a side of the river where it never was. Carl Gilbert, the only eyewitness participant to go on record, described a bridge.)

When the Escalante party arrived, the bridge was finished, herders and dogs had wrangled the lead sheep across the scary bridge, and the mass of the herd had started to flow single-file like water trickling from a dam about to burst, onto grass that sheep had never grazed before. Though at least two of the cattlemen were armed—Ben Lowe wore sidearms wherever he rode, and government hunter-trapper Tom Brent always had a scabbard rifle—no weapons were drawn. They delivered their message from saddle height. "Get those sheep back where they belong!" The "or else" was in tone and stance, the more menacing for being unspoken.

The herders had no authority to change their orders; sheep, men, and dogs milled uncertainly. The cattlemen wheeled and rode away, knowing Lathrop would get the word, confident he would heed advice weighted with threat. He didn't. The herd was brought across and drifted ten or twelve miles "into the middle of range where Escalante ranchers were wintering several hundred head of cattle."

Six men met at the Musser cabin to assess their situation and what to do about it.

Their situation was not the general one of cattlemen determined to keep sheep off cattle range on principle. It was specific. If those specific sheep ate that specific feed that specific year, they would all go broke.

By long-standing arrangement among themselves, Escalante cowmen had put precisely the number of cows down there that could winter through on the feed available in the coves and loops of lowland between the river and the cliffs. Grass does not replenish itself in Colorado wintertime; what's there in October is all there will be till spring. A band of sheep could mow off in weeks what was supposed to last the cows for months. If the sheep stayed, the cattle starved.

Escalante cattlemen couldn't move their stock up- or down-river — other cattlemen's herds were wintering above and below; they couldn't put their cows in ranch corrals and winter them on hay — by February any hay reachable by hoof or by haul was already spoken for. They couldn't move the cows back up to summer range; it was deep in snow.

And they couldn't go to law. Even if they did and won, they'd lose. Carl Gilbert explained: "They couldn't go to the sheriff because Lathrop hadn't violated any written laws. He'd pretty badly fractured the old Code of the West, at least from the cattlemen's viewpoint, but that was not enforceable in a court of law. Besides, then as now, legal suits took forever. In the meantime the cattle would starve.

"We decided to take our own action, not really concerned with whether it was legal or not. We intended to kill enough sheep to eternally convince Lathrop that the south side of the Gunnison was for cows."

One of them, John Hilkey, drew a line and fell out with Ben Lowe over it. "Killing sheep, all right. Men no!" Hilkey won, as Carl Gilbert acknowledges. "We planned carefully to avoid doing physical harm to any human."

The riders were Ben Lowe, 48, Don Musser, 30, John Hilkey, 35, Bill Gilbert, 43, and Gilbert's sons Zoe, 18, and Carl, 19. The men objected to Zoe and Carl because of their youth but Bill shut them up, speaking for his sons' ability to hold up their end, "Don't worry about those boys!"

On the night of March 7 the three Gilberts left their ranch on the North Fork (later known as Sawtell) and dropped down to the

Near Elk Horn Springs, the Canyon has burrowed into a tree-clad mountain. ▶

XVX to pick up John Hilkey, its owner at the time. The four of them trailed up out of the Canyon to the top of Sowbelly Ridge, where they were to rendezvous with Don Musser and Ben Lowe. The night was cold. Old, recrystallized snow, crunching under hoof, deepened as they climbed.

Ben and Don, at the rendezvouz place, had a fire going. When the men had warmed the chill out of their bones, they remounted and rode across the top of Boyce Gulch to Camp Ridge, and down the ridge until they rimmed out above the sheep bedground. Daybreak outlined Grand Mesa beyond the river. The men groped for positions in the dark, hunkered in the rocks, and waited. When it was light enough to locate the herders' tent (so as not to hit it and its human contents by mistake) they began shooting into the sheep.

"The sheep began milling. When a bunch would break from the herd, we shot the leaders to turn them back. Through it all we saw no activity around the tent, no sign of the herder.

"I don't know how many sheep were in the herd and don't know how many were shot. Newspapers reported the number killed at 200. I do know that I fired so many rounds through my rifle that the barrel got so hot I could hardly hold it.

"Most of the men were using ordinary 30-30 carbines, but my rifle was a .351 Winchester automatic, the only gun like it in the country. If I'd been very worried about committing a crime or getting caught, I would not have used that .351." In fact, all the men were so confident of being in the right and having the support of the community, they didn't even bother to pick up the evidence—empty shells and cartridge boxes identifiable by Delta store cost marks.

When they felt they had done enough damage to get the message across to Lathrop, the men remounted and rode home in broad daylight, arriving in late afternoon. They made no attempt to conceal their tracks, going or coming.

"Nothing happened. No law officers came into the Canyon to investigate, not even deputy sheriff Cash Sampson, who had been stock and brands inspector and deputy U.S. marshal." Nothing happened down at the sheep camp either. Lathrop skinned out the carcasses to retrieve some of his estimated $1,500 loss, and the herd went right on munching cattle grass.

So the "Night Raiders," as the papers called them, struck again. This time all Escalante ranches except Isaac Ward's were represented. Added to the original six were Oscar Huffington, Bert Shreeves, Tom Brent, and Harry Stockham, "son of the president of Delta's only bank and owner of a cattle spread over in Roubideau Canyon. Stockham feared that if sheep were allowed to breach the Gunnison River sheepline at Escalante they would soon overrun Roubideau.

"Bert Shreeves and Oscar Huffington prepared by going to Delta for new rifles and ammunition. I doubt that Oscar had ever owned a gun before."

Oscar's son Nelson says, "Dad owned a gun. Carl may have had Bert Shreeves in mind. Bert hadn't owned or used a gun since the time when he and Dad were young men hunting together, and Bert's gun went off accidentally and shot right between Dad's legs."

On the evening of March 24, nine men met at Bert Shreeves' place in the Lower Canyon, assembling after dusk at the corrals out of sight of the house.

From the Shreeves' place they rode downriver to McHugh to pick up Tom Brent, who was batching there, alone and free to invite them into the warm cabin where he had coffee ready. After midnight the ten men rode on downriver, then turned upcountry to approach the sheep camp from below. Silently in the dark, they edged up around the camp, took places, and waited for dawn.

"Don Musser and I worked our way carefully into some rocks above the herders' camp so that we could discourage any interference with the proceedings, and the other men positioned themselves around the herd. When it was light enough, someone signaled and the shooting began.

"When the shooting stopped, a man ran out of the herders' tent and began saddling a white horse, evidently to go for help. After he had the horse saddled, but before he could mount, Don and I shot and killed the horse and, I think, a packmule tied in the brush behind the camp.

"The man disappeared into the tent and stayed there.

"Don Musser and I kept watch over the camp until all the other fellows got to their horses and gave us a signal, then we made our way to our horses. Don and I were to stay for a few minutes, fire a few more shots so the herders would not rush out until after our men were out of reach.

"This time we rode up and over Camp Ridge to the southeast, avoiding the possibility of meeting anyone on the Escalante road. We were perhaps a little more nervous about the second raid, but I had used my .351 again."

Again no move from the law, but the *Daily Sentinel* printed an item that spooked the raiders. It reported that Ed Brown and several Mexican herders had made a stand against the attackers and had shot a horse from under its rider and were keeping horse and saddle until officers could arrive and identify the attackers by means of them.

"We figured that article was a trap to get someone to claim the story wasn't true. Either that, or Ed Brown was so scared he didn't recognize his own horse after the shooting was over."

The men who had taken part in the raids had a lot of burrs in their britches that they couldn't complain about without revealing who they were. It irked them to be called "Night Raiders," and when reporting ballooned into fiction, they were furious to see themselves accused of running whole herds of sheep off cliffs and of shooting at sheepherders.

But what rankled longest with Carl Gilbert were the aspersions cast on his marksmanship.

"All I can say is that had we intended to shoot at the herder, we wouldn't have hit the horse."

If there was any attempt to discover who killed the sheep, it was neither immediate nor obvious. But this time Howard Lathrop understood. He moved his sheep back to the north side of the Gunnison, and sheep have stayed on that side to this day.

Though there was no sign that the law was doing anything about the raids, Bill Gilbert took the precaution of putting his sons out of reach of consequences. Only days later Carl went to work for a cow outfit in Utah, and Zoe left for a similarly opportune job in Arizona. That is why when Eda Musser attended her first Escalante dance at the Gilbert home on the Fourth of July after her April wedding and the March sheep raids, the two Gilbert boys were not among the dancers.

Except possibly at that dance, Bill Gilbert carried a gun all that summer, his daughter remembered. "Father had sometimes carried a pistol in his chaps pocket, but that summer he strapped on a holstered gun."

Perhaps the wives didn't know, but Mrs. Gilbert knew enough to suggest they move. "Bill, if there's going to be that kind of trouble, let's go somewhere else." The Gilberts eventually did go, but it took more than fear of that kind of trouble to make Bill Gilbert quit. It took the deadly deep snow of 1919.

John Hilkey got out that same summer, moving his family to the Meeker-Rangely area even before he'd sold his place. The man who bought it was Cash Sampson.

Carl Gilbert concluded that the sale was taken as a put-up front for an inside investigation. "I'd surmise that the ranchers in the Escalante were suspicious that Sampson had been sent by the sheepmen to spy, to get evidence about the killings."

If it is true that "nobody talked," not even to wives, then apparently the wives had the intuition to guess, at least enough to be anxious. A few weeks after the second raid, Escalante women did something they had never done before and never did again: they organized a solidarity meeting.

The paper noted, "An Escalante Canyon resident says the ladies of that vicinity are arranging a 'good fellowship meeting at the school house to bring into one united body all the residents of that district to work for the good and advancement of the community.'"

Of course, there's a slim chance it was coincidental.

Neither Kel nor Eda attended the solidarity meeting; they were on their original honeymoon in Grand Junction.

And when Eda did come to the Canyon in May—coddled child of another world whom nobody expected to stick it out more than a few months—who would risk talking to her about the raids and the men involved in them if Kel didn't?

Perhaps Eda Musser was the only wife who didn't know.

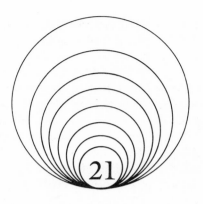

Cash Sampson

Only a few weeks after the Sheep War, Cash Sampson bought the Hilkey outfit in Escalante Canyon and put some cows up on mountain range. He owned it, as most cattlemen owned their ranches, in mortgage partnership with the bank. Canyon opinion was that the deal was merely a front to give him an "in" with neighboring ranchers; that he moved to the Canyon for no other purpose than to spy, to find out who had ridden in the raids, and most particularly to pin them on Ben Lowe.

"Cash Sampson was a lawman," Carl Gilbert wrote. "As far as I know, buying the Hilkey place was his first venture in the cattle business."

Well, maybe on that scale. But he had been running cattle for fifteen or twenty years outside the Canyon, so unobtrusively the papers took no notice of him at all. Facts about his early life are obtainable only from his obituary.

The facts have strange coincidences:

Cash Sampson and Ben Lowe were born the same year, 1868; in the same state, Missouri, though half the state apart; and both were members of large families with strong religious leanings. Both came to the Western Slope of Colorado in 1892; both cowboyed for various (but different) outfits during their early years here—Cash for Dillard, Mathews, and Huffington. Both took up homesteads and established cattle ranches south of town within three miles of each other and proved up on their claims the same spring. Both sold their ranches to move to Escalante, though in different years. Both died in the same moment of time in a duel that split Canyon loyalties for decades, and yet later a nephew of one married a daughter of the other.

There is, however, no evidence that the two ever knew each other before coming here, and no evidence that, living here as close neighbors in an era when neighboring was vital, they ever had more than a cool, nodding acquaintanceship.

Except for two characteristics they had in common—devotion to family, and a streak of stubbornness—they were as different as two men could be. While Ben was getting his head together after one of his shooting-up-Main Saturday nights, Cash was in the Presbyterian church listening to the sermon; while Ben was racing horses, Cash was fulfilling his duties as trusteee for Woodmen of the World Lodge; while Ben was training his sons to be crack sidearms marksmen, Cash was chaperoning his orphaned nieces to and from college. Cash provided absolutely nothing juicy for the papers to get their teeth into. If he hadn't gone to law, first as a plaintiff and then as an officer, there probably wouldn't be a riffle in history to show for Cassius Clay Sampson's life.

Cash Sampson went to law over the loss of twenty-two cows when a dam burst. His ranch on the Uncompahgre was near the mouth of Dry Creek, which had been dammed farther up by a private irrigation company. This was before the days of in-depth tests for soil strength and permeability and, though the farmers operating the scrapers heaped up the earth and tamped it down correctly, they failed to notice a hidden strata of gravel that cut the confining hillslopes on both sides. When Bonney Dam Lake built up enough pressure, that streak of gravel went out like sugar, and the lake descended Dry Creek all at once. It filled the Uncompahgre Valley, destroying crops, drowning countless animals, and washing out a quarter-mile of railroad track.

The irrigation company refused to accept responsibility.

The Denver & Rio Grande Railroad, shrugging its corporate shoulders, set about repairing the damage. Farmer victims did likewise—all but one. That one put a pitchfork through the throat of a director of the irrigation company.

Cash Sampson sued.

The district court awarded him damages. The irrigation company appealed. Seven years later the state supreme court awarded him $605 in damages plus 8 percent interest from the day of the Bonney Dam flood. In the meantime, while stubbornly pressing his case, Cash proved up on his homestead ranch, then relegated it to second place in his life by applying for the position of State Stock and Brand Inspector.

The State Brand Inspector's job was to apprehend cattle rustlers and horse thieves; the arena was generally railroad stockyards. Before the stockcars could be loaded and sealed, before the engineer got the signal to squirt steam to the pistons, every outgoing critter had to be checked by the inspector to see that its brand matched its bill of sale – or that there indeed was a bill of sale. In cases of wrong, forged, or missing bills of sale, the animals were impounded and the shipper was subject to arrest. If he resisted he could be shot – usually in incapacitating but unfatal areas of the body. To execute the latter maneuver successfully, the officer had to shoot before the shipper did.

As a law officer opposing the most dangerous class of men in the country, Inspector Sampson wore a badge and a gun. He could use a gun, quick and accurate, but it never looked quite right on him, belted a trifle high and too level, perhaps, like the way he wore his Stetson.

His district was large, with widespread shipping points that, according to newspaper items, kept him traveling most of the time, answering calls from shippers:

"Brand Inspector Sampson went to Placerville Monday where Patterson and Smith loaded four cars of horses for Saint Louis. Then to Sapinero where three parties shipped fifteen cars of cattle, then Cimarron, twenty-one cars cattle . . . C. C. Sampson says the district shipped more than three hundred carloads of steers to market since September."

Or calls from courts trying the cases of men he had arrested: "Cash Sampson returned from Ouray Wednesday where he convicted two men of horse and cattle rustling, altering and defacing brands . . . Cash Sampson went to Grand Junction Monday to appear as a witness in district court against a man recently arrested for theft of a valuable saddle."

One such arrest may have brought his first confrontation with Ben Lowe. A man came through town with two stolen horses, riding one and leading the other, which Sampson and the deputy sheriff recognized as being on their "hot list." They arrested the man and took him to the livery stable to deposit the horses before putting him in jail.

This was Ben Lowe's Main Street livery, which the city council had recently declared illegal; there was scuttlebutt that it intended to illegalize the replacement Ben was building on Dodge Street; so perhaps he wasn't feeling too kindly toward law in general. Or perhaps he had nothing to do with the fact that the prisoner escaped captors at his barn, galloping off into the sage. Much good it did. The stolen model had less horsepower than the official models, and Sampson had it by the reins in less than half a mile.

If Lowe had anything to do with this incident, it may have been in covert retaliation for an earlier one involving his brother Bert.

"Bert Lowe was arrested and brought before his honor, the complaint was made by Cassius Sampson that Mr. Lowe had been guilty of assaulting him." The assault consisted of a mere slap in the face, but it happened on Main Street on a Sunday afternoon in view of God and everybody, in typical Lowe fashion. A slap can be more assaulting than a slug if dignity is at stake—in this case, the dignity of the law.

"The assault was brought about over a horse inspection deal. Some time ago a shipment of horses was being made from the yards at Delta and one of the animals, a mare, was taken up by Inspector Sampson, he claiming that no bill of sale was at hand, and further that he had been notified by the owner at Telluride to locate the animal.

"Mr. Lowe informed Mr. Sampson that all inquiry in regard to the horse should be stopped, and emphasized his admonitions with a slap in the face."

Joining Cash in solicitude for the dignity of the law, the judge ruled "a total fine that with costs was something over $38, and besides Mr. Lowe was ordered by the court to keep the peace in the hereafter or more drastic measures would be taken."

In view of the generally accepted meaning of the term "the hereafter," popular opinion was that the judge had set himself a mighty long term of Lowe surveillance, and in unpleasant surroundings if it turned out the Lowe brothers spent the hereafter where people thought they would.

When Cash Sampson had been Brand Inspector for seven years, serving so well that his reappointment brought resounding approval from the stockmen whose property it was his duty to protect, he became dissatisfied with the job. He gave no reason for his resignation, but the exciting career of Doc Shores may have had something to do with it. Doc was a sheriff, a U.S. marshal, a Pinkerton man, a private detective for the Denver & Rio Grande, for Utah Fuels, for Globe Express, and for only Doc knew who else. He roamed the West after his current man – and collected big rewards.

At this time, while Cash was scuffling around in stockyard manure fingering brands on the rumps of horses and the ribs of cows to see whether the bar that made an "F" into an "E" had been recently burned in, Doc Shores was making spectacular arrests all over Sampson's own district – safe-blowers at Hotchkiss and Olathe, train robbers at Parachute, express office stickup men at Grand Junction. Romantic names and amounts – the capture of Packsaddle Jack, retrieval of $14,000 in payroll gold. Big time.

Moving toward a different field of law enforcement, Cash Sampson ran for sheriff, an office that, though it paid less in salary, positioned a man to collect on those thousand-dollar reward posters. He won with an all-time record vote.

The job proved to be even grubbier than checking brands. He arrested a man for having two wives, he arrested drunks, he arrested principals and promoters and gamblers in an illegal prize fight, he arrested an old man who plain lost track of where his house was and undressed and went to bed in the home of two unattended maiden ladies, he took the old man by train to the state asylum, he jailed drunks, he arrested a man for maintaining a tent of ill repute with his daughters as sole employees, he jailed bootleggers, rapists, and people who beat their kids with clubs.

They wouldn't stay jailed. Prisoners dug through the unfired local brick walls with their supper spoons or their fingernails – five through the south side, two through the east, one traditionalist filed the window bars. Toward the end of Cash's second year, the paper summed the summer: "nine felonies, nine jail-breaks, the jail is a sieve."

But Sheriff Sampson's nemesis was a black man named Charley Brown.

Charley Brown, billed as the Delta Shiner (shoe), and Guy Sprinkler, who, advertising himself as Kid Springer, were arrested midfight, along with promoters and spectators at a "smoker" in Austin. The law the sheriff had to enforce left a lot to his discernment – sparring for points (whatever that was) was legal; prize fighting (whatever that

Door of first Delta jail, less pervious to prisoners than later structures. ▶

was) was not. The sheriff, attending uninvited, watched one round to make sure he had a case, then arrested everybody in sight.

Having no money or property, Charley Brown sat out his fine in jail, using the time to plan a remedy for his financial state. When the current bootlegger dug out, and all around him squirmed through the hole, Charley stayed—his scheme required that he be a blameless victim.

Some weeks after his release the paper reported:

"Charley Brown, the colored shine artist, and J. Kada were held up at gunpoint in the alley back of Porter-Obert Hardware. Kada wanted to get the law, Charley didn't. Kada decided it was a frame —he'd given up $28 and other valuables, Charley only $6." The clincher was that the holdup man knew about, and asked for, a certain ring that Kada had recently lent Charley $10 on.

Charley was charged with complicity in a holdup.

This meant not just jail but the pen. Heretofore Charley had been arrested only for misdemeanors—fighting, in the ring or on the street. Facing real trouble, he dug out while he was still in a jail where it was possible. He managed the break successfully but without savoir faire, as the paper noted. "Abandoning all precedence," he perforated a wall other than the usual blind side next to the courthouse.

Three weeks later a man answering Charley Brown's description was reported to have killed himself at Whitewater. Sheriff Sampson investigated, though the paper pooh-poohed the idea in a quote that, though not intended as a compliment, acknowledged an innate and blessed racial optimism: "Who ever heard of a Negro committing suicide!"

The man wasn't Charley, but Charley had passed that way, getting as far as Price, Utah, where he was apprehended and held to be picked up by Sampson.

Cash Sampson almost got home with him. For some reason the prisoner was sitting some distance ahead of the sheriff when the train, after a stop at Fruita, began gathering speed again. Cash Sampson looked up to see Charley Brown diving through the coach window.

A witness reported, "I was looking down the car and saw a man suddenly lean out of the window, and the next thing I saw his heels disappearing through the sash. He landed full length on hands and face, rolled over three or four times, got up, shook himself like a horse, and began to run toward a pole fence. The train did not stop."

Sampson rushed to the rear platform, jumped and landed running, gun in hand. Though there was no chance he could overtake the man, who was a sprinter as well as a fighter, Cash Sampson did not shoot.

Perhaps the worst of serving as Delta County Sheriff was the complete lack of reward money. The only chance he had at it was when two convicts, a murderer and a burglar, escaped from a chain gang road crew. A couple of coal miners picked them up at Somerset and got the hundred-dollar reward. Cash got to escort them across the mountains to the penitentiary.

After a little more than a year and half as sheriff, Cash Sampson resigned, giving as reason that "financially as well as in some other minor respects the office has not been satisfactory." His application to be reappointed Stock Inspector was instantly accepted.

Thus it was that when 200 sheep were slaughtered north of Escalante Canyon, in country so broken it was hard to determine where the county line ran and which county had jurisdiction, the man with overall authority was called in to investigate, State Stock and Brand Inspector Sampson.

Riding with him was Deputy Sheriff Beaty, the same J. T. Beaty Ben Lowe had pulled a gun on during a stroll with friends up Eaton Avenue eight years before. Beaty had not been an officer then, but with Ben's gun leveled on him he had drawn his own, ordered Ben to drop his, and Ben had obeyed.

Consider the evidence Sampson and Beaty were studying–the hundreds of empty shells, some from a .351 Winchester, like no other in the country; the brands on the cattle grazing where they always grazed in winter, proclaiming just which owners had the most to lose if sheep were allowed to come in; the tracks.

The night riders had made no attempt to conceal their trail in the four trips they made in going and coming twice. Any experienced stockman could have followed track directly back to Escalante Canyon. Lathrop could have followed the killers of his sheep, but significantly didn't risk it. A skilled tracker could have followed each man back to his own corral. Tracks, to the lawmen of the Old West, were what fingerprints are to modern detectives. A hoof that falls slightly out of line because of the throw of a leg, overreach in one or both hind feet, an inside-feathered shoe shaped to prevent injury to the opposite leg in a horse that "brushes"–by such signs the tracker could read trail like reading lines on a page, could fill in missing facts like filling gaps in a crossword puzzle. Sampson, with his years of recognizing stolen horses by remembered details, probably could have named most of the horses that made those tracks, if not their riders.

Yet nothing was done.

If Sampson followed the tracks, nobody knew about it. Carl Gilbert believed Sampson didn't even come out to check on the killing. He blamed the apathy on the War, writing, "It was beginning to look like America would be drawn in, that American boys would be fighting in France. Everything else faded from importance."

That was in April; in May Cash Sampson resigned as Stock Inspector and bought the Hilkey ranch in Escalante Canyon.

It may all have been as simple and open as the paper stated: Cash Sampson and his brother Watt bought a large Escalante outfit—the Hilkey ranch, cattle, and mountain range. Watt Sampson was employed in Telluride where he would remain; Cash resigned his job to work full time with ranch and cattle. The coincidence of purchase so soon after the Sheep War may have been merely that the Hilkeys, apprehensive about their involvement in the killings, and wanting to leave the area fast, made Sampson a very good price.

Few in the Canyon believed these facts; some still don't. Speculation was fierce, if whispered. Had Hilkey sold out information as well as property? Had he been blackmailed into selling? Had Sampson really bought it, or was the ranch a front. Had he really resigned, or was he still a lawman in some secret capacity?

By what evidence exists, however, the resignation from all forms of law enforcement was complete. When Cash Sampson faced Ben Lowe over guns on June 9, 1917, it was as a private citizen.

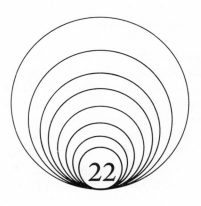

The Shoot-Out

Either Cash Sampson was still a lawman in some secret role, or his body and being—as distinct from his brain—did not accept the fact, after so many years behind the badge, that he no longer was. He kept on acting like one.

A year after his resignation, on the morning of June 9, 1917, he saddled and rode to the Calhoun Place on Kelso Creek to pay Calhoun's housekeeper, Mabel Campbell, for some baking she had done for him. He first stopped at the Cowger Place, where he gave Mattie Cowger a pearl-handled revolver. "I may not be back. I want you to have this," he told her. The Cowger outfit, run by widow and sons, was one of the small setups stockmen had tried to "discourage" out of existence.

Blanche Gilbert, who relates the incident, has this explanation for Cash's seeming premonition: "My Dad was having trouble over 'sleepered' calves. Sleepering is when a calf is earmarked, its ears notched in specific places around the rim with the code of its owner, but not branded. It was a quick, easy way to mark small calves on the range without the hassle of branding. Then at roundup time the sleeper calves were branded according to their earmarks.

"The earmark, pretty well covered by long hair, isn't as noticeable from the saddle as a brand, and a rustler could get by with earmarking a calf different from the brand of the mother it was sucking. Then at roundup the calf became officially his property when the crew branded it to match its earmarks. Sleepering was practiced by cowboys working for big outfits—that's how many of them started their own spreads, sleepering some of the boss's calves—and by un-scrupulous cattlemen against their range neighbors.

"My Dad was a Texan; he bought what they now call the Sawtell at the head of Spring Fork in 1911, and by 1916 had leased the Blumberg place and was running more cattle than any other Escalante rancher. He wasn't afraid of man or beast. He thought Ben Lowe was doing the sleepering and jumped him about it.

"When Ben denied it, Dad said, 'You and Bob Shreeves were the only ones riding down on the river this spring, and I know Bob Shreeves didn't do it. If I ever catch you doing that I'll kill you.'

"Cash Sampson had bought the Hilkey place just below us, and when Dad told him about the sleepering, and what he was prepared to do, Cash said he would take care of it. He said that rather than have any of the family men in the Canyon get hurt, he would take the responsibility."

But the-cause-and-effect link between an earlier Gilbert-Lowe confrontation and Sampson's June morning errands on Kelso Creek does not seem to be that direct and simple.

For one thing, there had been a third sheep raid, across the river at Kannah Creek. Since the riders in all three raids were still unknown, it could be suspected that the same men did the killing in all three. But the third raid was different, more selective—only purebred rams were slaughtered—perhaps indicating a leader who was learning by experience how to inflict most damage with least risk.

Furthermore, the weeks preceding the last day of Cash Sampson's life had included several unexplained trips away from the Canyon. In late April Cash turned all but ninety head of his cattle out on mountain range, and the next day left for Denver. A day or so after he got back, he took the train for an overnight trip to Grand Junction. And on this Saturday, June 9, he had only just returned to the Canyon after spending several days in Delta.

That last trip to Delta puts within the range of possibility one of the dozens of "I was in on it" stories that surfaced after the shooting. Most of these stories seem dismissable as rather pathetic fabricated brags; but young Claude Marsh, earnest in wanting to vindicate his benefactor Ben Lowe, at least had the time right.

"I knew it was going to happen. I was in the poolhall, and Cash Sampson came in and said he was going out to the Canyon to get Ben Lowe. Somebody said 'Better watch out Ben Lowe don't get you!'"

At 10:30 in the morning, having finished one of his errands, Cash Sampson stopped at the Musser Place for nooning before proceeding up Kelso Creek to pay Mabel Campbell for that bread.

Kel was holding down the ranch with the help of his hired man, Shorty Gibson. Eda was in town with the new baby.

"Cash helped me prepare the meal," Kel testified at the inquest. Shorty didn't. He sat and visited, it being part of a hired man's pay that he be able to sit down to a meal without having to help cook or clean up afterward. The food was simple and hearty—meat, milk, butter, and potatoes produced on the place. Home-canned fruit. Bread sliced from loaves Eda baked for Kel to take to the ranch when he came to town. Coffee from the pot always on the back of the stove.

Before the food was ready, three other horses pulled up at the yard. Ben Lowe and his two sons accepted Kel's invitation to join the meal. Like Cash Sampson, all three were armed, the two little boys, Robert, 11, and William, 9, sagging under the weight of .45's strapped to their slender hips. Ben's gun was in a shoulder holster— the gunbelt he usually wore was in town being repaired.

Whatever Kel and Shorty thought about four guests armed with heavy guns sitting around the table, they said nothing, though it wasn't usual. "Cowboys didn't wear guns as a rule," Blanche explains. "Revolvers were too big and heavy. It's cumbersome to work carrying them. A stockman would tie a rifle to the saddle if bear or mountain lions were getting to the calves, maybe a pistol tucked into his chaps pocket, but not a holster gun."

If Ben was wearing a jacket the shoulder holster and gun might have been invisible. During all the hashing and rehashing of the affair after its enigmatic end, no one ever suggested that this was the case, that Cash Sampson might have thought Ben Lowe was unarmed. And indeed it was unlikely—no one in his right mind would be wearing a jacket at noon of a torrid June day in the Canyon, and Ben was never known to go anywhere unarmed.

Conversation around the table was general, Kel Musser testified. Though it was noticeable that "Cash and Ben did not direct any remarks at each other, there was nothing to create suspicion that any trouble was brewing between them."

When touched by an inexplicable tragedy of magnitude, such as the murder of a President, everybody remembers throughout life precisely where he was and what he was doing at that moment. When the inexplicable tragedy is closer, involving friends and loved ones, the moment is not only indelible, it is a vortex—the terrible question "Why?"—dragging significance out of every detail.

The little boys, there, sitting hitched forward in their chairs because their legs were not long enough to reach the floor . . . had their father actually told them, as Nellie Walker said he did, "If anybody tries to kill me, shoot him"?

Eda's being gone . . . what if she'd been there in her kitchen to give guns the put-down, from her diminutive height ordering the men to get rid of their weapons, as on another occasion she would order a sheriff's posse?

If the presence of women in a community is a deterrent to violence in proportion to their numbers, as historians like to point out in writing about viciousness in all-male mining boomtowns, then the Canyon, always short of feminine influence, was especially vulnerable, being especially short of it on that June day. The women who wintered in town to put children in school had not yet returned to the Canyon. Others who customarily stayed in the Canyon chanced to be absent—four or five to have babies within call of a physician, three because the family ranch had sold and was temporarily or permanently under bachelor management. Mrs. Rogers was in town with appendicitis, the school-teacher, Miss Pearl Anderson, had gone to summer school. Ruby Lowe with a new baby girl was staying with her parents.

Accentuating the lack of feminine influence was an upsurge of male-orienting circumstances:

The land rush. Two months earlier the government opened millions of acres to homestead, quadrupling what a man might file on. The Old Wild West yeasted in male blood again—conquest. Grab the best before some bastard beats you to it. Grab all you're man enough to tame and hold onto.

The war. Four weeks earlier the United States declared war on Germany in what was to be the most fervently patriotic war of the nation's history. All men, draft age or not, measured themselves against a new yardstick—shooting and getting shot at—to find out just how much man they were.

Violence is a clench of mind. Tunnel vision. No solution exists except the one down the gunsight.

In the Musser kitchen, in the Canyon, in the world of the moment, influences toward some other solution were weak or missing, influences that by their mere presence could have shaken, shocked, or kidded the clench away.

Eda wasn't there, but she has some thoughts about it now: "Cash Sampson and Ben Lowe didn't like each other, but probably their quarrel would never have come to guns if people had let them alone. People egged them on. They'd tell Cash that Ben was out to get him before he could testify in the sheep killing, and they'd tell Ben that Cash had the goods on him for participating in it.

"In those days men who had violent natures, but didn't want to get into trouble themselves, took pleasure in egging lawmen on, building them up as big shots. Some officers became trigger happy and would shoot first and inquire later. I can't help wondering if that's what happened with Cash Sampson."

But Cash Sampson had carried a lawman's gun for twelve years without killing anyone. And Ben had been an outlaw (albeit a small-time and gentlemanly one) and a practicing quick-draw artist for even longer without harming anyone.

"The meal over, Mr. Lowe and his two boys left, headed for home, they said, riding down the road that follows the Canyon," Kel testified. About fifteen minutes after Lowe left, Sampson also headed out—not up Kelso Creek to pay Mabel, as he'd told Kel he intended, but downcanyon, saying he was going up on Flat Mesa to look for stock.

There is no Flat Mesa. If Sampson was giving some clue or signal in misnaming a feature of country he knew well, its meaning is lost.

Though Kel and Shorty testified there had been nothing to arouse suspicion, something was in the air that made the two men stand and watch Sampson out of sight, down slope after slope of the open park, through the shimmering heat of the June noon, and into the cedars. Shorty said, "If he keeps up at that clip he'll overtake Ben about a mile and a half down the road."

Ben Lowe and his boys had reached a place on the road almost exactly a mile and a half from the Musser ranch when Cash Sampson overtook them.

The place was the wildest section of the cliff-bottom talus ridges. Here the road dipped and twisted through a tunnel of half-dead cedars and sage; vision was barred in all directions by the gray shreds of bark and gray thickety twigs that cedars, able to die but unable

Lowe was thought to be riding to a hideout in some such cliff cranny.

to rot away, accumulate. Hardly denser along one side ran the jagged rick of a rip-gut fence. It was as if the two men, one traveling more slowly toward it than the other, had paced their horses, or their lives, to meet precisely here. Or perhaps it wasn't fated. Perhaps Ben had simply been too proud to run.

"Ben Lowe had one of his hideout cabins right there in the Canyon. Tucked down in the boulders back in one of the side crannies near Little Cottonwood," says Bonsal Huffington. "They think that's where he was heading, and that Cash suspected it and cut him off. I'm not old enough to know firsthand, but that's what was said. That Ben just didn't ride fast enough to reach his hideout."

"Ben Lowe and the boys had got pretty close to Little Cottonwood Creek," Oscar Huffington wrote in his diary for that day, "when Ben told the boys to go on, that he was going to wait for Sampson and have it out with him."

The cedar-sage jungle where Lowe and Sampson met. ▶

But that too was hearsay; the only witnesses were two little boys. They testified at the inquest, and so far as is known never spoke of it again as long as they lived.

According to the testimony, it was after Cash Sampson had overtaken them that Ben Lowe ordered the boys to ride on ahead because he wanted to talk to Sampson. When Bobby and Billie had ridden on about a hundred yards, out of sight around a bend, they heard loud quarreling and then a shot from Sampson's gun.

"How did you know it was Sampson's gun?" the coroner asked.

"Dad's gun has a louder report, makes more noise."

There was no other witness to challenge this statement that Sampson had fired the first shot, and their word was not doubted though it was well known that these children had outwitted the law more than once in shielding their adored father after one of his escapades.

The sound of four shots instantly followed the first, and, even as they turned and raced back, they heard Ben calling "Bobby! Bobby!" in a voice that gurgled horribly and choked off. If Ben was calling on his son to avenge him, as Nellie Walker said, there was no need—Cash Sampson lay on the ground a bullet through his head. Propping himself against a stump, Ben Lowe got off one more shot then slipped back lifeless, drowned in the blood that was filling his lungs.

Bobby, as if it were a task he had long prepared himself to carry out, took charge, sending his younger brother back to the Musser ranch for help, catching up his father's horse, which had bolted, sitting with the dead.

The child Billie arrived at the Forks, crouched in the saddle, sobbing. "Dad and Cash have killed each other. Down the road a mile and a half."

Kel, who himself was only twenty-two, rode over to get an older neighbor, Arthur Ward, to go with him.

"Well, I don't know," Ward said. "One of them might still be alive . . ." but he saddled and went along.

When a murder has been committed you do not touch anything at the scene of the crime; you call the authorities and you wait for them to arrive. That is the law.

The Canyon had its own law—common sense.

The shooting had occurred across the county line. To notify the authorities of the proper county was a six-hour ride to the nearest telephone. When notified, the Mesa County authorities must ride seventy miles to the Upper Canyon or find someone who owned an automobile or wait for the next day's train; in either of the latter cases there would still be the ride into the Canyon—the road down the Big Hill had not yet been made passable to cars.

Two days, not less than two. It was early afternoon of a scorching June day at the bottom of the Canyon heat trap. Men, stockmen who knew what happens to the bodies of dead cattle in a couple of summer days, could not allow such to happen to two friends.

Always a careful man, Ward was not sure about the consequences of removing the bodies, so Kel took the responsibility. Eda remembers, "We worried about that. It wasn't legal what Kel did, taking the bodies away, taking them into another county, and we knew Kel could get into trouble. But even if he'd waited for the authorities, what difference would it have made? Two men had killed each other. There were two victims, but no murderer to charge."

With Ward's help Kel made his own investigation, trying to find answers for all the questions he thought might be asked at the inquest. Four bullets were missing from the chambers of the two guns —one from Cash Sampson's, three from Ben Lowe's. The guns carried by Bobby and Billie had not been fired.

"I heard five shots," Bobby testified at the inquest, "but if only four bullets are missing, I guess I was wrong." The Canyon, throwing an echo from the cliff, got in its say.

Cash had taken a bullet through the head, which entered above the left ear and came out at the back of the skull, and another in the leg, entering at the knee and emerging back of the hip. The doctor who examined the bodies testified that Cash was already dead and had fallen from his horse when the bullet entered the leg. Ben's third shot had gone wild.

Ben Lowe had been shot once—in the back.

That fact was loaded with such terrible possibilities—Canyon hatreds and feuds for generations to come—that Kel searched the clues for some explanation more characteristic of the brave man Cash Sampson was known to be.

The bullet had not taken a straight back-to-front path. It angled, entering low on the right side toward the back and emerging near the left nipple, passing through the lungs but missing the heart, as the doctor testified in detail.

From that, along with tracks showing where Lowe's horse had whirled violently, it was conjectured that in the moment the quarrel turned from words to guns, Ben Lowe had whirled his horse and leaned forward to flash his trick shot from under the horse's neck; that Cash Sampson had seen the trick shot coming and fired; and that Ben, being bent forward and slightly turned away, had taken the bullet almost the length of his torso, back to front.

Had his famous trick cost Ben Lowe his life? Or, because his gun-belt happened to be in for repair, and he was not used to drawing from a shoulder holster, did he get off his first shot a thousandth of a second late?

Kel went back to the ranch for the wagon and to send Shorty Gibson on ahead by horseback to take word of the murders to the sheriff, who would notify Mesa County authorities. The four guns also came to town ahead of the bodies, on the saddle of Pete Campbell.

Once again in that viewless tunnel of dying cedars, Kel and Arthur Ward placed the bodies on straw and quilts in the wagon bed, covered them with tarps, and started the long, slow journey down the Canyon.

Word of the killings had preceded the wagon, whether surmised from Shorty's headlong ride, or whether he called it out as he passed. Perhaps the word even preceded him, a shock wave running ahead, like the wave of bad air that precedes a cloudburst flood down the Canyon slot.

People came to their gates to watch the wagon roll by, hats held in hands, murmuring to the drivers or to each other, "Our family was always friends with both." And later, "We attended both funerals."

The wagon began the climb up the Big Hill, became a dot crawling along the face of its immensity, and disappeared over the rim.

Sources

Most of the material in the book is taken from primary sources, unpublished memoirs and diaries, newspapers of the day, and the living memory of Canyon people whose cordial response in interviews and correspondence is deeply appreciated.

Interviews and Letters

Irma Surbeck Albin, Gertha Street Austin, Brown Blumberg, Louise Doty Blumberg, Fred "Kelly" Calhoun, George Calhoun, Bob Clark, Connie Hurst Clark, Lela Crabill, Don M. Crabtree, Eula Dills Craig, Maudie White Dannels, J. D. Dillard, Bill Fairfield, Louise Ireland Frey, Blanche Gilbert, Emily Blumberg Grooms, Harvey and Betty Head, Morgan Hendrickson, Harold Hilkey, Bonsal Huffington, Nelson and Annie Rudolph Huffington, Ray Hurst, Marie Shreeves Jones, Nellie Walker Jones, Seabron King, Ted Lockhart, Frankie Lowe, Jack McHugh, Fidel Martinez, Weston Massey, Pauline McKee Moeller, Earl Monroe, Jack and Bernice Hendrickson Musser, Kelso and Eda Baker Musser, Oliver Nutting, Lois Hillman Pritchard, James Rattzloff, Warren Reams, Walter Sawtell, Bert Shreeves, Jack and Velma Bowen Shreeves, Carl Smith, Cecil Smith, Richard C. Smith, Welland Smith, Esther Watts Stephens, Dorothy Stockmer, Irene Freyberg Smith Sylvia, Raymond Tyler, Hilda Walker, Frank Walker, Frank Ward.

Manuscript Materials

Blachly, Lou. Memoirs 1877–1965. Held by Harold and Ruth Bradley, Berkeley, Calif.

Burritt family memoirs, 1879–1906. Delta Public Library, Delta, Colo.

Cameron, Mary. Collection of interviews, clips and documents, U.S. National Forest Service, Grand Junction, Colo.

Dillard, J. D. Taped interview made by Judge Fred "Kelly" Calhoun. Delta, Colo., 1976.

Dillard, Jeff. Memoirs, 1964. Held by Dillard family. Excerpted in *Riding Old Trails,* by James Curtis. Grand Junction County Press, Grand Junction, Colo., 1976.

Huffington, Oscar. Memoirs and diary, 1880–1947. Held by Nelson Huffington, Delta, Colo.

Monroe, Earl D., Montrose, Colo. Old-timer interviews. Manuscript held by him, 1969.

Rockwell, Wilson. "Delta County, the Formative Years." Manuscript. Delta County Historical Society, Delta, Colo.

Sinnock, Scott. "Geomorphology of the Uncompahgre Plateau and Grand Valley, Western Colorado, U.S.A." Ph.D. dissertation, Purdue University, 1978.

Smith, Capt. Henry A. Diary and memoirs 1863–1920. Delta County Historical Society, Delta, Colo.

————. Government Records: Military service, disability, marriage, pension, and death benefits, of Capt. Henry A. Smith, 1862–1936. U.S. Army; Veterans Administration; Bureau of Pensions, Dept. of the Interior. Philadelphia and Washington, D.C.

U.S. National Forest Service Archives, Delta, Colo.

Books and Articles

Baars, Donald L. *Red Rock Country.* New York: Doubleday, 1972.

Bower, A. W. *Progressive Men of Colorado.* Denver: A. W. Bower & Co., 1905.

Clarke, J.S. *Clarke's Biographical History of Colorado.* Denver, Colo.: J. S. Clark. Co., 1919.

Curtis, James. *Riding Old Trails.* Grand Junction, Colo.: Country Press, 1976.

Dempsey, Jack. *Dempsey.* New York: Harper & Row, 1977.

Dillard, J. D. Letter-to-the-editor, *Colorado West.* Grand Junction, Colo., May 15, 1973.

Fairfield, Eula King. *Pioneer Lawyer.* Denver: W. H. Kistler Stationery Co., 1946.

Gilbert, Carl M. "The Delta County Sheep War." *Colorado West,* Grand Junction, Colo., Dec. 31, 1972.

Jocknick, Sidney. *Early Days on the Western Slope of Colorado.* Glorieta, N. Mex.: Rio Grande Press, 1913.

Johnson's Universal Encyclopaedia. New York: D. Appleton & Co., 1898.

Kreutzer, Bill. *Saga of a Forest Ranger.* Boulder, Colo.: University of Colorado Press, 1958.

Lathrop, Marguerite. *Don't Fence Me In.* Boulder, Colo.: Johnson Publishing Co., 1972.

Lavender, David. *One Man's West.* New York: Doubleday, Doran & Co., 1945.

Musser, Eda Baker, compiler. *Trails and Trials.* Privately printed, 1986.

Rockwell, Wilson. *Uncompahgre Country.* Denver: Sage Books, 1965.

Stearns Bros. Co. *With the Colors from Delta County 1861–1919.* Delta, Colo.: Stearns Printing Co., 1920.

Wood & Brache. *United States Dispensatory.* (Publishing data missing), 1833.

Newspapers

Daily Press. Montrose, Colo., 1898–1987

Daily Sentinel. Grand Junction, Colo., 1901–87

Delta Chief. Delta, Colo., 1883–85

Delta County Independent, intermittently *Delta Daily Independent* and *Delta County Independent.* Delta, Colo., 1885–1987

Delta County Laborer. Delta, Colo., 1890–1908

Delta County Tribune. Delta, Colo., 1908–32

Denver Post. Denver, Colo., 1902–45

Grand Junction News. Grand Junction, Colo., 1883

Index

Red Hole in Time was composed into type on a Compugraphic digital phototypesetter in eleven point Galliard with one and one half points of spacing between the lines. Galliard was also selected for display. The book was designed by Jim Billingsley, typeset by Metricomp, Inc., printed offset by Thomson-Shore, Inc., and bound by John H. Dekker & Sons. The paper on which the book is printed bears acid-free characteristics for an effective life of at least three hundred years.

TEXAS A&M UNIVERSITY PRESS : COLLEGE STATION